# Know Thyself Ideologically

# Know Thyself Ideologically

**Germinal Boloix**

Germinal Boloix
2020

Copyright © 2020 by Germinal Boloix
All rights reserved. This book or any portion thereof may not be reproduced or used in any manner whatsoever without the express written permission of the author except for the use of brief quotations in a book review or scholarly journal.

First Printing: 2020

Front Page: "Victory 2020"

ISBN 978-1-7771234-0-6

Germinal Boloix
email: gboloix@hotmail.com
Blog: gboloix.blogspot.com

# Dedication

To all those suffering Absurd (21$^{st}$ Century) Socialism without deserving it.

# Contents

Germinal Boloix ............................................................................. 3
**Acknowledgments** .................................................................... 9
**Preface** ...................................................................................... 11
**Introduction** ............................................................................ 15
**Chapter 1: Society** ................................................................. 20
**Chapter 2: The Extremists** .................................................. 31
**Chapter 3: The Moderates** ................................................... 48
**Chapter 4: The Unprogressive** ............................................ 59
**Chapter 5: Geopolitical Dimension** ................................... 74
**Chapter 6: Political System** ................................................ 82
**Chapter 7: Economic System** .............................................. 98
**Chapter 8: Personal Influence** .......................................... 112
**Chapter 9: Social Influence** ............................................... 123
**Chapter 10: Ideological Sphere** ........................................ 133
**Chapter 11: Pragmatic Sphere** .......................................... 143
**Chapter 12: Societal Evaluation Framework** .................. 160
**Chapter 13: Globalization Dimension** ............................. 168
**Chapter 14: Sociopolitical Summary** ............................... 179
**Chapter 15: Absurd Socialism in Venezuela** ................... 187
**Chapter 16: Sociopolitical Preference** ............................. 214
**Final Notes** ............................................................................ 227
**Bibliography** ......................................................................... 232
**Epilogue** ................................................................................ 235

# Acknowledgments

I want to thank all the people who influenced the completion of this book during so many hours of thinking, reading, and writing.

# Preface

This book is the last of a series of five inspired on the failure of Absurd (Twenty-first Century) Socialism in Venezuela. The first book was a story about a citizen suffering on his own the difficulties of absurd socialism's policies. The second was a digression on the subject, presenting a philosopher's perspective on socialism. The third was a compendium of failed communist and socialist experiences and their relation to absurd socialism. The fourth described the relationship between human nature and socialism, proposing a human nature framework for analysis. The fifth proposes a framework to describe sociopolitical systems and the influence of ideology. [Boloix 2017] [Boloix2018 ] [Boloix 2019a] [Boloix 2019b].

I remember several years ago when people asked about my political preferences, the answer was imprecise, 'the left' most of the time because the 'right' was unthinkable. The next question was, 'But what specific ideology from the left?' I did not know exactly which one because I had not made up my mind at the time. I sympathized with anarchism but in an unconvincing way, knowing that it was a Utopia. I knew socialism and communism were ideologies that failed around the globe but I was not exposed directly to any of them. Being liberal instead of conservative was also an alternative. It was at the end of my life's journey that I had exposure to absurd socialism in Venezuela and everybody knows what a disgrace it became. Today, I understand that people are prone to sympathize with aspirations belonging to different ideologies instead of just one. Therefore, people are characterized by a mixture of ideologies instead of just one. Using the trivia questions proposed in the book, I was able to characterize my preferences towards certain ideologies, in my case, moderate (liberalism) and less extremist, instead of unprogressive (fascism) or totally extremist (socialism, communism).

Why do I write this type of book? The answer is, "It is my duty," to let people know the reality of a flawed sociopolitical system. Absurd socialism demonstrated an absolute detachment from reality, penalizing the common citizen. Am I an expert on the subject? The answer is, 'Of course not, I am just proposing a new approach.' There is no way to become an expert on so many sociopolitical systems and those who consider themselves experts don't spend their time writing this type of book. Therefore, I am making a contribution to open the eyes of so many people that flirt with the idea that socialism and communism are still viable alternatives.

Since the beginning of my writings, it was clear that there is something strange about people's preferences for political systems. The title of the first book suggests a 'Knowledge Distorted Journey,' meaning that people are not clear about political systems, they have a distorted understanding and don't care much about the implications of their decisions. More precisely, people start to care only when things affect their lives, and of course, when it is too late to correct mistakes. Knowledge is distorted because political systems share similar human aspirations, some feasible and many unattainable, differing on the institutions implementing them and people must choose among conflicting proposals. To determine which should be the chosen ideology becomes a paramount project for any political system, it requires knowledge of many ideologies and the politicians' interpretations determine its adaptation to reality. Individuals have a harder time choosing their ideology, to simplify, they give preference just to one ideology to avoid complicating their life.

It was clear from the start of my journey that personal experiences have a profound impact on the expectations about socialist politics. I lived experiences under absurd socialism that marked me forever. It is one thing to read about the 'benefits' of socialism, how 'fair' it is to the masses and so on, and another to live such a disastrous experience; it includes sectarianism and bigotry penalizing the dissidents. People who have never lived under a socialist regime have no arguments to defend such a type of political system. Go live under such regimes, not precisely as a tourist, and you tell me later.

I never was a fan of socialism when I was young, even though at the time I thought socialism was a possible alternative. At the time, experiences around the world showed the existence of socialist societies accepted by the people living in them, thus making people believe that socialism could get a shot at governing a decent society. At the time, I was close to the left but in fact, I sympathized with anarchism, which at least is acceptable as a Utopia in comparison to socialism that does not deliver good results. I come from a worker's family that fought the civil war in Spain on the Republican side with anarchistic sympathies; by the way, anarchism is not a disordered ideology as usually claimed, it is oriented instead to highlight human-oriented values. As an adult, I understands that anarchism is a Utopia but it still remains a comfortable dream in front of the cruel socialist reality. My experience under absurd socialism in Venezuela was traumatic, it was incredible how a wrong approach was accepted by a sector of the population, primarily those that have nothing to lose independently of the political system in power. After many years of suffering absurd socialism, I was intrigued by the kind of support the excluded population gave to the regime. I started some research on the subjects of socialism and communism, finding both approaches basically similar, even though in practice they may look different, one imposing the party-state and the other simply the state. How come in Venezuela people were blindfolded with absurd socialism whereas the world already knew a lot about how bad socialism and communism are. Many people in Venezuela don't recognize how dangerous a socialist or communist system really is. A few still believe absurd socialism is the solution to their difficulties while the corrupt regime maintains power.

After some reflection, I have determined that socialism, communism, and all their derived newcomers are definitely Utopia. It is impossible to justify those approaches unless they are cataloged as such. For example, take the Soviet Union, China, Vietnam, North Korea, and Cuba and the evaluation is that the original aspirations never were accomplished. The regimes changed all their principles and produced a monstrous society without human values that asphyxiates the population. The original aspirations were impossible to implement, they represented a Utopia never to be accomplished. I prefer anarchism, recognized as Utopia, rather than socialism and communism that consider themselves as the salvation of humanity without proof.

Ideologies provide a mechanism to understand the world, through beliefs and theories inspiration for political action gets developed. Ideas and ideologies influence political life and as a result, society gets tangible benefits. Sociopolitical systems represent the implementation of ideologies in society, they involve traditional political systems and social systems, as well as their interactions. Ideologies reflect a set of aspirations that must be supported by solid institutions. A social institution is a specific pattern of relations between members of a society, the relations between them, and the organizational structures that emerge out of their interaction. Aspirations are very important, the problem is that trying to implement them generates a chain reaction that usually backfires and produces unexpected and negative results. I am going to be using traditional names for ideologies and political systems, liberalism, socialism, communism, capitalism, and so on, to refer to the integrated view of sociopolitical systems.

Most of the time people sympathize with a particular ideology thinking that it presents a clear approach and that it is feasible. Most, if not all, ideologies present a superficial view of the world, and things are not so clear at all when they are applied in a particular situation. The worst cases of doubtful ideologies belong to the extremist ones, socialism, communism, absurd socialism, and anarchism. This book presents a mechanism to relate current ideologies and governments to aspirations or institutions that implement them. People and governments do not belong to one specific ideology but to a group of aspirations, associated with several ideologies, hoping to implement some through adequate institutions.

The book starts with a general understanding of societies, followed by a survey of sociopolitical systems organized in terms of the extremists (Communism, Socialism, Absurd Socialism, Anarchism), the moderates (Social Democracy, Liberalism) and the unprogressive (Conservatism, Capital Democracy, Fascism). Next, the sociopolitical framework is presented in terms of dimensions (Geopolitical, Societal, Globalization), characteristics, and features. It continues with the steps to define questions that can be organized according to social features, sociopolitical systems or the framework itself. An example evaluation of absurd socialism using the framework is presented.

Even though the book describes most sociopolitical ideologies and proposes a framework to compare different aspects, its inspiration was the failed absurd socialism doctrine. It is worthwhile to understand most sociopolitical ideologies to understand the place of absurd socialism. Knowing many ideologies allows a blueprint of comparison. Absurd socialism is going to be mentioned frequently in the following chapters, hopefully, readers around the world will be aware of the calamities caused by such a socialist wrongful approach.

The worst problem with ideologies is that implementing unfeasible aspirations provokes unexpected consequences affecting the lives of millions of people. Just implementing a misinterpreted human equality aspiration produces a chain reaction involving political, social, and economic difficulties. It is the job of citizens to react against such unfeasible aspirations and accept only realistic transformations of society.

My only concession is that ideologies are full of aspirations, people tend to sympathize with some, and get associated with those that present the most attractive aspirations. People should associate themselves with realistic aspirations instead of specific ideologies. The learning experience of this book is that people sympathize with a mixture of aspirations from several ideologies instead of just one. This suggests that ideologues should devise new ideologies integrating the positive aspects of existent ideologies instead of forcing people to accept obsolete ideologies containing many flaws.

# Introduction

The song "Emmenez Moi" by Charles Aznavour is a good analogy to symbolize why people prefer fantasy (socialism) to reality (capitalism, democracy). Fantasy makes people believe socialism is an acceptable alternative and reality makes them come down to earth. Let us check some of its lyrics:

> Emmenez-moi au bout de la terre
> Emmenez-moi au pays des merveilles
> Il me semble que la misère
> Serait moins pénible au soleil

The English translation would look like this:

> Take me along, a long way from here
> Take me along to a faraway shore
> When you're poor it's easy to bear
> With sunshine and soft summer air

People should know by now that going to places with better climates doesn't mean a better life, the sun, the heat, mosquitoes, poverty, ignorance, and crime abound and make them lose interest on a mythical warm and sunny life.

The political interpretation of the song would be:

> Take me along, a long way from capitalism
> Take me along to my dreamed socialism
> When you're poor it does not matter
> What type of political system you live in

Socialism plays with people's emotions proposing an unattainable better life. With socialism, as with warm paradises, the mirage of fantasy attracts many followers but reality brings them down. In the world, millions of people already understand that socialism is not a good alternative, once socialism takes to power the life of citizens worsens.

Socialism has been a failure in every opportunity their supporters have taken power, the proof is that today, even after several experiences demonstrating its non-viability, socialism penalizes not only the middle-classes but also those at the lower echelons of society. It is possible to demonstrate that socialism annihilates society because it is based on ideologies that do not understand humans, it forces on everybody a homogeneous view of the world, it projects a struggle against injustice in abstract terms, it suggests equality between humans without analyzing how humans behave, and it imposes the view of a fantastic human collectivization alternative. How can an idea which has failed so many times, in so many different variants and so many radically different settings, still be so popular?

Part of the reason is that socialists have long been very effective at distancing themselves from real-world examples of socialism in action. Socialist ideology stays on a pedestal, above the crude reality, meaning it is untouchable, it is perfect, it is mythical. Curiously, socialism is only supported in the abstract, in its idealistic form, it is not supported in any actual example of a socialist system in action. For example, the former Warsaw Pact countries, Maoist China, North Vietnam, North Korea, Cuba or Venezuela are abundantly criticized by socialists. Socialists have successfully distanced themselves from the over two dozen failed attempts to build a socialist society.

The most recent example of criticisms is Venezuela, there was an enthusiastic endorsement, followed by retroactive disowning. 'Venezuela-mania' started around 2005, and socialists claimed that this time would be completely different: '21st-century socialism' would be democratic bottom-up socialism, which had nothing in common with the authoritarian top-down socialism of ancient years. With Venezuela's descent into economic chaos, political unrest, and authoritarianism, Venezuela-mania began to fade not long after Chavez's death. After a period of silence, socialists began to explicitly dispute the socialist credentials of 'Chavismo.' Venezuela is joining a long list of countries that never were 'really' socialist.

Contemporary socialists take it as given that historical examples of socialist states never were really socialist. What is the difference between 'real socialism' and 'unreal socialism'? What is it about the versions of socialism practiced in so many failed states, that makes them all 'unreal'? What would they have had to change to move into the 'real socialism' category?

Real socialism, they claim, should be democratic socialism from below, socialism that democratizes economic life, and ensures that wealth and power are evenly shared. Real socialism puts ordinary working people – not technocrats, dictators or party elites – in charge. Contemporary socialists assume that the autocratic, stratified character of previous (and remaining) socialist regimes was deliberate. Socialist politicians could have established worker-run grassroots democracies, but chose not to do so. They could have established systems in which power would be vested in the hands of ordinary workers, but they did not want to. According to them, establishing an authentic workers' democracy, then, is merely a matter of political will. Contemporary socialists appear to assume that a democratized, participatory version of socialism would not just be more humane, but also economically more successful. Autocratic socialism failed, but democratic socialism would have worked just fine, in terms of economic performance.

Socialism is nonetheless here to stay and that is the reason why books like this one are so necessary. Most of us instinctively dislike the market economy. Anti-capitalism is a 'default opinion,' which comes naturally and effortlessly to us. Whatever its achievements, capitalism feels wrong. It is counter-intuitive. Even the most prominent free-market thinkers, such as F. A. Hayek, James Buchanan or Milton Friedman, did not start their careers as free-marketeers.

But while socialism cannot be attained, it can be easily projected onto actually existing societies, by being so abstract and nebulous. For the same reason, that projection can just as easily be ended. This is what Western intellectuals have been doing for almost a century. Thirty years ago, Hayek wrote about 'intellectuals' vain search for a truly socialist community, which results in the idealization of, and then disillusionment with, a seemingly endless string of "utopias." Since then, this string has only grown longer. [Hayek 1994]

Socialism has always been portrayed as the solution to all democracy and capitalism problems. Socialists use to criticize the mistakes of democracy and capitalism suggesting a new society where people should not be egotistic, sharing resources for the good of the people. One of the big defects of socialism is not knowing how wealth is produced, socialists run against private property and towards the supremacy of the state, thinking it is a good idea to run a centralized society. Additionally, socialists count with the support of part of the population that believes that work and effort are not necessary to progress in society.

The reception of socialist experiments usually follows a three-stage pattern. Socialist experiments often go through an initial honeymoon period, during which they have, or at least seem to have some initial successes, and during which their international standing is relatively high. This honeymoon never lasts long. At some point, the model's failures become more widely known in the West, and the respective country's international standing deteriorates. Western socialists shoot the messenger; they act as if the critics of the system were somehow responsible for the system's failure. Outside forces and/or members of the old, discredited elites are accused of 'undermining' socialism. But there comes a point when the system's failures become so obvious, and its international reputation becomes so irreparably damaged, that defending it becomes a lost cause. This is the third and final stage. Small sects of true believers continue to defend the system, but mainstream intellectuals fall silent on the issue.

The debate about whether socialism is a good idea that has just been distorted and/or badly implemented in practice, or whether the idea itself is flawed and could not have turned out very differently, is not new. It is fair to say that for now, proponents of the former view have won the debate. Where that question is explicitly asked in surveys, the results speak for themselves. Around four out of five East Germans, but also nearly every other West German, agree with the statement that socialism is a good idea that has just been badly implemented.

This book proposes a framework to evaluate sociopolitical systems, it is open to several applications and different circumstances, oriented to countries, regions or continents. It can be applied to ideologies, countries, and regions. It can be used to evaluate the performance of a government, to compare different sociopolitical systems, to describe a particular sociopolitical system and many more viewpoints. The framework starts with an understanding of the Geopolitical dimension surrounding countries and regions, it follows with the Societal dimension at the local level and concludes with the Globalization dimension that involves a worldwide view. Each dimension can be decomposed into characteristics and features. A series of questions define the direction of the evaluation towards ideologies, governments, countries, or regions; some of the questions are presented in the form of trivia. The population to be interviewed includes the common citizen, selected sections of the population or politicians experts on the matter at hand.

The book is divided into three parts. The first part presents an introduction about the general characteristics of societies, followed by a description of the principal sociopolitical systems organized on the extremists, the moderate, and the unprogressive. The extremists include socialism, communism, absurd socialism, and anarchism. The moderate, liberalism and social democracy. The unprogressive, conservatism. capital democracy, and fascism. Notice that the traditional view of left, center, and right has been modestly rearranged.

The second part of the book presents the sociopolitical framework. It is composed of three dimensions, geopolitical, societal, and globalization. The geopolitical dimension includes geographical, environmental, ethnic or political conflict, personal and national idiosyncrasies, and political development. The societal dimension presents the local view of the political system, the economic system, the personal influence, the social influence, the ideological sphere, and the pragmatical sphere. Finally, the globalization dimension includes political, economic, and social considerations at the worldwide level, international trade considerations, international organizations, the effects of global environmental changes, and populism and its global effect.

# Chapter 1: Society

Early humans lived in relative isolation, they lived in bands and knew each other, including nearby groups. Each band hunted, gathered and manufactured almost everything it required, from meat to medicine, from sandals to sorcery. Different band members may have specialized in different tasks, but they shared their goods and services through an economy of favors and obligations. One villager may have been particularly adept at making shoes, another at dispensing medical care, so villagers knew where to turn when barefoot or sick. A piece of meat given for free would carry with it the assumption of reciprocity – say, free medical assistance or a pair of shoes. [Harari 2014]

Modern humans live in relative and limited companies. People live surrounded by a limited amount of companions, it is not true that people interact with thousands of other people. In a society, the activities are organized, that is what makes the difference. People still live in bands but organized according to required productive or non-productive activities. According to sociologists, a society is a group of people with common territory, interaction, and culture having diversity and using the principle of division of labor to organize themselves.

Territory: Most countries have formal boundaries and territory that the world recognizes as theirs. However, a society's boundaries don't have to be geopolitical borders, such as the one between the United States and Canada. Instead, members of society, as well as nonmembers, must recognize particular land as belonging to that society.

Interaction: Members of society must come in contact with one another. If a group of people within a country has no regular contact with another group, those groups cannot be considered part of the same society. Geographic distance and language barriers can separate societies within a country.

Culture: People in a society share aspects of their culture such as language or beliefs. Culture refers to the language, values, beliefs, behavior, and material objects that constitute a people's way of life. It is a defining element of society.

Diversity: Diversity is an important characteristic of any society and it requires an organization to implement. Human societies are not just groups of cooperating people: they are communities of persons, who live in mutual judgment, organizing their world in terms of moral concepts that arguably have no place in the thoughts of some other primates.

Division of Labor: Division of labor is a vital factor in the maintenance of human societies. It is a concept that requires organization, clustering of groups of people to perform specific activities. It also gives people the time to participate in non-productive activities instead of living only for survival.

Society is organized along with social groups which consist of several people who interact, exchange, and identify with one another. A society is composed of several groups interacting through the group's representatives or individuals. The only characteristic of a society that we can be certain of is its incessant transformation. People have become used to changes, and most of us think about the social order as something flexible, which can be engineered and improved at will.

Any attempt to define the characteristics of modern societies is akin to defining the color of a chameleon, the society changes over time influenced by knowledge, beliefs, and needs. There are many ways to characterize a society, thus, a set of variations upon the theme are presented:

- Society consists of individuals. (Liberalism, Anarchism)
- Society does not consist of individuals; it expresses the sum of connections and relationships in which individuals find themselves. (Communism, Socialism)
- Society does not consist of individuals; it does not even express the sum of connections and relationships in which individuals find themselves: it is the expression of the connections and relationships which emerged from a past that is no longer present and have to be conveyed to a future that is not yet present. (Conservatism)

Imagined Communities

An imagined community is a community of people who don't really know each other but imagine that they do. Such communities are not a novel invention. Kingdoms, empires, and churches functioned for millennia as imagined communities. Like the nuclear family, the community could not completely disappear from our world without any emotional replacement. Markets and states do so by fostering 'imagined communities' that contain millions of strangers, and which are tailored to national and commercial needs. Markets and states today provide most of the material needs once provided by communities, including tribal bonds.

The two most important examples for the rise of such imagined communities are the nation and the consumer band. The nation is the imagined community of the state. The consumer band is the imagined community of the market. Both are imagined communities because it is impossible for all customers in a market or for all members of a nation really to know one another the way villagers knew one another in the past. Consumerism and nationalism work extra hours to make people imagine that millions of strangers belong to the same community, that they all have a common past, common interests, and a common future. This isn't a lie. It's imagination. Like money, limited liability companies and human rights, nations and consumer bands are inter-subjective realities. Imagined communities exist only in people's collective imagination, yet their power is immense. [Harari 2014]

The nation does its best to hide its imagined character. Most nations argue that they are a natural and eternal entity, created in some primordial epoch by mixing the soil of the motherland with the blood of the people. Yet such claims are usually exaggerated. Nations existed in the distant past, but their importance was much smaller than today because the importance of the state was much smaller. A resident of medieval Nuremberg might have felt some loyalty towards the German nation, but she felt far more loyal towards her family and the local community, which took care of most of her needs. Moreover, whatever importance ancient nations may have had, few of them survived. Most existing nations evolved only after the Industrial Revolution. [Harari 2014]

<u>To Live in Society</u>

Are current societies an aberration for grouping human beings? Are there any other alternatives to associate them? These are important questions that philosophers and sociologists should answer. Living in a society, people have rights and deserts, and sustainability becomes an important consideration to thrive. People want to have opportunities to make a living and contribute to the rest of the population. Failed states become the enemy of the citizen, they become the burden for a satisfactory life.

Sociologists consider many countries as Pluralistic Societies, meaning they are built up with many ethnic groups. As societies modernize, they attract people from countries where there may be economic hardship, political unrest, or religious persecution. Since the industrialized countries of the West were the first to modernize, these countries tend to be more pluralistic than countries in other parts of the world. Immigrants arrived in waves from Europe and Asia and helped create the pluralism that makes these countries unique.

Living together in society has advantages and disadvantages. Some advantages are related to the availability of multiple services, finding the easy company, having more producers of goods, and the sharing of common resources. Some disadvantages are obeying rules which conflict with the freedom of the individual, paying taxes, the lack of privacy, the increase of competition, and the increase of pollution. Good and bad attitudes towards society are subjective and difficult to identify.

Rules, Laws, Rights, and Deserts

It is important for everyone to follow rules and obey laws. Laws create fairness and protect the health and safety of all individuals. They protect our freedom and democracy. We must obey laws or pay consequences. Good citizenship for adults also means serving on political activities, jury duty, and paying taxes. When rules and laws are unfair, a good citizen must collaborate to reverse those rules or laws.

Rule of law and rule by law are totally different concepts. The rule of law refers to a state of constitutionalism where the law (nor parliament) is supreme and where all government's power is subject to the law. Rule by law means the opposite. It refers to a police state in which the government invokes the law (indeed creates law) to "justify" excessive use of government force. During a period of tyranny, leaders need to be visionaries, with prophetic voices, who are able to rise above the present crisis and take a principled stand against the rule by law.

When we refer to rights, deserts, and duties; what we owe to each other; and such fundamentals ideas as freedom, justice, and impartial spectator, we are making use (directly or indirectly) of the concept of person, which provides the shared perspective from which we address virtually all such issues. Human communities are communities of persons, and this is the point of agreement from which our disagreements begin. That is due which is deserved, and that is deserved which may be rightly and justly inflicted. In short, punishment is a moral idea, to be unpacked in terms of those concepts of justice, desert, and responsibility that Nietzsche was supposed to be explaining. [Scruton 2017]

## Societal Sphere

People need to be fed, accommodated, and cared for according to their needs and contributions to society. Each age has different requirements to contribute to society; infants don't contribute, they demand a lot; mature people contribute the most; senior people contribute and demand sparingly. Health issues get a say regarding contribution, some people are not in a good physical or mental condition to participate, they deserve some consideration. Ideally, everybody would benefit of the activities performed by others in a society, however, some benefit more than others.

A society requires productive human activities to make it viable. In general, it requires economic, educational, technological, social and cultural activities to serve the needs of the people. The organization is the key for a society to thrive because humans are used to live in very small groups, primarily the family, and not used to live in complex communities. How to organize a society depends on the beliefs, needs, and desires of the population. People can organize around the same interests, same objectives, same locations, same political ideas, same religion, and so on. It is unnatural to organize everybody around the same criteria because people are different and get motivated by specific activities. Private enterprises, public institutions, non-profit organizations, volunteer organizations, clubs, associations, and so on, are examples of organizations that help citizens to pursue their dreams.

Opportunities

The most important activity in a society is the economy. People need jobs to make a living. Society must guarantee opportunities to find a job, get accommodation, and nourish the families of every citizen, as well as to receive the best services regarding health, education, and recreation. Depending on the society, the opportunities and services would be supplied by multiple organizations including the government. The government must define the policies to guarantee the participation of the whole population and the liberation of the forces of the free-market.

Entrepreneurship

Entrepreneurship is the act of creating businesses while building and scaling it to transform the world by solving big problems like initiating social change, creating innovative products or presenting a new life-changing solution, and in most cases generating a profit. Entrepreneurship is what people do to take their career and dreams into their hands and lead it in the direction of their own choice. It's about building a life on your own terms. Entrepreneurs are able to take the first step into making the world a better place, for everyone in it.

Manufacturing

Most industries would make a product with tools and/or machines by effecting the chemical, mechanical, or physical transformation of materials, substances, or components, usually repeatedly and on a large scale with a division of labor. Manufactured items are often different from other similar goods in one or more aspects, and are sold commonly using a particular brand name.

Primary industries involve getting raw materials, e.g., mining, farming, and fishing, available to the consumers. Many of these industries would come from the private sector whilst others are public enterprises. The government has a role in regulating or defining the constraints on these industries. Agriculture, Fisheries and Oceans, Natural Resources are institutions that belong to the government to help the entrepreneurs.

Secondary industries involve the process of manufacturing, e.g., making cars and appliances out of steel and electronics. Most of them come from the private sector and others from public industries financed by the state.

Services

Many enterprises are founded to help or do work for someone else. These are tertiary industries providing services, e.g., teaching and nursing. In this area, there is room for private enterprise and public enterprise. Banks and Financial Businesses come from the private sector in most cases. However, the government has a role in defining the characteristics of these enterprises. Normally, governments are primarily related to National Defense, Public Safety, Public Education, Public Welfare, and Health Care.

There are quaternary industries involving research and development, e.g., Information Technology, Artificial Intelligence, Auditing, Accounting, and Management services. Many of these enterprises come from the private sector with some influence from the government.

There are several services supplying a public need such as transport, communications, or utilities such as electricity and water that can be administered by the private sector but in many cases, it is the government who takes them under its umbrella.

### Infrastructure Management

Governments have some implications on services such as Public Land Administration, Administering Utilities, Establishing Post Offices, and Building Roads. They can hire the private sector or any other type of organization to run or complete the projects.

### Technology

The application of scientific knowledge for practical purposes, especially in industry, including the branch of knowledge dealing with engineering or applied sciences, and machinery and equipment. For example, advances in computer technology are helpful to develop enterprises that aim at highly sophisticated technologies. The private sector has some participation in this area and the government can create opportunities for these developments.

### Social Activities

Any society needs to develop social activities such as Arts, Literature, Music, Culture, and Folklore. There is room for many organizations to participate in this area, including volunteers, non-profit organizations, the private sector, and the government.

### Recreational Activities

Humans need recreational activities to overpass boredom and combat routine. A healthy mind requires some time to relax performing an amusing activity. Volunteers, non-profit organizations, private enterprises, and the government can participate in many events.

### Sport Activities

It is well known that a 'healthy mind in a healthy body' guarantees productivity. People need to participate in physical activities to improve their overall health patterns. Gymnastics, Sports, and Trail activities must be readily available to the whole population. The government has a role to increase opportunities for participation. Volunteers, the private sector, and non-profit organizations are also able to contribute in this area.

## Culture

After the Agricultural Revolution, human societies grew ever larger and more complex, while the imagined constructs sustaining the social order also became more elaborate. Myths and fictions accustomed people, nearly from the moment of birth, to think in certain ways, to behave in accordance with certain standards, to want certain things, and to observe certain rules. They thereby created artificial instincts that enabled millions of strangers to cooperate effectively. This network of artificial instincts is called culture. [Harari 2014]

Culture is the means by which society connects its members with the problems of being human. We already know what some of those problems are – death, loneliness, and significance. These are problems that everyone has, of course, regardless of income or educational status. The only choice we have is whether we want to try to face them or ignore them. [Huenemann 2009]

Can culture alter human behavior to approach altruistic perfection? The answer is no. "If it were all so simple!" Aleksandr Solzhenitsyn wrote in the Gulag Archipelago. "If only there were evil people somewhere insidiously committing evil deeds, and it was only necessary to separate them from the rest of us and destroy them, society would become a paradise. But the line dividing good and evil cuts through the heart of every human being. And who is willing to destroy a piece of his own heart?" [Wilson 1978]

Every culture has its traditional beliefs, norms, and values, but these are in constant flux. The culture may transform itself in response to changes in its environment or through interaction with neighboring cultures. But cultures also undergo transitions due to their own internal dynamics. Even a completely isolated culture existing in an ecologically stable environment cannot avoid change. Unlike the laws of physics, which are free of inconsistencies, every man-made order is packed with internal contradictions. Cultures are constantly trying to reconcile these contradictions, and this process fuels change. [Harari 2014]

A cultural idea – such as belief in Christian heaven above the clouds or Communist paradise here on earth – can compel a human to dedicate his or her life to spreading that idea, even at the price of death. The human dies, but the idea spreads. According to this approach, cultures are not conspiracies concocted by some people in order to take advantage of others (as Marxists tend to think). Rather, cultures are mental parasites that emerge accidentally, and thereafter take advantage of all people infected by them. [Harari 2014]

## Citizenry

It is interesting to highlight that people would like to do whatever they want without any interference. People do not like to be accountable for what they do. Maturity makes people understand that anything they do is observed by others and there are consequences for their decisions.

Immature people always complain about this constant interference on their own affairs, they have not yet reached the enlightened stage. Society should help prepare those people to adapt to possible interference and help regulate their behavior towards better comprehension and empathy.

A citizen is a member of a community, state, or nation that contributes to the prosperity and well-being of the population. Citizens have rights and responsibilities. For example, family members have to take care of each other, students in a classroom of a school must be learning and contributing, and members of a community, state, and nation must contribute with their good behavior and effort to produce the goods and services necessaries for survival. Being a good citizen means:
- Following rules and laws
- Being responsible and respectful
- Helping others

A good citizen must contribute to the well-being of the society and must be vigilant to the injustices committed by the state. Citizens must know what procedures to follow to claim for their rights. When governments are not performing, citizens must elevate their voices to facilitate an environment for change. And citizens must cooperate with their peers or neighbors who are in distress because of difficulties or injustices.

## Natural and Imagined Order

The first millennium BC witnessed the appearance of three potentially universal orders, whose devotees could for the first time imagine the entire world and the entire human race as a single unit governed by a single set of laws. Everyone was 'us,' at least potentially. There was no longer 'them.' The first universal order to appear was economic: the monetary order. The second universal order was political: the imperial order. The third universal order was religious: the order of universal religions such as Buddhism, Christianity, and Islam. [Harari 2014]

A natural order is a stable order. There is no chance that gravity will cease to function tomorrow, even if people stop believing in it. In contrast, an imagined order is always in danger of collapse, because it depends upon myths, and myths vanish once people stop believing in them. In order to safeguard an imagined order, continuous and strenuous efforts are imperative. Some of these efforts take the shape of violence and coercion. Armies, police forces, courts, and prisons are ceaselessly at work forcing people to act in accordance with the imagined order. If an ancient

Babylonian blinded his neighbor, some violence was usually necessary in order to enforce the law of 'an eye for an eye.' When, in 1860, a majority of American citizens concluded that African slaves are human beings and must, therefore, enjoy the right of liberty, it took a bloody civil war to make the southern states acquiesce. [Harari 2014]

However, an imagined order cannot be sustained by violence alone. It requires some true believers as well. Prince Talleyrand, who began his chameleon-like career under Louis XVI, later served the revolutionary and Napoleonic regimes, and switched loyalties in time to end his days working for the restored monarchy, summed up decades of governmental experience by saying that 'You can do many things with bayonets, but it is rather uncomfortable to sit on them.' A single priest often does the work of a hundred soldiers far more cheaply and effectively. Moreover, no matter how efficient bayonets are, somebody must wield them. Why should the soldiers, prison guards, judges, and police maintain an imagined order in which they do not believe? Of all human collective activities, the one most difficult to organize is violence. To say that social order is maintained by military force immediately raises the question: what maintains the military order? It is impossible to organize an army solely by coercion. At least some of the commanders and soldiers must truly believe in something, be it God, honor, motherland, manhood or money. [Harari 2014]

## Sociopolitical Systems

Ideologies include communism, socialism, liberalism, libertarianism, populism, religious fundamentalism, ecologist, feminism, humanism, conservatism, and fascism. As can be seen, some labels are repeated for different purposes; communism, socialism, and capitalism are often interpreted as political or economic systems. It is not the purpose of this book to unravel the distortions of so many ideologies.

Some authors identify political systems such as Authoritarian, Libertarian, Totalitarian, Oligarchy, Plutocracy, Monarchy, Republic, Communism, and Democracy. Also, other authors identify economic systems such as traditional economies, command economies, free-market economies, and mixed economies. Additionally, the economic system is associated to communism, socialism, and capitalism.

I am using the more traditional names for political systems to designate sociopolitical systems. Sociopolitical systems are systems composed of both social elements and political elements as well as their interactions. Understanding many issues of society requires an understanding of social systems and the political realm. Processes of change originate in society and over time galvanize into political movements. Most sociopolitical systems never have been implemented as originally conceived by their ideology, they are adapted solutions involving a mixture of approaches according to the idiosyncrasies of different cultures. Among many alternate sociopolitical systems, socialism, communism, liberalism, conservatism, fascism, ecologist, populism, anarchism, humanism, capitalism and democracy, represent a fair sample.

In the next chapters, I am proposing a framework to structure and evaluate sociopolitical systems. The sociopolitical framework is composed of three dimensions: geopolitical, societal, and global economic. Each dimension is organized with several characteristics. The geopolitical dimension includes geographical, physical resources, and environmental considerations; as well as, ethnic, linguistic, religious, cultural, and regional composition of the population. The societal dimension includes the political system, the economic system, the personal influence, the social influence, the ideological sphere, and the pragmatical sphere. The global economic dimension includes primarily economical considerations worldwide, the historical evolution of those factors, and the expectations for the future. Each characteristic is decomposed into features such as institutional structure, social measures to help the population, administrator's honesty, corruption, equality, freedom of the people, freedoms of markets and speech, human rights considerations, and so on.

Traditional political systems based on known classification schemes look like this:

The Left: Communism and Socialism
The Center: Social Democracy and Liberalism
The Right: Conservatism and Capital Democracy
The Unclassified: Absurd Socialism, Anarchism, and Fascism

I am proposing the following taxonomy for sociopolitical systems in the book:

The Extremists: Communism, Socialism, Absurd Socialism, and Anarchism
The Moderates: Social Democracy and Liberalism
The Unprogressive: Conservatism, Capital Democracy, and Fascism

## Chapter 2: The Extremists

Humans can create whatever sociopolitical system they want. The problem is not just to create, anybody can, the problem is to create a viable approach. Socialists argue that if humans have created capitalism, humans can create socialism, however, the difference is that capitalism has existed for hundreds of years and socialism has no proof of viability. Is socialism the right solution? Socialism has already been implemented in many countries, and all those experiences have had disastrous consequences. Clear examples are the Soviet Union, China, North Korea, Cuba, and Venezuela.

The extremists want to change the world without analyzing what happened over seventy thousand years. They believe everything up to now is bad and they have to change it. The evolution of humans tells a reality that is impossible to erase but the extremists want to distort that history. In this respect, I agree with conservatives that history tells us part of the story. Extremists should start by recognizing the evolution of humans first and then decide what can be improved.

The song by Aznavour tells us a bit about this emotional human paradigm, always willing to change the world without analyzing what has happened over the years.

> Ils viennent du bout du monde
> Apportant avec eux des idées vagabondes aux reflets de ciels bleus
> De mirages
> Traînant un parfum poivré de pays inconnus
> Et d'éternels étés où l'on vit presque nus
> Sur les plages

The English translation looks like this:

> They come from the end of the world
> Carrying with them vagabond ideas to reflect the blue skies
> Of mirages
> Trailing a peppery perfume of countries unknown
> And eternal summers where one lives almost nude
> On the beaches

The extremists represent a mirage, everything looks so good but misery is hidden behind the invented paradise.

## Socialism and Communism

The criterion of socialism and communism – the standard by which it judges entities, institutions, and events – is that debts are owed to the self as constituted by society. Socialism and communism interpret that we are not mere selves, but selves in a situation, in a society – and that it is to these selves that a debt is owed. The self is no longer merely selfish, but self-constituted by its existence in society. If the criterion of liberalism is that debts are owed to the self, the individual, then socialists and communists have a much more complicated task, which is to explain the significance for politics of the suggestion that the self is socially constituted because it is an abstract concept that equalizes the whole society.

The real truth is that socialism and communism have no arguments to demonstrate they are better approaches than capitalism and democracy. It has been tried in the Soviet Union, Yugoslavia, Albania, Poland, Vietnam, Bulgaria, Romania, Czechoslovakia, North Korea, Hungary, China, East Germany, Cuba, Tanzania, Benin, Laos, Algeria, South Yemen, Somalia, the Congo, Ethiopia, Cambodia, Mozambique, Angola, Nicaragua, and Venezuela, among other countries. All their arguments are taken from unreal views of the world: people cooperating willingly without prejudices, the eternal undefined total equality among human beings, the injustice to the poor and the proletariat.

A classless society based on cooperation and equality can't be built following the premises of socialism and communism. Equality considerations should be defined around society requirements and not on individual differences, humans are unique and diverse, they deserve independence. The case for equal educational opportunities, equal pay for the same abilities and performance, independent of sex or race, are examples of society's requirements on equality. Current socialist and communist regimes have demonstrated that after so many years in power, the problems of the people become even worse in those regimes.

Communism and Socialism are the same approaches, they have been tried many times with different interpretations and unsuccessful results. A pure capitalistic system never has been tried either, capitalism is primarily an economic system working usually under democracy. Only four sociopolitical systems have had some tangible results in the world, Liberalism, Conservatism, Social Democracy, and Capital Democracy. Absurd Socialism is a wrongful interpretation of socialism with fascistic and anarchistic inclinations. Many other ideologies can be associated with sociopolitical systems, such as Ecologism, Feminism, Religious Fundamentalism, Populism, and Humanism. However, they are in one way or another integrated into the main approaches. For example, humanism demonstrates a case of a possible ideology but is integrated into any sociopolitical system, human considerations have to be included in all.

## **Communism**

The communist political order is structured according to the most fundamental debt owed to the social self, an invention of communists to justify any state wrongdoings against individuals. The pure thought of communism is that only the social self has infinite credit, everything else is an instrument of that credit, and it is debt about this credit. Worst of all, communists demonstrated their hate against capitalism by alienating any individual entrepreneurship. Communists seek to shift the balance between individualism and collectivization indicating that the right of the individual is subject to the right of the rest of the society, and the authority of the party-state is in charge of limiting individual possibilities. Communism eliminates differences making everybody equal to the rest, it is a trap to look fair and just to everybody but in the end, people get minimum benefit from this aspiration.

Communism is a political and economic system where the state represents the population and decides for them, it uses the communist party as the instrument to justify all their decisions. In a communist system, the community must obey these decisions independently of how logical they are because punishment is its way of life. In the communist economic system, the party-state owns the factors of production and manages all resources, it defines what people eat, where they live and work, and how many hours of rest they deserve. The means of production are labor, entrepreneurship, capital goods, and natural resources.

The party-state owns all businesses on behalf of the workers, which in effect means the government has a monopoly of productive activities. The government rewards company managers for meeting the targets detailed in the plans. In communism, central planners replace the forces of competition and the laws of supply and demand that operate in a market economy, as well as the customs that guide the economy.

Communism is inspired by Marxism and its concepts of alienation and class struggle. Its historical view is related to the notion of historical materialism expressed by Marx. Alienation, according to communists, refers to the unjust nature of worker's treatment in capitalism which prevents them to develop skills, talents, and understanding. Workers are alienated by producing goods they don't need and benefit unknown capitalists. In capitalism, worker's labor becomes just another commodity to be sold at the best offer. Class, on the other side, is defined in terms of economic power, that of the Bourgeoisie and that of the Proletariat. The bourgeoisie exploits the proletariat creating class struggle and conflict.

<u>The Communist Party</u>

The communist party is the most powerful institution of communism. To function, it follows the principle of "democratic centralism" where alternatives are discussed at all levels and the final decision is taken by the party-state leadership. People must follow strictly the decisions emanated from the leadership, any disobeying is severely penalized. Democratic centralism is associated with central planning and a command economy. The leaders create a plan that outlines their choices, and it is executed through laws, regulations, and directives. The goal of the plan is to give to "each according to his need." The central plan also seeks to increase the nation's economic growth, secure national defense, and maintain infrastructure.

In communist experiences, democratic centralism may appear to be straight forward convenient. It is described as something facilitating open discussion and then unity around the final policy. In practice, it is highly centralized and dictatorial, providing leaders with a paramilitary structure. Any criticism of the leadership and its prevailing policy can be denounced as activities to help the enemy class which is always menacing the status quo. In 'democratic centralism' lower bodies are subordinate and submit to the higher organs, and informal contacts across the base of the party or members are outlawed as 'factional activity.'

In addition to the process of democratic centralism, there are professional bureaucracies inside the party, staffed by a narrow group, in reality, appointed by the leadership from the top; these professionals are selected according to their loyalty to the party. Party practice amounts to a militaristic discipline and the execution of orders is mandatory. Any type of internal elections amounts to the nomination by the leadership, a reduced group. The promotion of staff also depends on the leadership, anybody being submissive and obedient can reach high positions. In the end, it is a hierarchy that mimics 'bourgeois society,' with low power of decision and the elected representatives (parliamentarians, for example) will be low in the structure and under the purview of superiors at the party.

Communist countries use to have free health care, education, and other services which usually have low to average quality. It is impossible to provide better services to a community when the resources are limited and diluted to help everybody. The only way for a communist country to prosper would be by integrating with a capitalist economy, such as the case of capitalism integration in China. Another possibility is the availability of natural resources providing a constant flux of funds to finance the huge cost of providing free services to the population, such as the case of Venezuela. Even with unlimited oil income, Venezuela was incapable of sustaining free services programs; it is the only case in the world of a country that could not maintain its basic services because of the huge amount of corruption.

Marxism

Marx said, "From each according to his ability, to each according to his need." This meant that people would work at what they love and do well, happily contributing with their skills for the good of all, and the economy would prosper because they would work harder than in capitalism. Marx was mistaken because he did not take into consideration human nature; humans are diverse and imperfect, prone to random behavior. Read the book 'Human Nature against Socialism' [Boloix 2019b] describing why communism doesn't take into consideration human nature.

A summary of what a communist system represents can be found in Marx and Engels ten goals of Communism:
1. Abolition of property in land and application of all rents of land to public purposes.
2. A heavy progressive or graduated income tax.
3. Abolition of all rights of inheritance.
4. Confiscation of the property of all emigrants and rebels.
5. Centralization of credit in the hands of the state, by means of a national bank with State capital and an exclusive monopoly.
6. Centralization of the means of communication and transport in the hands of the State.
7. Extension of factories and instruments of production owned by the State; the bringing into cultivation of waste-lands, and the improvement of the soil generally under a common plan.

8. Equal liability of all to work. Establishment of industrial armies, especially for agriculture.
9. Combination of agriculture with manufacturing industries; gradual abolition of all the distinction between town and country by a more equable distribution of the populace over the country.
10. Free education for all children in public schools. Abolition of children's factory labor in its present form. Combination of education with industrial production, etc.

Communism as many other leftists approaches never has been implemented in its aspiration scope. Countries calling themselves communists are in their imagined stages of constructing communism, without admitting that communism is unattainable. For communists, fifty years of no results mean 50 more years to keep trying and the cycle repeats itself over and over. It is a pity that communism still exists in some countries, the misery suffered by the population is unacceptable; it is preferable to die standing, fighting communism than to accept hopelessly a despairing future.

<u>Classless Society</u>

Karl Marx formed his idea of class struggle in the 1840s, it is the basis of much economic analysis, political debate, and social organizing efforts today. Marxism's concepts of alienation and class struggle are in the center of some political ideologies. Class was defined in terms of economic power, that of the Bourgeoisie and that of the Proletariat. The bourgeoisie exploits the proletariat creating class struggle and conflict.

Marx "theorized" a classless society, where the interests of wealth accumulation and labor exploitation no longer constituted the objectives of administering the means of production. Marx perceived a higher level of civilization by introducing more justice but at the same time drew upon egalitarian societies of hunter-gatherers as the warrant for how a classless society could be possible. According to communists, the resulting society, to be attained in an undefined future, would be stateless as well as classless and the production geared to human needs instead of capitalist's greed. This final stage would become a paradise on earth.

A society involves how a group of people utilizes, manipulate, and organize the means of production. Archaeology allows the understanding of how early humans organized themselves, how early humans maintained their survival without technology, knowledge, language, or order. Early humans lived primarily in woodlands, where fruits and nuts could be scavenged with easy, hunting was a rare practice. In a society characterized by hunting and gathering, there was not much room for other human relations to form. Everyone was focused on hunting/scavenging enough food to stay alive and moving in the right direction to meet shelter before nightfall. In this type of world, all were responsible for their survival.

However, no one was completely alone: families of a few dozen humans roamed their respective geographies in groups, working together to hunt superior predators, scavenge resources, traverse new terrains, and settle down. These "societies" worked together for the general welfare of the group and saw each other as nothing more than human beings. This familial unit - according to an overwhelming majority of historians - was the only instance of an egalitarian society in human history.

## **Socialism**

The socialist political order is almost a carbon copy of communism, it is structured according to the most fundamental debt owed to the social self, an invention of socialists to justify their totalitarian approach against the population. In socialism only the social self has infinite credit, everything else is an instrument of that credit, and it is debt about this credit. For socialists, history has only one meaning, the exploitation of the workers by capitalists. In socialism, the party has a lesser impact on the decisions affecting the population, it is the state the one that decides for the people. Socialism also promotes the influence of the strong man, a charismatic character that monopolizes the attention of the masses. The similarities between socialism and communism are so amazing that it is difficult to distinguish one experience from the other. Most communist countries were created using the military path, and the power of the party was fundamental. Most socialist countries followed a concealed process using existing democratic institutions to undermine the constitution and twist democracy towards socialism.

Over the past hundred years, there have been more than two dozen attempts to build a communist or socialist society. All these attempts to build the 'dreamed' society have ended with varying degrees of failure. There has to be a reason why those attempts did not build an acceptable society, all of them becoming tyrannies; the root cause is the ideology.

It is important to point out that when socialism is used under the democratic umbrella, for example, social democracy, it is feasible to benefit the population and still maintain the possibility of correcting mistakes. The welfare system is around all of us, most democratic and capitalistic systems also allow benefits to the population. Social programs have been available in most capitalistic countries. Therefore, capital democracy and social democracy are two approaches that complement each other and differ basically on the level of welfare or entrepreneurship incorporated.

However, when socialism takes power using democratic institutions, it starts following the route towards autocracy and things begin to change for the worst. Socialist regimes have no other choice than dictatorship because they must force the population to accept unpopular measures. In authoritarian socialistic regimes, the population has no say on public policy; decisions are taken, overwhelmingly, by the state, party in power or the dictator in charge. Therefore, beware of socialism taking power using democratic institutions, it is just a facade to totalitarianism.

Socialism is a state-based society and its argument rests on the assumption that the public sector is driven by altruistic motives, and that therefore, whatever is done by the state is done with 'the common good' in mind. This is the ultimate socialist assumption that is debatable. It has been demonstrated time and again that self-interest behavior exists in the public political sphere as much as anywhere else. For example, senior civil servants trying to expand their budgets and their remit to improve their prestige; rent-seeking by special interest groups; political privileges; 'jobs for the boys' tendencies, and so on.

Socialism is primarily characterized by a populist approach confronting social classes, usually 'The People' against 'The Elite.' The People, also known as 'working people' or 'ordinary people,' are a homogeneous group with common, and easily identifiable, economic interests and preferences. There is, therefore, a very easy solution to most of the economic and social problems of society, get rid of current Elites, and replace them with champions of The People. This is a simplified version of Marxist class theory, in which social classes, not individuals or more specific groups, form the main unit of analysis. However, social class is just one dividing line among many. On virtually all the important issues of our time (emigration, immigration, the housing crisis, 'austerity,' welfare reform, etc.), the dividing lines run across social classes, not between them.

Additionally, socialism has always led, and must always lead, to an extreme concentration of power. By abolishing market signals and competition, socialist economies deprive themselves of vast amounts of knowledge. But they also deprive themselves of something else, an extremely effective way of dispersing and limiting power. As Hayek said, 'the competitive system is the only system designed to minimize the power exercised by man over man.' In a socialist economy, the state becomes the main employer, the main landlord, the main supplier of goods and services, the main financial intermediary, etc.

'Extending democracy to the economy' and 'democratizing every aspect of society' are nice soundbites, but what does that mean in practice? What would an institutional framework which fulfills those aspirations look like? What is the impact of implementing certain aspiration? Socialism is an ideology of radical democracy, it seeks to empower civil society, using the supreme power of the state, to allow participation in the decisions that affect our lives. And a huge state bureaucracy can be just as alienating and undemocratic as corporate boardrooms, so we need to think hard about the new forms that social ownership could take.

It is better to look for international best practice on a policy-area-by-policy-area basis, we can always find at least one decent real-world example in any given area. Learning from international practice in each policy area is, of course, easier said than done. But searching for solutions in this way would certainly be more fruitful than chasing after the next socialist utopia. Motivated reasoning is a powerful force. We can always find an excuse to protect a cherished belief if we look hard enough. And we can always find flaws in ideas that we dislike if we look for mistakes.

The socialist ideology emerged with force in the mid-19th century as a reaction to the rise of early capitalism and the economic inequality it induced. However, Christians were the first promoters of socialist ideas, which by themselves are not bad, but placed into the context of society are rather harmful. Common possessions were looked upon by many of the first Christians as an ideal to be aimed at. The disciples of Jesus 'were of one heart and one soul: neither said any of them that ought of the things which he possessed was his own, but they had all things common.' [Brown 2009]

Throughout history, socialists have disagreed over how a change should come about. Some promote a change through revolution whereas others look for a parliamentary solution. The choice of revolution, even if possible, is discouraged in most societies. The tendency is to use democratic institutions to reach power and use that power to twist constitutions according to the socialist's desires, looking to perpetuate in power and force the population to accept the newly created status quo.

It is a common misunderstanding that socialism failed because a socialist economy expects people to work primarily for the common good rather than their good and that most people were not altruistic enough to do that. This is not true. In practice, socialist economies never relied on altruism. There were statutory work norms, there were production quotas, there were differences in pay, and there were performance-related material incentives. Socialist economies were not leisurely places. Socialism's relative failure, and capitalism's relative success, had much more to do with capitalism's capacity to generate economically relevant knowledge. [Niemietz 2019]

Views on Socialism

Socialism has had the most success in the form of critique. If anarchism is the negative moment of liberalism, then critique is the negative moment of socialism. Its greatest achievement has been its 'understanding of the intrinsic defects of a capitalist mode of production.' However, the choice between 'pure' socialism and 'pure' capitalism was always an illusion, as all economic forms have, in different ways, blended features of both systems. Indeed, modern socialists tend to view socialism not so much as an alternative to capitalism, but as a means of harnessing capitalism to broader social ends.

Another approach treats socialism as an instrument of the labor movement. Socialism, in this view, represents the interests of the working class and offers a program through which the workers can acquire political or economic power. Socialism is thus really a form of 'laborism', a vehicle for advancing the interest of organized labor. From this perspective, the significance of socialism fluctuates with the fortunes of the working-class movement worldwide.

Socialist Aspirations

Real socialism means to 'convert the means of production into the property of freely associated producers' and thus the social property of people who have liberated themselves from exploitation by their master, as a fundamental step towards a broader realm of human freedom. Or 'giving workers ownership over the means of production.' These are nice aspirations but they are also highly abstract aspirations, they are not tangible descriptions of economic systems. What do they mean? What would be the impact of implementing them? Which set of institutions would deliver them? How would those institutions work? How would we monitor whether they deliver what they ought to deliver, and how would we correct them if they do not? [Niemietz 2019]

When contemporary socialists talk about 'extending democracy to the economy' and 'democratizing every aspect of society', they are not being dishonest. That is their aspiration. But the point they miss is that this has always been the aspiration, and the promise, of socialism. There never was a time when socialists aspired to create stratified societies, in which power would be concentrated in the hands of a technocratic elite. Much less did they aspire to create police states that relied on terror, torture, forced labor and mass murder for their very survival. Socialist experiments ended up that way, but they were not intended to be that way. [Niemietz 2019]

How can an idea which has failed so many times, in so many different variants and so many radically different settings, still be so popular? [Niemietz 2019]

Democratic collective ownership can work perfectly well – but only in small, homogeneous, voluntary communities with simple economies. The classic example of this is the Israeli kibbutz. In a kibbutz, one can meaningfully say that the community, as a whole, organizes its economic affairs collectively and democratically. Democratic collectivism requires small, homogeneous communities, characterized by a high degree of internal agreement on aims and means. And even then, such communities can only coordinate a very limited range of activities. [Niemietz 2019]

Critics of socialism are perfectly aware that contemporary socialists have no intention of bringing back forced labor camps, mass executions, show trials, forced confessions, the Stasi or the Berlin Wall. But no socialist project ever started with that intention. The intention is to draw attention to the fact that these systems were not just randomly oppressive. They were all oppressive in similar ways. There are recognizable, recurring patterns of oppression under socialist regimes, and they are intimately linked with socialist economics. [Niemietz 2019]

**Absurd Socialism**

Absurd Socialism or 21st-century Socialism is a variant of socialism that introduces some tyrannical, populist, fascist, and corrupt ways of government. It is a mixture of Marxism, Fascism, and Anarchism. Absurd

Socialism seeks Public Ownership of the means of production by attacking first its capitalist political enemies and taking from them industries and land to demonstrate its power. In this approach, the unique consideration of history comes from Marxism's class struggle, the poor are the unique survivors, growing evermore. The state moves slowly to intervene in most industries according to its needs. One important characteristic of Absurd Socialism has been that it prospers within an environment abundant in natural resources. These societies require huge amounts of income from natural resources because they are not able to overcome their ideological difficulties to sustain average living standards. Absurd socialism takes the worst from anarchism by disorganizing the means of production and the worst of fascism by orienting its efforts to serve the poor at the expense of the rest of the population.

The absurd socialism political order is structured according to the most fundamental debt owed to the social self, an invention of socialists to confuse the population; this social self becomes a class interpretation where only the poor gets consideration, annihilating the rest of society. Only the poor have infinite credit, everything else is an instrument of that credit, and it is debt about this credit. This preference for a class over the rest of the population is one of the determinants to define the ideology as fascistic. Absurd socialists seek to shift the balance between individualism and collectivization indicating that the right of the individual is subject to the right of the rest of the society, and the authority of the state can limit individual possibilities. Merits and hard work are not appreciated in absurd socialism, if people contribute with a minimum performance, begging most of the time, that is enough for the absurd socialist state.

The similarity of Absurd Socialism with Fascism is outstanding, both regimes are different from military dictatorships and authoritarian regimes but they seek to enlist rather than exclude the masses. Both involve economic systems in which the state controls the private entities that own the factors of production. Economic activities like production, exchange, distribution, and consumption have greater importance. The laws of demand and supply are weakened and a consequence is that the economy has difficulties to prosper. They collapse the distinction between the public and private sphere. They eliminate the private sector interests by absorbing it into the public good.

Absurd Socialism and Fascism help only those who align with the national values. They may use their power to rig the system and create additional barriers to entry. This includes laws, educational attainment, and capital. In the long term, this can limit diversity and the innovation it creates. Both ignore external costs, such as pollution. This makes goods cheaper and more accessible in some cases but it also depletes natural resources and lowers the quality of life in affected areas.

Absurd Socialism points to a Classless Society where only the poor have the right to improve its economic situation, therefore, the middle class and the rich will eventually disappear. In a society governed by absurd socialists, if they dispose of abundant natural resources, there is a mirage of the bonanza that last the time the natural resources are in its peak. After that, the country enters a crumbling spiral that impoverishes the masses. Absurd Socialism is a lousy planner trying to control all the economic activities but incapable of accomplishing results. Absurd Socialism is incapable of establishing a powerful public industry because they lack the knowledge to design adequate strategies.

Absurd Socialism creates a State Responsible for the Basic Necessities of Life. Food, shelter, clothing, health, education, and employment are abundant while there is enough income from natural resources. In this economic system, the opposition to the status quo is discriminated from public established needs.

Absurd Socialism claims that Socialism Provides Equal Opportunity. Every individual will be taken into service independently of his skills, talent, and ability because success is not among its objectives. It is only the abundant income from natural resources that guarantees the survival of an absurd socialist population. The state becomes a complete welfare system thanks to the huge income from natural resources.

Absurd Socialism seeks No Competition and Limited Choice of Consumer Products. The state, with abundant income from natural resources, is in charge of importing most products and forcing free entrepreneurs to collapse. The state has major control over the import and production of goods as well as services. Moreover, since absurd socialism focuses on necessities of life, choice in consumer products is limited and only confined to the essentials. When the income from natural resources decreases, the population is incapable of getting even the essentials.

Absurd Socialism utilizes the Pricing Mechanism to maintain low prices for the population. The pricing process does not work freely but works under the control and regulation of the state. In a socialist economy, prices have vital importance. In absurd socialism, price control is a tool to constrict the small entrepreneur still surviving.

Margarita Lopez Maya has written an article called "Populism, 21st-century socialism and corruption in Venezuela" [Lopez 2018] where she presents some characteristics of Absurd Socialism in Venezuela.

One characteristic is the creation of populism. Populism has been considered a universal way of making politics attractive when there is a set of unmet demands and/or a critical situation in a society that produces high levels of uncertainty in the population. Populism is consolidated through the figure of a charismatic leader who interprets the moment in terms of a Manichean discourse of good and bad, the guilty and the victims, oligarchs and *the people*.

Populists follow some fixed views, discourse, and actions to gain support. This produces the ongoing erosion of institutional accountability mechanisms typical of liberal representative regimes. This populism is reinforced by a socialist-statistic ideology that sought to build institutions of direct democracy as an alternative to liberal representative democracy. These institutions are of a collectivist type, and without political intermediaries and lacking independence, crystallized into the structure of a *communal state*.

Populists use to govern together with his relatives and close friends as well as military colleagues, outside the rule of law, making use of public goods for the benefit of his private interests. Under that rule, liberal democratic institutions have been utterly destroyed and the lack of institutional checks and balances has resulted in unprecedented levels of impunity and corruption proliferation.

Populism tends to recruit, for state operations, staff members linked to the leader by ties of blood, loyalty, and affection. This governing style contributes even more to the expansion of corruption, as well as to the penetration of criminal organizations in the state and the national territory.

Venezuela under absurd socialism is one of the most corrupt countries in the world. The country is also increasingly seen as a *criminal state*, run by groups and mafias dedicated to drug and human trafficking, money laundering, gold and arms smuggling, among other illicit businesses. These features – which the government denies and denounces as part of discourse within an 'economic war' against the Revolution – are deepening amid the country's social and economic catastrophe, suggesting the eventual collapse of its petro-state.

## **Anarchism**

Anarchism is a radical, revolutionary leftist political philosophy that advocates for the abolition of government, hierarchy, and all other unequal systems of power. It seeks to replace what its proponents view as inherently oppressive institutions – like a capitalist society or the prison industrial complex – with non-hierarchical, horizontal structures powered by voluntary associations between people. Anarchists organize around a key set of principles, including horizontalism, mutual aid, autonomy, solidarity, direct action, and direct democracy; a form of democracy in which the people make decisions themselves via consensus.

Anarchism claims that the most fundamental debt is owed to the individual self. However, anarchism considers society as the recipient of this individual debt; it means society gets benefits from an individual's satisfaction. The pure thought of anarchism is that only the self has infinite credit, everything else is an instrument of that credit, and it is debt about this credit which gets transferred indirectly to society. The anarchist seeks 'to indicate the right of the individual to shape his destiny, regardless of any authority which might seek to limit his possibilities.'

In the first place, anarchism states that the individual is the sovereign and he is the sole determiner of everything. Any sort of intervention in his affairs will be treated as harmful and undesirable. So anarchism may be regarded as an extreme form of individualism or liberalism. Both do not recognize the importance of state or any other organization.

Secondly, the anarchist theory of individualism is different from common usage. It never says that the individual is a completely isolated unit and selfish. Rather, it says that he is cooperative minded.

Third, anarchism believes that the development of the inherent qualities of the individual is possible only through the recognition of his sovereign status. The meddling of any other authority or organization can achieve the opposite goal. This is because according to the anarchist thinkers the individual is quite reasonable and he understands what is good and what is bad. So the individual should be left alone and, if done so, that will generate the greatest welfare in society.

Fourth, there are some extreme anarchists, and Max Striner (1806-1856) is one of them. He says that each person should be given unrestricted freedom to do whatever he likes because in this way he can develop his intellectual capacity and contribute to society as a result.

In the fifth place, a thorough study of anarchism reveals that it is in strong opposition to collectivism and communism because they do not recognize individuals' worth and freedom. Collectivism does not say that individuals are capable of making a remarkable contribution to the progress of society. This view has been held by Benjamin Tucker (1854-1939). Tucker advocates no compromise with collectivism or communism.

In the sixth place, anarchism has laid great confidence upon the reasonableness of individuals. The doctrine stresses that there shall be laws and regulations in any society but the individuals will on their own accord obey these laws.

Seventh, it envisages all-round social progress but the only actor of this process will be the individual and not the state.

The anarchists have been found to strongly support the federalization of society which visualizes that there shall not be any single authority in a society, rather, there shall be multiple centers. This multiplicity of centers implies the decentralization of power in all its manifestations.

There is an anarchist theory of revolution. Almost all the anarchists are in favor of changing society through revolution. Because they believe that compromise or reforms could not be relied upon to change society radically. This extremist position reveals the lack of maturity of anarchist thinkers.

By advocating that in the future society there shall be cooperation and harmony, anarchists have dismally failed to understand the proper nature of man. The basic tendency of individuals is selfishness and, in this context, harmonious society cannot be set up. The most important aspect of anarchism that has impressed quite a very good number of men of the academic and political world is the freedom of choice and the absence of central coercive authority in a society.

Max Stirner, for example, rejects any kind of limitation on the action of the individual, including social structures that may evolve spontaneously – for example, parental authority, money, legal institutions (for example, common law), and property rights; Proudhon, on the other hand, argues in favor of a society of small enterprising cooperatives. The cooperative movement often attracts those with collectivist leanings but who seek to move away from the potentially authoritarian model of typical socialism. In contrast, libertarian thinkers who support the free market have proposed anarchic solutions to economic and political problems: they stress the voluntary nature of the market system as a moral as well as an efficient means of distributing resources and accordingly condemn state failure to provide adequate resources (health care and education but also police and defense services); the so-called public goods and services, they assert, ought to be provided privately through the free market.

So the core principle of anarchism is its rejection of the state. But what is the state? It's typically at this point in discussions of anarchism that fine details fall by the wayside, as many seem to take the dictum that 'anarchism opposes the state' as a broad decree for its followers to resist all forms of social organization – a prospect which many find disturbing. This notion of anarchism, however, is inaccurate. By rejecting the state, it doesn't mean the absence of any institutions or the absence of any form of social organization. 'The state' really refers to the professional apparatus of people who are set aside to manage society, to preempt the control of society from the people.

To summarize, anarchists believe that the state needs to be rejected or resisted and that the state consists of special groups of people that have gained sovereignty over the rest of society. Anarchism involves the abolition of all government and the organization of society on a voluntary, cooperative basis without recourse to force or compulsion. Anarchism is another political system seeking the impossible egalitarian society.

# Chapter 3: The Moderates

Liberalism and social democracy are placed as moderates in the political spectrum because they imply a balance between the extremes of socialism-communism and conservatism-capitalism. Liberalism and social democracy differ on the criterion of whom the debts are owed to. Liberals point out to the self, the individual, whereas social democrats point out to the self socially constituted. Liberalism considers the social self indirectly because it allows the individuality criterion to expand to the social self; everybody knows that liberalism contributes to society, the individual collaborates. However, social democracy demonstrates ambivalence between the individual and social self because it tries to demarcate from socialism making exceptions regarding the individual self. Social democrats have a much more complicated task to explain the applicability for politics of two irreconcilable concepts.

## **Liberalism**

The liberal claim is that the debt is owed to the self, the individual. The pure thought of liberalism is that only the self has infinite credit, everything else is an instrument of that credit, and it is debt about this credit. The liberal seeks 'to indicate the right of the individual to shape his destiny, regardless of any authority which might seek to limit his possibilities.' However, as it was already expressed, liberalism also expands the criterion to include the social self.

Liberal systems are constitutional in that they seek to limit government power and safeguard civil liberties, and they are representative in the sense that political office is gained through competitive elections. It is very important for liberalism to allow changes when the government is not performing; to enact those changes, the constitution must be written to avoid misinterpretations. The political cultures of most western countries are built upon a bedrock of liberal-capitalist values. Ideas such as freedom of speech, freedom of religious worship and the right to own property, all drawn from liberalism, are so deeply ingrained in western societies that they are seldom challenged openly or even questioned.

Marxists, for instance, have suggested that liberal ideas simply reflect the economic interests of a 'ruling class' of property owners within the capitalist society; they portray liberalism as the classic example of 'bourgeois ideology.' On the other hand, thinkers such as Friedrich Hayek have argued that economic freedom – the right to own, use and dispose of private property – is an essential guarantee of political liberty. Hayek, therefore, claimed that a liberal democratic political system and the respect for civil liberties can only develop in the context of capitalist economic order.

This is reflected in the belief that liberalism gives priority to 'the right' over 'the good.' In other words, liberalism strives to establish the conditions in which people and groups can pursue the good life as each defines it, but it does not prescribe or try to promote any particular notion of what is good. The moral and ideological stance of liberalism is embodied in a commitment to a distinctive set of values and beliefs. The most important of these are the individual, freedom, reason, justice, tolerance, and diversity.

The individual

A belief in the primacy of the individual is the characteristic theme of liberal ideology. Whether human nature is conceived of as being egoistical or altruistic, liberals are united in their desire to create a society in which each person is capable of developing and flourishing to the fullness of his or her potential. Kant expressed a similar belief in the dignity and equal worth of human beings in his conception of individuals as 'ends in themselves' and not merely as a means for the achievement of the ends of others.

Freedom

Individual liberty is for liberals the supreme political value and in many ways the unifying principle within liberal ideology. It also allows individuals to pursue their interests by exercising choice, the choice of where to live, who to work for, what to buy, and so forth. John Stuart Mill argued that 'the only purpose for which power can be rightfully exercised over any member of a civilized community, against his will, is to prevent harm to others.'

Classical liberals have believed that freedom consists of each person being left alone, free from interference and able to act in whatever way they may choose. This conception of liberty is 'negative' in that it is based upon the absence of external restrictions or constraints upon the individual. However, modern liberals accept the criticisms and respond through the necessary laws that guarantee fairness for all.

### Reason

The central theme of the Enlightenment was the desire to release humankind from its bondage to superstition and ignorance, and unleash an 'age of reason.' To the extent that human beings are rational, thinking creatures, they are capable of defining and pursuing their own best interests. In the liberal view, the expansion of knowledge, particularly through the scientific revolution, enabled people not only to understand and explain their world but also to help shape it for the better. In short, the power of reason gives human beings the capacity to take charge of their own lives and fashion their destinies.

Reason, moreover, is significant in highlighting the importance of discussion, debate and argument. While liberals are generally optimistic about human nature, seeing people as reason-guided creatures, they have seldom subscribed to the Utopian creed of human perfectibility because they recognize the power of self-interest, egoism, and human nature.

### Justice

Justice denotes a particular kind of moral judgment, in particular one about the distribution of rewards and punishment. In short, justice is about giving each person what he or she is 'due.' The narrower idea of social justice refers to the distribution of material rewards and benefits in society, such as wages, profits, housing, medical care, welfare benefits, and so on. Liberal justice is seen to demand respect for individual rights. So long as individuals acquire or transfer their wealth justly, the resulting distribution of wealth, however unequal, must be just. Those with more ability or who have worked hard, have 'earned' their wealth and deserve to be more prosperous than the lazy or feckless.

Consequently, liberals fiercely disapprove of any social privileges or advantages that are enjoyed by some but denied to others based on factors such as gender, race, color, creed, religion or social background. Rights should not be reserved for any particular class of person, such as men, women, whites, blacks, Christians, Islamic, the wealthy or the poor.

Liberals subscribe to a belief in the equality of opportunity. Each and individual should have the same chance to rise or fall in society. The game of life, in that sense, must be played on an even playing field. This is not to say that there should be equality of outcome or reward, that living conditions and social circumstances should be the same for all. Liberals believe this type of social equality to be undesirable because people are not born the same. They possess different talents and skills, and some are prepared to work much harder than others. Liberals believe that it is right to reward merit, ability and the willingness to work – indeed, they think it essential to do so if people are to have an incentive to realize their potential and develop the talents they were born with. Equality, for a liberal, means that individuals should have an equal opportunity to develop their unequal skills and abilities.

Tolerance and diversity

The liberal social ethic is very much characterized by a willingness to accept and, in some cases, celebrate moral, cultural and political diversity. Indeed, pluralism or diversity can be said to be rooted in the principle of individualism, and the assumption that human beings are separate and unique creatures. However, the liberal preference for diversity has more commonly been associated with tolerance.

Tolerance means forbearance, a willingness to allow people to think, speak and act in ways of which we disapprove. This was expressed by Voltaire in his declaration that, 'I detest what you say but I will defend to the death your right to say it.' Tolerance is both an ethical ideal and a social principle. On the one hand, it represents the goal of personal autonomy; on the other, it establishes a set of rules about how human beings should behave towards one another.

Sympathy for tolerance and diversity is also linked to the liberal belief in a balanced society, one not driven by fundamental conflict, one that looks for solutions through negotiation. Although individuals and social groups pursue very different interests, liberals hold that there is a deeper harmony or balance among these competing interests. For example, the interests of workers and employers differ, workers want better pay, shorter hours and improved working conditions; employers wish to increase their profits by keeping their production costs – including wages – as low as possible. Nevertheless, these competing interests also complement one another, workers need jobs, and employers need labor. In other words, each group is essential to the achievement of the other group's goals.

The Liberal State

All individuals would recognize that it is in their interests to sacrifice a portion of their liberty to set up a system of law; otherwise their rights, and indeed their lives, would constantly be under threat. Respecting and obeying government and law means gratitude for the safety and security that only a sovereign state can provide.

The social contract argument embodies several important liberal attitudes towards the state in particular and political authority in general. In the first place, it suggests that in a sense political authority comes 'from below.' The state is created by individuals and for individuals; it exists to serve their needs and interests. Government arises out of the agreement, or consent, of the governed. This implies that citizens do not have an absolute obligation to obey all laws or accept any form of government. If the government is based upon a contract, made by the governed, the terms of this contract can be reviewed. When the legitimacy of government evaporates, the people have the right to rebellion and the government must yield.

In the second place, the social contract theory portrays the state as an umpire or neutral referee in society. The state is not created by a privileged elite, wishing to exploit the masses, but out of an agreement among all the people. The state, therefore, embodies the interests of all its citizens and acts as a neutral arbiter when individuals or groups come into conflict with one another. For example, if individuals break contracts made with others, the state applies the 'rules of the game' and enforces the terms of the contract, provided, of course, each party had entered into the contract voluntarily and in full knowledge. The essential characteristic of any such umpire is that its actions are, and are seen to be, impartial. Liberals thus regard the state as a neutral arbiter among the competing individuals and groups within society. Therefore, the state is not above the individual.

Liberalism involves an enthusiasm for freedom, tolerance, individualism and reason, on the one hand, and disapproval of power, authority, and tradition, on the other. It involves 'the idea of limited government, the maintenance of the rule of law, the avoidance of arbitrary or discretionary power, the sanctity of private property and freely made contracts, and the responsibility of individuals for their fates,' complicated by 'state involvement in the economy, democracy, welfare policies, and moral and cultural progress.'

Liberalism recognizes that its emphasis on the self is only a means of judging an order, but is not by itself sufficient to enable that order to exist. The liberal must postulate the existence of an external order. Liberalism cannot take some sort of order for granted, and so has to insist on the necessity of an order external to the self, but without which the self cannot exist. This order is the law. Perhaps the best way to express this is to say that the liberals always divide the world into three, first, what is intrinsically necessary (the self), second, what is necessary to support that intrinsic necessity (a system of standards, rules, laws), and third, what is contingent (everything else, including all other beliefs, practices, and institutions). Kant makes it clear that such an order is founded upon 'three principles, firstly, the principle of freedom for all members of a society (as persons); secondly, the principle of the dependence of everyone upon a single common legislation (as subjects); and thirdly, the principle of legal equality for everyone (as citizens).'

What does liberalism achieve? 'People are not freed from religion; they receive the freedom of religion. They are not freed from the property; they receive the freedom of property. They are not freed from the egoism of trade; they receive the freedom to trade.' Politically, liberalism 'rests on a certain view about the justification of social arrangements.' This view is that everything has to be 'capable of being made acceptable to every last individual.' So, 'social and political order is illegitimate unless it is rooted in the consent of all those who have to live under it, the consent or agreement of these people is a condition of its being morally permissible to enforce that order against them.'

## Social Democracy

Social democracy is a reinterpretation of socialism, therefore, debts are owed to the self as constituted by the community. Social democracy tries to integrate the debt to the individual self with the debt to society. This explains why social democrats have a much more complicated task to explain the significance of politics integrating both types of debts. The close relationship between socialism and communism and how related they are with social democracy was presented in "Socialism and Failed States" [Boloix 2019a].

Socialism is based on a contradiction, that the system that enforces moral virtues leads to poverty (socialism) while the system that encourages vice leads to prosperity (capitalism). Social democracy tries to integrate both viewpoints with a trade-off between being moral and being practical. Social democracy becomes a "third-way" compromise between the moral ideal of socialism and the practical necessity of capitalism. But there is another explanation to this dilemma, the apparent contradiction between moral and practical should be re-examined. Social democracy is intended to be practical and moral at the same time.[Merino 2010 – Robert W. Tracinski]

As with liberals, social democrats generally view society as equal to the sum of its parts. In other words, society is what people make of it. People are social beings, and society is where people achieve their fullest potential. A society is formed with people who *naturally* come together in social settings to have a better life. However, social democrats strongly reject an individualistic view of society such as might be seen in both liberal and conservative ideologies.

Social change is not only possible but necessary in the social democratic view. Greater equality, stronger bonds of community, etc., are all things which social democrats see as important concepts. However, they tend to understand that change is gradual and incremental. Social democrats are strongly critical of society when it is divided, they would argue artificially divided, into classes or groups based on socioeconomic position, access to education, gender, etc. Society is a place where all people are equal, and any society that does not promote that value is neither a good nor a just society. However, like socialism, social democracy doesn't define equality in precise terms.

For social democrats, the state has a central role to play in promoting a good, just, and healthy society. Because of their firm belief in democracy, social democrats see the state as representative of the will of all, and as such it must take the lead in upholding society's values. In this way, the state is an instrument of social change. They differ sharply with Marxists who see the state as an instrument of oppression. However, social democrats have a limp leg because they still maintain the old dream of a totalitarian society awake; for social democrats, socialism is the next stage, to be followed by the final communist stage suggested by Marx.

Social democrats, like liberals, have generally supported the institutional model of social welfare. Social welfare is a fundamental part of society, and as the democratic expression of society, it is the responsibility of the state to guarantee access to resources to meet basic needs. Whereas liberals see the institutional welfare model as something needed to deal with the distributive failings of capitalism, social democrats have traditionally seen the model as part of the gradual movement toward a more just society. Liberals might see the model as an unfortunate necessity; social democrats see it as integral to the proper development of society and therefore one in which a democratic state plays a pivotal role.

In many countries, the welfare state was to be established as an instrument to reform capitalism. However, the changes wrought by globalization have necessitated a major reconsideration by social democrats of the role of capitalism and indeed of the welfare state. The result has been an acceptance that capitalism is not gradually disappearing, and the realization that there needs to be some other way to improve capitalism. Social democrats have always had an ambivalent but generally benign view of the role of the market in society. Social democracy assumed that the expansion of democracy would lead to the gradual elimination of capitalism. However, they went to great lengths to distance themselves from any perspective that saw the overthrow of capitalism as the primary goal.

Rather than a system, social democracy is a way of regulating society and of putting the market economy at the service of the people. It accepts the market economy, because it is the most effective means to regulate, manage, and allocate resources, stimulating initiative and rewarding effort and work. But it discriminates the market society, although the market produces wealth in itself, it generates neither solidarity nor values, neither objectives nor meaning. So, social democrats are not just left-wing liberals, they are socialists. And to be a socialist is to affirm that the political should take precedence over the economy.

Cooperation and Community

Community sharing is sometimes referred to as fraternity, fellowship, or solidarity. It is part of the rejection of a competitive market system that was a major component of traditional social democracy and socialism in all its various forms. Cooperation also includes the notion of altruism, in which people offer help to others without a sense of getting something back in return. Social democrats have always had a strong sense of community, expressed through a larger notion of society and also about cooperation.

Community building emphasizes support networks, self-help and the cultivation of social capital as a means to generate economic renewal in low-income neighborhoods. Fighting poverty requires an injection of economic resources, but applied to support local initiative. Community-building initiatives concentrate upon the multiple problems individuals and families face, including job quality, health and child care, education, and transport.

Equality/Inequality

The social democratic case for equality represents both the desire for equality of outcome (which is favored by the Marxists) and equality of opportunity, which has support from liberals. The argument for equality has generally been based on a rejection of the consequences of inequality, for example, economic inefficiency, social disruption, poverty (or social exclusion as it is sometimes called), and natural justice. The welfare state was often seen as a way of reducing inequality and moving toward a more equitable society. As support for the welfare state has waned, social democrats place a greater emphasis on equality of educational opportunity.

Freedom/Liberty

Social democrats have a conception of freedom that accepts liberal and even some conservative notions, but also includes the notion that people are not free if they do not have the resources *to do* certain things. Where a conservative might see freedom as the absence of constraint, social democrats would think that this is insufficient. First, they would argue that freedom requires a concern for equality. The greater the inequality of economic resources, the less free some people (the less well-off) will be. Second, political freedom must also mean economic freedom. Fear of being without work, of having no power in one's workplace, of having no workplace protection, means people are not free. Lastly, they argue that freedom is the result of government action. If the government is not prepared to provide some measure of support for the freedom found in the law, then people are not free.

Survival Needs

For social democrats, the issue of need has largely been one of determining which needs are universal or basic and which are of a secondary order based perhaps on some normative process. We can find some social democrats who have tried to develop some general criteria that can be applied to a discussion of basic needs. Food, shelter, and health care are often mentioned.

Also included is the notion of autonomy. Without autonomy or the freedom to be able to decide and choose, human beings are arguably deprived of a need as basic as physical health. It is no use being healthy without the ability to realize the aspirations or objectives which make us human; secondary needs are necessary, such as being able to develop oneself in various ways, to communicate and to become engaged with other human beings.

Views on Poverty

To understand the social democratic view of poverty, one has only to look at one way of describing it: social exclusion. Poverty for social democrats is not simply the lack of money, it is the whole range of issues that arise when people are not actively engaged in society. Because work is seen as a major defining way in which people become engaged, to be out of work is to be not engaged. People are excluded based on ethnic and racial characteristics, because of a physical impairment, or age. If we accept the social democratic view of human nature (active creators through participation in society) and the human need for autonomy, then we can easily see the problems caused by poverty in this context. Poverty prevents people from being able to participate.

Social democrats define need as normative, in the sense that they believe that the development of a poverty line is important, it is a measure of how well society is meeting the needs of its members.

Social Justice

Social justice is a significant component of the social democratic ideology. It is by appealing to principles of fairness and justice that social democrats provide justifications for the collective actions they see as necessary to control the excesses of capitalism. Social democrats argue strongly that the problems created by a market society by losing badly in the competitive system (the aged, those without educational opportunities, the disabled, etc.) can, in fact, be averted through collective action.

Traditional social democratic imperatives for action called for methods, of which the welfare state was one for reforming capitalism. The difference between social democratic reforms and liberal reforms was that social democrats wanted their reforms to be part of a process that led to the transformation of capitalism into something else. Liberal reforms were designed to protect the fundamentals of capitalism itself. However, current social democratic thinking has moved away from the notion of transformation by gradual reform and, as we have seen, has tried to come to some accommodation with capitalism.

There is an explicit attempt to reformulate social democracy in such a way that it becomes the new common sense defined in terms of the ambition to combine a dynamic market economy with the requirements of a decent and cohesive society. It involves a rejection of both the new right and the old left, rejecting market individualism and state collectivism.

The Nordic Model

What is 'the Nordic model'? On the British left, the term is often used in the sense of 'a heavily interventionist, state-dominated economy, which stops just short of being fully socialist.' The Nordic economies are not 'more mixed economies.' The difference between them and Venezuela is not a difference in degree. It is a qualitative difference, namely the difference between a large state and an interventionist state. The Nordic states are large, but they are not particularly interventionist. The Nordic economies are characterized by high taxes and high levels of public spending, but they are otherwise relatively liberal market economies.

This means that relative to most other developed economies, the Nordic economies are not heavily regulated, the state is not an active participant in economic life, and it does not try to direct economic activity. Nordic governments do not interfere heavily in wage and price-setting processes, and they do not engage in an activist industrial policy. They privatized many formerly state-owned enterprises long ago.

Socialists tend to say that they embrace the Nordic Model but it does not mean they support the Nordic-style social democracy, or its continental cousins, i.e. Dutch or German social democracy. Socialists are not social democrats. A rhetorical embrace of 'the Nordic model' counts for little if it is coupled with a rejection of all the features that make the Nordic model work.

The Nordic countries generally score very high on indices such as the Economic Freedom Index or the Ease of Doing Business Index – except in those subcategories that are specifically related to the tax burden.

The difference between socialism and social democracy is perhaps clearer in countries such as the Netherlands, Germany, and Sweden, which have (or used to have) a major social democratic party and a major socialist party side by side. There, a socialist party would not simply be the more radical version of a social democratic party. Rather, such parties might have similar positions on taxation and welfare spending, while differing sharply on issues such as nationalization, price controls, allowing the profit motive, and so on. [Niemietz 2019]

## Chapter 4: The Unprogressive

Conservatism, capital democracy, and fascism are placed as the unprogressive in the political spectrum because they represent an eccentric view opposing absolutely socialism and communism and distancing themselves from liberalism and social democracy. Fascism represents a combination of capitalism and totalitarianism without a solid ideological basis. Conservatism and capital democracy agree on the criterion – the standard by which it judges entities, institutions, and events – that debts are owed to the self but accept the concept of the self socially constituted. For conservatives, the history and the status quo are important factors whereas capital democracy leans toward innovation. Some disadvantages of conservatism are that it associates moral, social and cultural diversity with disorder and instability whereas capital democracy represents a more open-minded type of society. Capital democracy, of course, involves some disadvantages such as those notions of 'greedy,' 'selfish,' 'corrupt,' and 'divisive' society.

Fascists consider the debts owed to the nation, the race, the elite or the class. For fascism, history and the status quo are relatively unimportant and innovation and knowledge are not in their agenda; promotion of historical events is performed just to consolidate its power. The disadvantages of fascism are that it associates moral, social and cultural diversity with disorder and instability. Fascism is naturally tyrannical to maintain a submissive society.

<u>Evolution of Capitalism</u>

We take it for granted that living standards rise over time. For most of history, they did not. For hundreds of thousands of years – almost all of human history – people's living standards were essentially static or increased only at an imperceptibly slow pace. This trend only really began with the advent of industrial capitalism in the mid-nineteenth century which was a game-changer in world history. Before the advent of industrial capitalism, virtually the whole of the world's population lived in abject poverty, it would not even have made sense to measure poverty, because such a measure would not have shown anything interesting. [Niemietz 2019]

In the mid-nineteenth century, there were only about 1.3 billion people in the world, virtually all of whom lived in poverty. Today, there are about 7 billion people and the global poverty rate has fallen below 10 percent for the first time in history. It means that today around 1 billion people still live in poverty but around 6 billion people are living better. It means capitalism has not done such a bad job as pictured by socialists.

For most of history, average life expectancy was below 30 years. This was partly the result of extremely high infant mortality rates, but life expectancy among those who survived infancy was still well below 50 years. It was only with the spread of industrial capitalism that life expectancy began to rise systematically over time, at first only in the Western world and then elsewhere. Globally, the average life expectancy is now over 70 years. [Niemietz 2019]

Life was 'nasty, brutish and short', consisting mainly of backbreaking labor. The concept of 'leisure' only arose with industrial capitalism. In the 1870s, non-agricultural laborers in what was then the industrialized part of the world still worked for an average of around 60 hours per week. The length of the average working week then dropped to under 50 hours by the mid-twentieth century. Combined with increases in holiday time, this led to a decrease in the annual number of hours worked per employed person. One can always find exceptions, but, by and large, people become more prosperous, and better off in all kinds of ways, to the extent that their governments adopt free-market policies.

So why does a system, such as capitalism, which has produced, and which keeps producing, many benefits, arouses widespread and passionate hatred? Why do people so easily dismiss all the massive gains that capitalism delivers and obsess over its shortcomings? Why are people so desperate for an alternative that they are prepared to give the most horrendous systems a free pass (at least for a while), provided it is not capitalist? Why are (or were) so many well-meaning observers willing to turn a blind eye to Gulags and Laogai, but incandescent with rage when large companies earn a profit, or when some people earn a lot more money than others? [Niemietz 2019]

Our minds, and especially our moral intuitions, have evolved over hundreds of thousands of years, during which our ancestors lived in small tribes of hunter-gatherers. Our minds are, therefore, in many ways, poorly adapted to a modern environment, and this is particularly true in the economic sphere. They are adapted to the economic life of tribal society – not to an economy based on the division of labor and coordinated by anonymous mechanisms.

Of course, nobody would argue that we should organize a modern society in the same way as a hunter-gatherer tribe. We all know that a modern economy is infinitely more complex than a mammoth hunt. But, in essence, that is what socialism is, it is an attempt to turn economic life, once again, into a consciously directed group effort. The tribe gathers around the campfire, its members work out what their common needs and priorities are, they agree on a way to fulfill them and put it into action. The drafting of a Five-Year Plan, then, is just a more sophisticated version of the campfire gathering. [Niemietz 2019]

But whether anti-capitalism is hardwired into us, or whether it has other origins, it is safe to say that anti-capitalism comes easily, effortlessly and naturally to us. Appreciation of the market economy, in contrast, is an acquired taste. It is hard to think of a prominent free-market thinker who was already a free-market thinker at the beginning of their career. F. A. Hayek, of all people, was initially sympathetic to socialism. So was James Buchanan, a co-founder of the Public Choice School. Milton Friedman was initially sympathetic to Keynesianism and New Deal – type economic interventionism. These economists certainly understood their opponents' moral intuitions, because these had once also been their own. This understanding was rarely mutual. [Niemietz 2019]

Historically, a capitalist society is characterized by the split between two classes of individuals – the capitalist class, which owns the means for producing and distributing goods (the owners) and the working class, who sell their labor to the capitalist class in exchange for wages. The economy is run by individuals (or corporations) who own and operate companies and make decisions as to the use of resources. But there exists a "division of labor" which allows for specialization, typically occurring through education and training, further breaking down the two-class system into sub-classes (e.g., the middle class).

Companies exist to make a profit. The motive for all companies is to make and sell goods and services only for profits. Profits are not only motivated by greed but they also accomplish at least three important objectives, allow entrepreneurs to make a living, invest in research and development, and create new developments generating jobs. Companies do not exist solely to satisfy people's needs. Even though some goods or services may satisfy needs, they will only be available if people have the resources to pay for them.

## Conservatism

The criterion of conservatism is, even if contradictory, that we owe a debt to the self as constituted by its existence not only in society but also according to history. Conservatism, understood as a 'disposition,' is 'to prefer the familiar to the unknown, the actual to the possible, the limited to the unbounded, the near to the distant, the convenient to the perfect.' Conservatives argue that there is no obligation to change the world because human imperfection, on the one hand, and unforeseen consequences, on the other, make it impossible to know that any change will be for the better. If we do change anything, it should be in terms of the considered judgments of the past, for the reason that we cannot depend on our own experience.

Conservatives look backward, not forward, and so look to the very traditions that liberalism and socialists put into question. This is why they are less securely secular than liberals or socialists. Even if a conservative is not religious, he tends to respect religion because it guarantees God's support. Conservatism expects far less of the future or even the present than does liberalism or socialism because even when it is not religious, it locates eschatology in, and only in, religion. Unlike the liberal or the socialist, who attempts to liberate man from tradition, the conservative seeks no liberation from tradition but complete submission.

The conservative, in general, distrusts argument because it simplifies what should not be simplified. This is why the conservative argument usually takes the form of negation or reaction. Against the positive assertions of liberals and socialists, the conservative issues rebuttals, and otherwise defends what he can in silence. Conservatism appreciates the status quo, therefore, it cheers for capitalism.

A central and recurrent theme of conservatism is its defense of tradition – values, practices, and institutions that have endured through time and, in particular, been past down from one generation to the next. Conservatives, for several reasons, believe that customs and institutions should be preserved precisely because they have survived the test of history. Conservatives also venerate tradition because it generates, for both society and the individual, a sense of identity, a belief in order, authority, and discipline. Established customs and practices are ones that individuals can recognize; they are familiar and reassuring. Tradition thus provides people with a feeling of 'rootedness' and belonging, which is all the stronger because it is historically-based.

Change, on the other hand, is a journey into the unknown: it creates uncertainty and insecurity and so endangers our happiness. Tradition, therefore, consists of more than political institutions that have stood the test of time. It encompasses all those customs and social practices that are familiar and generate security and belonging, ranging from the judiciary's insistence upon wearing traditional robes and wigs to campaigns to preserve, for example, the traditional color of letterboxes or telephone boxes.

Conservatives prefer to base their thinking upon experience and history rather than abstract principles, but this preference is itself based upon specific beliefs, in this case about the limited rational capacities of human beings. Human imperfection is understood in several ways. In the first place, human beings are thought to be psychologically limited and dependent creatures. In the view of conservatives, people fear isolation and instability. They are drawn psychologically to the safe and the familiar, and, above all, seek the security of knowing 'their place.' Such a portrait of human nature is very different from the image of the self-reliant, enterprising, 'utility maximizer' proposed by early liberals. The belief that individuals desire security and belonging has led conservatives to emphasize the importance of social order and to be suspicious of the attractions of liberty. The order ensures that human life is stable and predictable; it provides security in an uncertain world. Liberty, on the other hand, presents individuals with choices and can generate change and uncertainty.

For conservatives, the individual cannot be separated from society but is part of the social groups that nurture him or her: family, friends or peer group, workmates or colleagues, local community, and even the nation. These groups provide individual life with security and meaning. As a result, traditional conservatives are reluctant to understand freedom in terms of 'negative freedom,' in which the individual is 'left alone.' Freedom is rather a willing acceptance of social obligations and ties by individuals who recognize their value. Freedom involves 'doing one's duty.' The free market has exposed the extent to which conservatism had already been influenced by liberal ideas. Conservatives see society as an organism, a living entity. Society thus has an existence outside the individual, and in a sense is before the individual; it is held together by the bonds of tradition, authority and common morality.

Conservatives have thus feared moral and cultural pluralism, arguing, for instance, that multicultural societies are inherently unstable. Instead, conservatives call for a common culture and shared values. Such a culture may nevertheless be fashioned from a variety of sources, important ones including tradition, family, and religion, in the form of 'traditional values,' 'family values' and 'Christian values.'

Conservatives believe that authority is necessary and beneficial as everyone needs the guidance, support and security of knowing 'where they stand' and what is expected of them. Authority thus counters rootlessness and anomie. This has led conservatives to place special emphasis upon leadership and discipline. Leadership is a vital ingredient in any society because it is the capacity to give direction and provide inspiration for others. Discipline is not just mindless obedience but willing and healthy respect for authority. Authoritarian conservatives go further and portray authority as absolute and unquestionable.

For conservatives, the property is an asset that possesses a deep and at times almost mystical significance. Those who work hard and possess talent will, and should, acquire wealth. The property, therefore, is 'earned.' The ability to accumulate wealth is an important economic incentive but also holds a range of psychological and social advantages. The property provides security, ownership gives people a sense of confidence and assurance, something to 'fall back on.' The property, whether ownership of a house or savings in the bank, provides individuals with a source of protection. Conservatives, therefore, believe that thrift – caution in the management of money – is a virtue in itself and have sought to encourage private savings and investment in property.

Property ownership also promotes a range of important social values. Those who possess and enjoy their property are more likely to respect the property of others. They will also be aware that property must be safeguarded from disorder and lawlessness. Property owners, therefore, have a 'stake' in society; they have an interest, in particular, in maintaining law and order. In this sense, property ownership can promote what can be thought of as the 'conservative values' of respect for law, authority and social order.

Conservatives, however, are not prepared to go as far as laissez-faire liberals in believing that each individual has an absolute right to use their property however they may choose. Conservatives have traditionally argued that all rights, including property rights, entail obligations.

Property is not an issue for the individual alone but is also of importance to society. The rights of the individual must be balanced against the well-being of society or the nation. In the case of national interest, conservatives believe that when government intervention in the economy is required, then the freedom of the businesses must be curtailed.

Conservatives are keen to demonstrate their commitment to democratic, particularly liberal-democratic, principles. There is a tradition within conservatism that has favored authoritarian rule. The preservation of order can provide people with safety and security. Revolution, and even reform, on the other hand, would weaken the chains that bound people together and would lead to a descent into chaos and oppression. The values that conservatives hold most dear – tradition, order, authority, property and so on – will be safe only if policies are developed in the light of practical circumstances and experience.

## Capital Democracy

The criterion of capitalist democracy is that we owe a debt to the self in the same way as liberalism proposes but directing it towards the commercial-oriented society. History has lesser importance for capital democrats and they are ready for change, excepting the profit motive which they consider untouchable. Capital democracy, understood as a 'disposition,' is 'to prefer the new to the old, the future to the past, the unbounded to the limited, the distant to the near, the convenient to the perfect.' Capital democrats are always ready to change the world provided capitalism continues to thrive. Anything can be changed, science, technology, and experience justify any improvements to capitalism.

A capital democracy puts entrepreneurship in front of any other objective in society. Such a government incorporates businessmen into the traditional parliamentary structures to impulse new developments and create more jobs. Considerations of culture and tradition are set aside, giving priority to the commercial society. To combat poverty, capital democrats would devise mechanisms incorporating the poor into entrepreneurship. In a capitalist democracy, work is the main driver of prosperity, everybody must work hard.

Capitalist societies believe markets should be left alone to operate without government intervention. However, a completely government-free capitalist society exists only in theory. Even in the United States, the poster child for capitalism, the government regulates certain industries. By contrast, a pure capitalist society would allow the markets to set prices based on demand and supply to make profits.

True capitalism needs a competitive market. Without competition, monopolies exist, and instead of the market setting the prices, the seller is the price setter, which is against the conditions of capitalism. Another characteristic of capitalism is the ability to adapt and change. Technology has been a game-changer in every society, and the willingness to allow change and adaptability of societies to improve inefficiencies within economic structures is a true characteristic of capitalism.

Capitalism in its purest form is a society in which the market sets prices for the sole purpose of profits and any inefficiency or intervention that reduces profit making will be eliminated by the market. There is no real example of a purely capitalist society, governments have been always there, even before any attempt at capitalism, therefore, wealth distribution policies and taxation have been always there. Governments use to serve the interests of participating citizens, and their variety determines what policies people support.

The most important aspects of a capitalist system are private property, private control of the factors of production, accumulation of capital, and competition.

Private Property

The right to private property is a central tenet of capitalism. Citizens cannot accumulate capital if they are not allowed to own anything, nor can they buy or sell things. As long as the owner stays within the parameters of the law, which generally are broad in capitalist systems, he may do what he wants with the property he owns.

A private citizen may purchase a property from another private citizen at a price that is mutually agreed upon and not dictated by a government. In a capitalist system, the free market forces of supply and demand, rather than a central governing body, set the prices at which property is bought and sold.

Factors of Production

In capitalism, private enterprise controls the factors of production, which include land, labor, and capital. Private companies control these factors and set prices and production at levels that maximize profit and efficiency. A common indicator of whether the factors of production are privately or publicly controlled is what happens to surplus products. In a capitalist system, it is held by the producer and used to achieve additional profit. Part of the profits go to research and development, as well as making a living for the entrepreneur.

The centerpiece of a capitalist system is the accumulation of capital. In a capitalist system, the driving force behind the economic activity is to make a profit. Capitalists see amassing profits as a way to provide a powerful incentive to work harder, innovate more and produce things more efficiently than if the government had sole control over citizens' net worth. This financial incentive is the reason capitalist economies see innovation as going hand-in-hand with their market system.

Competition

Competition is another vital attribute of a capitalist system. Private businesses compete to provide consumers with goods and services that are better, faster and cheaper. The principle of competition forces businesses to maximize efficiency and offer their products at the lowest prices the market will bear, lest they get put out of business by more efficient and better-priced competitors.

A natural connection exists between liberal democracy – the combination of universal suffrage with entrenched civil and personal rights – and capitalism, the right to buy and sell goods, services, capital, and one's labor freely. They share the belief that people should make their own choices as individuals and as citizens. Democracy and capitalism share the assumption that people are entitled to exercise agency. Humans must be viewed as agents, not just as objects of other people's power.

Capital democracy is an economic system in which the means of production are privately owned and individuals are responsible for their own lives. Business organizations produce goods for a market guided by the forces of supply and demand; governments elected by the people are limited to protecting the community and maintaining order through the enforcement of contracts. Underlying capitalism is the presumption that private enterprise is the most efficient way to organize economic activity. Adam Smith expressed this idea in his Wealth of Nations (1776), extolling the free market in which the businessman is "led by an invisible hand to promote an end which was no part of his intention."

The marketplace is the center of the democratic capitalist system. It determines what will be produced, who will produce it, and how the rewards of the economic process will be distributed. From a political standpoint, the market system has two distinct advantages over other ways of organizing the economy: (a) no person or combination of persons can control the marketplace, which means that power is diffuse and cannot be monopolized by a party or a clique; (b) the market system tends to reward efficiency with profits and to punish inefficiency with losses. Economists often speak of capitalism as a free-market system ruled by competition. But capitalism in this ideal sense cannot be found anywhere in the world. The economic systems operating in Western countries today are mixtures of free competition and governmental control.

Let us point out the relationship between democracy and capitalism. Nobody saw more clearly than De Tocqueville that democracy as an essentially individualistic institution stood in an irreconcilable conflict with socialism, "Democracy extends the sphere of individual freedom," he said in 1848; "Socialism restricts it. Democracy attaches all possible value to each man; socialism makes each man a mere agent, a mere number. Democracy and socialism have nothing in common but one word: equality. But notice the difference: while democracy seeks equality in liberty, socialism seeks equality in restraint and servitude" [Hayek 1994]

The individual is always the most important entity, without it, there is no collectivity. Independently of how alienated people feel about capitalism, it is a system that allows variety; those that work hard may live better, those that are lazy should live poorer. Those who believe in social welfare can find ways of applying it within capitalism, and the individual has a bit of freedom to decide its destiny, not depending on the state to make his choices.

Capitalism versus Socialism

Despite its long list of failures, socialism remains far more popular than capitalism. The case for capitalism is counter-intuitive, to most of us, capitalism simply feels wrong. Socialism, in contrast, chimes with our moral intuitions. Socialism simply feels right. Being a socialist is a 'default opinion,' which comes easily and naturally to us. Appreciating the benefits of a market economy, in contrast, takes some intellectual self-discipline. Common associations with capitalism include 'greedy,' 'selfish,' 'corrupt,' and 'divisive' (but also 'innovative'). Common associations with socialism include 'For the greater good,' 'Delivers most for most people' and 'Fair.' The most common negative association with socialism is 'naïve,' a trait which is not all that negative, and which some may find endearing. [Niemietz 2019]

Capitalism's relative success has much more to do with capitalism's capacity to generate economically relevant knowledge. Market prices have proven to be an indispensable way of collating and disseminating information about conditions of supply and demand. Market prices are determined by the buying and selling decisions of thousands, if not millions or billions of people, who are acting upon their knowledge of their preferences, and of any information they possess that is relevant to the transaction. [Niemietz 2019]

Planned economies, such as socialism, have no way of replicating this knowledge-collecting and knowledge-disseminating function of market prices. They, therefore, deprive themselves of vast amounts of information, which must lead to worse economic decisions. Another indispensable feature of market economies, which no socialist economy has yet been able to replace, is the fact that market competition is an ongoing trial-and-error process, coupled with extensive feedback mechanisms [Hayek 1994].

People do not know, from the outset, how to organize a successful enterprise or industry (let alone an entire economy). They find out by trying lots of different things, with most of them failing, but some succeeding and the latter ones getting more widely adopted. A market economy is a testing ground, in which different business ideas, different management styles, different organizational models and different industry structures can be tried and tested in competition with one another.

## **Fascism**

Fascism is not supported by any coherent philosophical system, instead, it is a product of mass politics motivated primarily by nationalism. Fascism can also be driven by populism and racism and there are examples of disastrous consequences (i.e., Hitler and Mussolini). It searches unity, purity, and nationalist mobilization, promoting unquestioned devotion to the community and its leader. There are no historical considerations in fascism, only the fantasy of considering the masses as indispensable in the transformation of society. The economic system is directed by the state and it controls the private entities that own the factors of production. A central planning authority directs company leaders to work in the national interest. Under fascism, national interests supersede all other societal needs. It subsumes private people and businesses into a vision of the good of the nation.

The fascist political order is structured according to the most fundamental debt owed to the national self (or the race, or the poor class) according to the leader's vision. Fascism considers the nation as the recipient of all that debt; it is clear that the importance of the nation (race or class) is an invention to manipulate the population. Fascism also involves a dark side regarding the importance of the leader or the elite; any fascist society requires a strong and charismatic man to guide the population. The pure thought of fascism is that only the national (race or class) self has infinite credit, everything else is an instrument of that credit, and it is debt concerning this credit which gets transferred to society. The fascist seeks to promote the right of the individual to shape the destiny of the nation, the state is the unique authority which might seek to limit individual possibilities for the benefit of the nation.

Fascism is an extreme form of authoritarian rule linked to fanatical nationalism. Under Fascism, the mission of citizens is to serve and the government's job is to rule. It turns the traditional social contract upside down, instead of citizens giving power to the state in exchange for the protection of their rights, power begins with the leader, and the people lose their rights. Citizens are required to do exactly what leaders say they must do, nothing more, nothing less. [Albright 2018]

Fascism usually grows under difficult times when people are dissatisfied with the current state of affairs. A fascist leader exploits discontent by promising a prosperous society without class struggle where workers, students, soldiers, and business people would unite and form a common front against the world. A fascist leader claims to speak for a whole nation or group, is unconcerned with the rights of others and is willing to use any means, including violence, to achieve his goals. Fascists use the notion of a single party, speak with one voice, control every state institution, and call the resulting structure a triumph of the popular will. [Albright 2018]

Fascism uses nationalism to override individual self-interest. It subjugates the welfare of the general population to achieve imperative social goals. It works with existing social structures, instead of destroying them. It focuses on "internal cleansing and external expansion," it adores violence and seeks to materialize the final victory of their chosen race or nation or class over what it saw as its inferior opponents. This can justify the use of violence to rid the society of minorities and dissidents.

Fascist movements and regimes are different from military dictatorships and authoritarian regimes. They seek to enlist rather than exclude the masses. They often collapse the distinction between the public and private sphere. They eliminate the private sector interests by absorbing it into the public good. They convince conservatives and businessmen to follow them to handle the communists and protect the social and economic order. At the same time, the radical party members are looking for a "permanent revolution" that would succeed in maintaining the fascist regimes longer in power.

For fascism to extend its reach from the streets to the high offices of state, it must secure backing from multiple sectors of society. Primarily from common people, of course, because they are the majority, and having the majority on one's side is a pretty good idea for winning elections. The other sector is wealthy, to create tyranny out from the fears and hopes of average people, money is required, and so, too, ambition and twisted ideas. It is the combination that kills. In the absence of wealthy backers, we likely never would have heard of Mussolini or Hitler. What makes a movement fascistic is not ideology but the willingness to do whatever is needed – including the use of force and trampling on the rights of others – to achieve victory and command obedience. [Albright 2018]

It is worth remembering, too, that fascism rarely makes a dramatic entrance. Typically, it begins with a seemingly minor character – Mussolini in a crowded cellar, Hitler on a street corner, Chavez on TV after his coup d'etat saying "By now, we couldn't" - who steps forward as events unfold. Fascists advance when small aggressions remains unopposed and grow into a large one, when what was objectionable is accepted, and when contrarian voices are drowned out. [Albright 2018]

The Economy in Fascism

In fascism, the factors of production are owned by individuals as in the case of capitalism, however, it is the state in charge of defining what the entrepreneurs must do. In communism and socialism, the factors of production are owned by everybody, represented by the state. In fascism, the factors of production are important to build the nation, compared to capitalism that works for profit. Socialism and communism use the factors of production to be useful to the collectivity.

In fascism, the state demands from each according to its value to the nation, compared to socialism and communism that values people according to their abilities and capitalism according to the markets. In fascism, each one gets according to its value to the nation, compared to socialism that rewards according to his contribution and needs, communism according to its needs, and capitalism according to its income, wealth or borrowing abilities.

Fascism and Central Planning

A central planning authority cannot get accurate, detailed, and timely information about consumers' needs. That happens naturally in a free market economy, but central planners set wages and prices. They lose the valuable feedback these indicators provide about supply and demand.

Fascism allocates resources following the central plan, the same socialism and communism do. Fascism integrates private and public interests in a common plan to serve the nation. Capitalism on the other side allocates resources according to the laws of supply and demand.

Fascist economies are good at wholly transforming societies to conform to a planner's vision. They have many of the same benefits of any centrally planned economies and mobilize economic resources on a large scale. They execute massive projects and create industrial power.

Fascism aids only those who align with national values. They may use their power to rig the system and create additional barriers to entry. This includes laws, educational attainment, and capital. In the long term, this can limit diversity and the innovation it creates. Fascism ignores external costs, such as pollution. This makes goods cheaper and more accessible. It also depletes natural resources and lowers the quality of life in affected areas.

Fascism Vs. Capitalism

Fascism and capitalism both allow entrepreneurship. A fascist society restricts it to those who contribute to the national interest; entrepreneurs must follow the orders of the central planners. They can become very profitable, but not because they are in touch with the market.

Fascism, like capitalism, does not promote equality of opportunity. Those without proper nutrition, support, and education may never make it to the playing field. Society never will benefit from their valuable skills.

Fascism Vs. Socialism

In both fascism and socialism, the government rewards companies for their contribution. The difference is that socialist governments own the companies in strategic industries such as oil, gas, and other energy-related resources.

Fascist governments allow private citizens to own property. The state may own some companies, but it is more likely to establish cartels of business within the industries. It hands out contracts, thereby co-opting business owners to serve the state.

## Fascism Vs. Communism

In the past, fascism gained power in countries where communism also had become a threat. Business owners preferred the fascist leader because they thought they could control him. They were more afraid of a communist revolution where they lost all their wealth and power.

Fascism organically unified national community, embodied in a belief in 'strength through unity.' The bourgeoisie attempts to cling on to power by lending support to fascist dictators. Fascism addresses the soul, the emotions, the instincts. Intrinsically propagandists interested in ideas only to elicit an emotional response and spur the masses to action. Fascism saw itself as a creative force, a means of constructing a new civilization through 'creative destruction.' A community shaped not by the calculations and interests of rational individuals but by innate loyalties and emotional bonds forged by a common past.

According to fascists, society is formed of three kinds of people, the supreme leader with unrivaled authority, the 'warrior' elite distinguished by its heroism, vision and its capacity for self-sacrifice, and the masses, weak, inert and ignorant, whose destiny is complete obedience.

# Chapter 5: Geopolitical Dimension

Let me continue with the analogy of Charles Aznavour's song Emmenez Moi to stress the contradictions of socialist regimes.

> Prenant la route qui mène à mes rêves d'enfant
> Sur des îles lointaines où rien n'est important
> Que de vivre
> Où les filles alanguies vous ravissent le coeur
> En tressant m'a-t-on dit de ces colliers de fleurs
> Qui enivrent

The English translation would look like this:

> Taking the road which carries me to my childhood dreams
> On distant islands where nothing is important
> Only to live
> Where the languished girls charm your heart
> Braiding, as someone told me, with these garlands of flowers
> Making you dizzy

Let us take the socialist road where nothing is important but to live and doing the less possible effort. Living a supposedly easy life pleasing the desires of the heart. And very far away from capitalism that demands work and effort. Socialism is a dreamer's panacea, people think things are going to be better with such unfeasible sociopolitical systems instead of recognizing approaches that have given a decent result over the years.

There are many considerations when evaluating sociopolitical systems, conceptual, geographical, religious, political, cultural, economic, ideological, and personal are just a few examples. An overall geopolitical and historical background is necessary to understand the intricacies of sociopolitical evolution. The "Political Map of Europe," the "American Dream," the "Latin American Belt," "The Arab Stretch," "The Asian-Pacific Rim," "The African Renaissance," represent several possible areas of concern. Here, the history of events, the overall size of the population and the timing of both nation formation and the establishment of a democratic political system determine the geopolitical structure.

Regarding general economic conditions, both the level of development and the basic class structure of the societies concerned enter the equation. Some indicators are the national product per capita; the level of urbanization; the span of literacy; the amount of industrialization; and data corresponding to the main social classes. The particular ethnic, linguistic, religious and regional composition of the population together with the possible existence of overarching structures which bridge the gap between such cleavages.

The political culture's most relevant concerns include the overall 'national' identity; the existence of strong cultural influences which characterize the 'community system;' attributes such as the extent of secularization, egalitarianism, tolerance and the acceptance of violence in the social sphere. The level of political interest and information; political participation; the dominant patterns of conflict resolution (competitive or consensual) and decision-making (authoritarian or participatory); the extent of 'closed-minded' and 'egoistic' orientations; and the resulting degree of overall democratic legitimacy.

An overview of issues regarding internal regional considerations is required. The strength of the major interest groups (rural, commercial, employers, trade unions); the existence of important social movements, militias or anti-system parties; the overall fragmentation of the party system; and the incidence of clientelism, populism, or corporatism forms of interest mediation.

The specific features of the sociopolitical system have to be identified as well as which tendencies are extended on the population. Among these are the general system type; the vertical separation of powers (e.g. independence of the judiciary); the horizontal separation of powers (centralized or federal); the electoral system (proportional or majoritarian); the stability of governments; the strength of the bureaucracy and the repressive apparatus; the social security system; the political role of the military; and, as an important normative criterion, the guarantee and observance of civil rights and political liberties.

The local conditions related to the region define the interactions and include such factors as economic or political characteristics, cultural influences and specific historical conditions (e.g. revolutionary movements, the consequences of World War II, the possession of colonies). Examples of large-scale changes include social revolutions (e.g., the French Revolution of 1789, the Russian Revolution of 1917, or the Chinese Revolution of 1949), nation-building, economic transformation and development (e.g., the shift from a rural economy to a capitalist-industrial economy), political development (especially democratization), among others.

## Geopolitical Dimension

The geopolitical dimension is evaluated at the local level, it includes geographical, physical and natural resources, environmental and political considerations; demographic information about the population, including ethnic, linguistic, religious, educational, and cultural considerations; and the historic-political evolution.

<u>Geography</u>

Geography contributes to the understanding and response to global economic change through the focus on place and space – in this context, the effects of place (location) and space (the connections between locations at different scales) on economic change and development. Geographers go beyond regional estimates of production costs and product markets to understand the complex relationships among regional political, social, and environmental conditions and processes.

Contemporary geographical issues and events have both a spatial and temporal dimension. This means that they occur in a particular context and time frame. They might, for example, be a local community-based issue (such as a development proposal) that is a focus of peoples' attention for just a short time, or an environmental issue that affects the whole planet (for example, global climate change) which may be of concern for generations.

Some examples of contemporary geographical issues and events include air and water pollution, child labor and exploitation, coastal erosion, coal seam gas extraction, drought, endangered species, famines, flooding, food security, global climatic change, global inequalities, global terrorism, deforestation, human rights, impacts of tourism, effect of mining, natural hazards, and disasters, population growth, population movements (eg. refugees), poverty, rights of Indigenous people, salinity, soil erosion, unemployment, urban developments, waste disposal, water quality.

<u>Environment</u>

As the twentieth century draws to a close, there is growing concern that humans are irreparably degrading the physical environment that supports them. A wide range of human activities contributes to this problem, including the pollution of air, land, and water as a result of industrial and agricultural activities. In many parts of the world, the quality of the air has declined to the point that plant and animal communities are threatened, as well as human health. The heavy use of fertilizers and pesticides in agriculture and the expanding quantity of waste that must be stored on or near the Earth's surface are impairing the quality of the land.

Climate change is an environmental concern that involves enormously complex interactions among the atmosphere, hydrosphere, and biosphere. These interactions vary significantly across spatial scales. Thus, geographic perspectives that consider place and scale are essential for understanding the potential effects of climate change.

Ethnic Conflict

During the past two decades, ethnic conflict has undermined the existing social and political orders of many cities, countries, and world regions. Conflicts between ethnic groups are manifest at a variety of scales, and in some cases, they are precipitating major humanitarian crises. Consequently, ethnic conflict has increasingly attracted the attention of scientific and policymaking communities. Efforts are being made to understand the causes and consequences of ethnic conflict, and policymakers are grappling with ways of mitigating intergroup hostilities.

Health Care

Geography has an important role to play in addressing questions about health care. Health care services are provided in particular places; effective decisions about where a particular service should be located must take into consideration the spatial organization of people, health problems, and related services. By focusing attention on location efficiencies, a geographic analysis can point to specific ways of providing needed health care services cost-effectively and, in many instances, can point to better ways of providing critical health services.

Education

One of the greatest challenges facing society in the late twentieth century concerns education. The need to improve the skills of the labor force and to meet the challenges of democratic citizenship in a fast-changing, increasingly complex world present enormous educational challenges. What do tomorrow's citizens need to know to function effectively in a world characterized by both a globalized economy and changing local circumstances? What should schools be teaching students who may well hold several different kinds of jobs during their lives? What educational experiences can promote personal enrichment in an age of television, telecommunications, computers, and hypermobility?

Geography must be a part of any serious effort to meet the educational challenges implicit in these questions. Students need to be exposed to ideas and perspectives that cut across the physical-human divide, that consider how developments in one place influence those in other places, that focus attention on how local circumstances affect understandings and activities, and that foster an appreciation for the diversity of peoples and landscapes that comprise the Earth's surface.

Social Idiosyncrasy

Idiosyncrasy is a term that can be used in several contexts, primarily personal and social. At the personal level, it defines the peculiarity of people; people's attitudes, people's feelings, reactions, behavior and so on. People are characterized by patterns of relationships (social relations) between individuals who share a culture and institutions; a given society may be described as the total sum of relationships among its constituent members. In the social sciences, a society often evinces stratification or dominance patterns in subgroups.

How 'the spirit of cooperation,' 'the notion of fairness' or even 'social democracy' is going to be translated to specific combinations of stratified characteristics in the society – this type of family, this level of interpersonal trust, this pattern of industrialization, this form of corporate governance, these skills, this infrastructure, these policies, these policy institutions, and so forth? It is possible to connect a particular structure of the family with a particular form of corporate governance and a particular pattern of party-political competition. Yet the connections are historically contingent or, more generally, sensitively dependent upon initial conditions.

National Idiosyncrasy

Idiosyncrasy defines the particularity of nations and the people living in them. What institutions matter, what policies are convenient, how globalization impacts society and so on. Institutions matter in ways and for reasons that both reflect and impact upon their broader environment including actors, other institutions, and even themselves.

At the level of nations, there is an idiosyncratic nature of national diversity. Countries have remained distinctive despite the many common forces acting upon them. There are 'differences' between countries that are important to economic performance, international competitiveness, institutional adaptation, or democratic stability.

Countries will develop idiosyncratically or not at all. The point is not simply that countries are different in certain respects. Rather it is that even similarities across countries are likely to have arisen for different reasons, along differing trajectories, and with different implications or effects. In regions such as the European Union, it is difficult to translate one national context to another, 'the spirit of co-operation,' 'the notion of fairness' or even 'social democracy,' is difficult to integrate without considering national idiosyncrasies.

Idiosyncrasy affects several policies at different levels. Wage-bargaining institutions, monetary authorities (including central banks), distributive policies, tax regimes, political ideologies, and patterns of party-political competition constitute the focus of concern for macro-analysis. Corporate governance, supply networks, infrastructure, labor organization, labor market regulations, and skills development provide a meta-layer for attention. Social capital, interpersonal trust, popular values, and the economics of the family lie at the micro-layer. Bracket a set of necessary or indicative features for analyzing particular problems. Wage bargaining and unemployment, central banks and inflation, social capital and democratic stability, and so forth.

Natural Resources

Natural resources are usually either renewable or non-renewable. The former refers to those resources that can renew themselves in time. These include living resources like forests or non-living ones like wind, water, and solar energy. Non-renewable resources are those that can no longer be tapped once the available stock at a site is exhausted. Once we use them, there isn't anymore. Mineral resources are non-renewable. Fossil fuels, which are formed from the fossilized remains of prehistoric organisms, are also considered non-renewable.

Without natural resources, the whole budget has to rely on what the economy of the specific country generates and the economy in some countries tends to be rather poor and unstable. A more recent source of income for some corrupt states is drug trafficking, instead of oil, to maintain its influentials happy.

Political Development

It is unclear what is the effect of ideas on the evolution of political thinking compared to material needs. Some authors believe material forces define changes but ideas that are driven materially through the practices of individual political agents can and do have an impact upon political history. Irrigation, for example, has been theorized as a prime mover for the evolution of urban state formations. The debate over this theory rarely addressed the role of ideas in the development of hydraulic works. Yet, if irrigation is important in social evolution, it is due at least in part to the fact that some leaders saw benefits to their power by expanding and/or intensifying hydraulic systems.

Some theories explain the evolution of political order based on three "institutions": the state, the rule of law, and the mechanisms of accountability. These may perhaps be better understood as three equilibria factors that society strives to reach: The first entails the central control of violence by the state. The second requires the establishment of an objective law by which rulers are effectively bound and that they cannot change arbitrarily to suit their purposes. The third, democratic accountability, is close to *inclusion*: the development of modern universal citizenship through which all groups, not just elites, gain a voice in decision making and control. For all three to be sustainable, economic development is indispensable. [Fukuyama 2014]

Fukuyama makes a compelling argument that England's successful modernization path went through three stages: Economic development produced societal development, which in turn led to political development. Not all development paths successfully lead to stable and prosperous states or necessarily result in happy endings. Liberal democracy "cannot be said to be humanly universal, since such regimes have existed for only the last two centuries in the history of a species that goes back tens of thousands of years." There is no end of history because there is no end to human nature. So decay, no less than progress, is also a perennial feature of human history, but it is especially threatening in a world where the demands placed upon states exceed their capacity.

Fukuyama doesn't seem to accept the crucial distinction between institutions as the rules of the game (both formal and informal) and organizations as the players, groups of individuals engaged in purposeful activity. Yet viewing the state as an organization (even if one grew monstrously out of proportion) and not as an institution has some advantages. For instance, it makes it easier to explain why similar state structures result in such different levels of performance across various institutional contexts. (An institutional context cuts across both state and society, which reciprocally shape each other.) Also, given Fukuyama's contention that patrimonialism is inherent in human nature, it makes sense to think that every organization starts as being patrimonial; the autonomy of the state from private interests grows as the "owners" of the organization expand to include all the citizens of a state. Therefore, society must develop sufficient controls to prevent any particular person or group from using the organization (the state) for private advantage using patronage, clientelism, or other institutions.

Fukuyama contends that creating an autonomous bureaucracy is the key to success, but it is unclear how this can be achieved in a country that already holds elections and in which parties compete for public spoils by politicizing the government in turn. By my estimation, however, this is the most common situation in the world today, found in 86 countries (those that Freedom House rates as Free or Partly Free, but where corruption is the main governance norm according to the World Bank's Control of Corruption scale). There is no autonomous bureaucracy in these countries, only total collusion between elected and appointed officials in support of preferential social allocation.

He holds that change occurs only due to great accidents and that in between these sharp disjunctures gradual adaptation occurs. Fukuyama acknowledges the role of accidents but then warns that they should not prevent supporters of change from working hard to prepare for their windows of opportunity.

# Chapter 6: Political System

## Societal Dimension

The societal dimension is organized according to the following characteristics, the political system, the economic system, the personal influence, the social influence, the ideological sphere, and the pragmatic sphere. Each characteristic includes a series of features. The following paragraphs describe each characteristic.

In the following chapters offer a description for each characteristic:
- Political System
- Economic System
- Personal Influence
- Social Influence
- Ideological Sphere
- Pragmatical Sphere

## Political System

Politics is not deterministic and cannot be predicted because it is chaotic, there are too many factors involved in the possible outcomes. Level one chaos does not react to predictions about it, there is no relationship between the predictions and the outcomes. The weather, for example, is a level one chaotic system, its predictions are separated from possible outcomes. Level two chaos is a chaos that reacts to predictions about it, and therefore never can be predicted accurately, any prediction can affect the outcome. Markets and politics are level two chaotic systems, so many forces are at work and their interactions are so complex that extremely small variations in the strength of the forces and the way they interact produce huge differences in outcomes. [Harari 2014]

Usually, making predictions about politics can affect paths contrary to the expected outcome. A political regime that does not perform is predicted to fall but those predictions can have an effect allowing the regime to react and apply populist measures to counteract the storm of political forces opposing it. Let us take the case of Venezuela, there is a regime that does not perform and everybody would predict it is going to fall anytime. The regime starts conversations with the opposition to get an agreement, simulating they are interested in solving the problems. Time passes by, the regime applies several economic policies that seem promising, to gain time and remain in power, standing the heat without solving the difficulties. It is the people who suffer the consequences of a bad regime that only cares to stay in power. Many politicians criticize Sovietologists for failing to predict the 1989 revolutions and castigate Middle East experts for not anticipating the Arab Spring revolutions of 2011. This is unfair. Revolutions are, by definition, unpredictable. A predictable revolution never erupts. [Harari 2014]

So why study political history? Unlike physics or economics, political history is not a means for making accurate predictions. We don't study politics to know the future but to widen our horizons, to understand that our present situation is neither natural nor inevitable and that we consequently have many more possibilities before us than we imagine. For example, studying how Europeans came to dominate Africans enables us to realize that there is nothing natural or inevitable about the racial hierarchy and that the world might well be arranged differently. [Harari 2014]

<u>Sociopolitical Institutions</u>

There has been a broad recognition among economists in recent years that "institutions matter," poor countries are poor not because they lack resources, but because they lack effective political institutions. We need to understand the origin of institutions. There are three categories of institutions, the first, the state is the centralized source of authority holding an effective monopoly of military power over a defined piece of territory. Peace is kept by the state's army and police. Second, social rules are formalized as written laws, known as the rule of law, to protect the citizens. Property is owned by individuals and their rights are enforced by courts and legal systems. Third, societies limit the power of the state forcing rulers to comply with the law and holding them accountable to parliaments, assemblies and other bodies representing the population. [Fukuyama 2011]

Governments do many things, establishing and operating school systems, maintaining public order, fighting wars, and so on. To carry on so many disparate activities, societies have specialized structures, institutions or agencies, such as parliaments, bureaucracies, administrative agencies, political parties, interest groups, legislatures, executives, courts, and so on. These structures perform functions, which in turn enable the government to formulate, implement, and enforce its policies. The policies reflect the goals and the agencies provide the means to achieve them. The problem comparing political systems is that similar structures may have very different functions. For example, Britain and China have similar types of political structures. However, these institutions are organized differently in the two countries. More importantly, they function in dramatically different ways.

Aspirations and Institutions

Who does not appreciate a better society? Who does not admire a better human? Who does not dream of an economic system without pressures? Who does not respect the self-determination of the individual? Everybody does, however, solutions must be viable, charlatans abound and some retrograde ideologies have become the more distrusted alternatives.

Political ideologists, primarily, socialists and anarchists, tend to escape into abstraction and talk about lofty aspirations rather than tangible institutional characteristics. Those aspirations are presented as expected outcomes and are not supported by institutional structures. They are not analyzed for feasibility, their impact can be worse than expected. Enabling people to 'organize together to chart new destinations for humanity,' 'empowering civil society,' and 'allowing participation in the decisions that affect our lives' are fine aspirations, but they are just that. How do we evaluate the feasibility of aspirations?

Aspirations are desires and many of us have good desires for a better society, however, knowledge and intelligence are required to make transformations. Aspirations must be analyzed first of all for feasibility and then presented under institutional structures that define objectives, procedures, and evaluation methods. Aspirations are not enough, feasibility and the design of institutions to attain results is obligatory. Finally, aspirations must be evaluated to determine whether the institutions are delivering what is expected.

Some ideologies promote unproven statements. According to them the problems of societies are originated in the capitalist approach. For example, sustaining that capitalists are guilty of all the disgraces of humanity. War? Capitalists are the ones to blame, and it's human nature to fight. Racism? Capitalism promotes racism, and it's human nature to fear "outsiders," or "dissimilar." Women's oppression? Capitalists are misogynistic, and men and women are "naturally different."

Generally, the distinction between institutional characteristics of a system and observable outcomes is straightforward enough. Institutional characteristics are the features of a system over which policymakers have direct control. They can be introduced when the political will is there, and they can be abolished when the political will is not there. 'Tariff-free trade' is an institutional feature. A government can introduce tariff-free trade, namely by abolishing tariffs. 'A high GDP per capita', in contrast, is an outcome. A government cannot 'introduce' a high GDP per capita, it can only implement policies that might result in a high GDP per capita. Similarly, 'private ownership of the main means of production' is an institutional characteristic. 'A high employment rate' is an outcome. 'Freedom of contract' is an institutional characteristic. 'A high life expectancy' is an outcome. 'Voluntary exchange of goods and services between consenting adults' is an institutional characteristic. 'A low rate of absolute poverty' is an outcome. 'Universal suffrage' is an institutional characteristic. 'A high level of voter engagement in politics' is an outcome. And so on. [Niemietz 2019]

We can define a political and/or economic system in terms of its institutional characteristics and any sensible definition must be outcome-neutral. Whether the system we favor produces the outcomes we would like to see remains to be seen. It may, or it may not. If it does not, we cannot claim that the system was therefore not 'real.' 'Extending democracy to the economy' and 'democratizing every aspect of society' are nice soundbites, but what do they mean in practice? What would an institutional framework which fulfills those aspirations look like? Trying to implement those aspirations would not produce an unexpected result that jeopardizes the intended desire?

Political institutions develop often slowly and painfully as societies strive to organize themselves to master their environments. Changing circumstances require political systems to adjust but human nature tends to help the conservation of institutions because stakeholders oppose fundamental change. [Fukuyama 2011]

But there is one outcome that some political systems constantly mistake for an institutional characteristic, the idea that under the 'real' ideology, workers are in control of their economic life. Some political systems seem to see working-class control as something that can be introduced at any time given the political will. They seem to see it as akin to universal suffrage: if a government wants every adult citizen to have the vote, all they need to do is give every adult citizen the vote. And in such political systems' worldview, if a government wants 'the working class' to be in control, all they need to do is give 'the working class' that control.

This assumption is never explicitly spelled out. Those systems never have fulfilled these aspirations, but this is not for a lack of trying. The usual explanation of socialists and communists' failures is that this time the outcome was not attained but in 50 years more it will be. If ideologies were supported by institutional structures it would be possible to evaluate their implementation and in case of failures look after better approaches.

Governments are organized following some political models. A popular model defines three powers, Executive, Legislative, and Judicial. These powers are in charge of performing the duties of the state. There are many tasks expected from the government, among them, Establish Courts, Make and Enforce Laws, Administer Ministries, Managing Municipalities, managing the Federal Government, establishing Financial Budget and borrowing, chartering Banks and Corporations, controlling Foreign Affairs, and Conducting Elections.

The government is in charge of defining policies regarding Taxes, Employment, Immigration, and the Environment. Climate Change is a popular subject these days that is getting ample relevance. The government is in charge of regulating many areas of society according to the needs of the population. However, the government should abstain from meddling in such crucial factors as the economy which requires some degree of independence. The government should work in harmony with several other enterprises, private industry, non-profit organizations, and volunteer groups to allow the construction of a prosperous society.

## Democracy

Democracy is a system of government characterized by the participation of the population in the decisions of the state. Through independent institutions, basically through three powers, the executive, the legislative and the judiciary, the state is controlled by timely institutional intervention to recover society's balance and promote stability. Each of the powers has clearly defined scopes of participation for the good of the people. In a democracy, the executive power has to build up a consensus to approve its actions; an executive independent viewpoint is not permitted, in other words, the executive power is not authoritarian like in a dictatorship.

Liberal democracy is more than majority voting in elections; it is a complex set of institutions that restrain and regularize the exercise of power through law and a system of checks and balances. A common error is to assume that the winner of an election has a license to do whatever he wants. In many countries, democracy was accompanied by the systematic removal of checks on executive power and the erosion of the rule of law. Examples of dismantling democratic institutions have been Russia, Venezuela, and Iran which manipulates elections, control the media and clamp down on opposition activities. [Fukuyama 2011]

In a true democracy, leaders respect the will of the majority but also the rights of the minority – one without the other is not enough. This means that constitutional protections for the individual must be defended, even when those protections become inconvenient to the party on top. Hitler said, "... once we possess constitutional power, we will mold the state into the shape we hold to be suitable." [Albright 2018]

There is absolutely no proof that human well-being inevitably improves as history rolls along. There is no proof that cultures that are beneficial to humans must inexorably succeed and spread, while less beneficial cultures disappear. There is no proof that Christianity was a better choice than Manichaeism, or that the Arab Empire was more beneficial than that of the Sassanid Persians. [Harari 2014]

Today, about half the nations on earth can be considered democracies – flawed or otherwise – while the remaining 50 percent tend toward authoritarianism. Consider that a majority of people in the world have below average standard of living, they lack full-time jobs, youth unemployment is high, wages have stagnated in the last 40 years. The current climate is reminiscent of that which a hundred years ago gave birth to Italian and German Fascism. [Albright 2018]

The best way to promote democracy is by promoting prosperity. The most reliable means to a good life for ordinary people remains the presence of institutional incentives in the form of dependence on a big coalition that compels power-seeking politicians to govern for the people. Democracy aligns incentives such that politicians can best serve their self-interests, especially their interest in staying in office, by promoting the welfare of a large proportion of the people. [Bueno 2011]

In a democracy, people have the freedom and the right to assemble. They have also the means through which to coordinate and organize. Governments ruled by a large coalition produce lots of public goods, including a free press, free speech, and freedom of assembly. Democrats provide the policies people want because otherwise, the people will protest. [Bueno 2011]

Democracies have a great advantage over socialism and communism that when things go wrong, the incumbent government can be blamed and voted out. The example of greater tolerance, free elections, accountable government, and respect for human rights, plus substantially higher living standards, has a profound effect. The political system itself is preserved as a result of the exercise of democratic accountability. An authoritarian regime that is driven to relying on economic performance for legitimacy faces special difficulties when that performance weakens. It was through simply being there as a better alternative to communist rule that democracies prevailed in the battle of ideas. [Brown 2009]

In democracies, politics is an arms race of ideas. When seeking office, proposing policies that the voters like is a convincing argument. Coming to power and staying in power are very different things. Politicians are trying to satisfy their coalition in the short run, but democrats must be responsive to the people when governing. It pays to want to do more (as opposed to less) even if the economic consequences are damaging down the road (when the leader is no longer in office). [Bueno 2011]

Coming to the office and staying in the office are the most important things in politics. And candidates who aren't willing to cheat are typically beaten by those who are. Since democracies typically work out myriad ways to make cheating difficult, politicians in power in democracies have innovated any number of perfectly legal means to ensure their electoral victories and their continued rule. [Bueno 2011]

Elections

The primary motivation of a politician is to be re-elected, and sooner or later they accept that their surest path to re-election is to be part of a successful team with a popular leader. Lone wolves can survive, but they do not thrive outside the pack. Governments have many strategies to stay in power combining managing the money, the rivals, and the population. Additionally, there is another activity in the government's survival guide, somewhat surprisingly, called "elections."

Most countries have elections, but some governments usually rig them. Today, election rigging is more sophisticated than simply burning or stuffing ballot boxes. The use of sophisticated digital systems makes rigging easy. Marshaling an impressive vote total is designed to show to others, both within the population but also elites within the regime that any resistance is futile. It's a way of signaling strength, that belonging to the regime is the only possible choice.

However, when elections are rigged, the voice of the people is neutralized, and only the elite class is in charge of the country. The first thing to avoid rigged elections is to have an honest electoral system that does not blackmail voters. An electoral system that can be audited by local and international organizations, a transparent system that does not allow doubts. Bad governments tend to avoid international witnesses to elude criticisms.

Elections in some countries play with people's needs. Even if people don't agree with the government, they vote for it, they fear to lose their survival benefits, such as food, medicines, and supplies. Do people vote in rigged elections? Usually, they are forced to vote, however, it doesn't matter because things never change and politicians may be evil; additionally, a vote in several million doesn't count, therefore, for some, there is no need to vote. Yeah, that is learned helplessness.

For some governments, elections are not about picking leaders. They are not about gaining legitimacy. How can an election be legitimate when its outcome is known before the vote even occurs? Rigged elections are a warning to powerful politicians that they are expendable if they deviate from the leader's desired path. This notion can be extended to governments where the leader is in control of the Electoral Entity. [Bueno 2011]

Democracy and Authoritarianism

We don't need to appeal to civic spirit to explain why people have so much better life in a democracy than in an autocracy. Higher levels of education are accessible to everyone when the coalition is large; education is basic when the coalition is small. Health care is for those who are loyal when the coalition is small; babies and the elderly are not excluded from health care when the coalition is large. Good water is for everyone when the coalition is large; otherwise, it is only for the privileged. And most importantly, freedom to say what you want and to dissent when you don't get is abundant when the coalition is large and is scarce in the extreme when the coalition is small. [Bueno 2011]

Democratic politics is a battle for good policy ideas. If the leader rewards cronies at the expense of the broader public, as it is done in a dictatorship, then the leader will be out on his ear so long as he relies on a massive coalition of essential backers. This happened to Winston Churchill. After six hard years of war, rationing, and sacrifice, he offered the policies of continued austerity to make Britain great again. These policies had little appeal after the war. Clement Atlee offered to promote the National Health Service and the creation of a welfare state over reestablishing international dominance. Atlee won the battle for good ideas. [Bueno 2011]

Mussolini observed that in seeking to accumulate power, it is wise to do it in a manner of one plucking a chicken feather by feather, so each squawk is heard apart from every other and the whole process is kept as muted as possible. Around the globe, fascism is creating stirrings, the discrediting of politicians, the emergence of leaders who seek to divide instead of uniting, the pursuit of political victory at all costs, the invocation of national greatness, and so on. They are signposts that should alert us are the altered constitution that passes for reform, the attacks on a free press justified by security reasons, the dehumanization of some masked as a defense of virtue, or the hollowing out of a democratic system so that all is erased but the label. Undemocratic practices are on the rise, some violent, some not. [Albright 2018]

Repressive governments from across the globe are learning from one another. Among several strategies to destroy democracy, how to rig a constitutional referendum, how to intimidate the media, how to destroy political rivals through phony investigations and fake news, how to create human rights commissions to cover up human rights violations, how to co-opt a legislature, and how to divide, repress, and demoralize opponents so that no one believes you will ever be defeated. In 1933, shortly after Hitler took power, Mussolini said, "The idea of fascism conquers the world. I have already given Hitler many good ideas. Now he will follow me." [Albright 2018]

The trend of Latin American autocratic and authoritarian governments using democracy as a tool in the process of creating socialist dictatorships exposes critical flaws of democracy as a system of government. The replication of these regimes reveals not only the personal ambition or abuse of power of the leaders, but also the eventual dissembling of democratic values (freedom of expression), principles (separation of powers), and institutions (free vote) that once inspired, and are synonymous with the notion of democracy. [Gaona 2018]

## State Control

The main theories of the state are represented by Hobbes, Locke, and Rousseau. They proposed three interpretations of the social contract theory that are still valid today. Hobbes' contract is one in which the people unconditionally surrender their rights to the government. In Locke's case, people conditionally delegate their power to the government and make the rulers accountable to them. Rousseau is most radical in enthroning the people and making the people themselves the rulers. Hobbes stands for legal sovereignty, Locke supports political sovereignty, and Rousseau, popular sovereignty.

The state represents the society's political organization, or the body politic, or more narrowly, the institutions of government. The state is a form of human association distinguished from other social groups by its purpose, the establishment of order and security; its methods, the laws, and their enforcement; its territory, the area of jurisdiction or geographic boundaries; and finally by its sovereignty. The state consists, most broadly, of the agreement of the individuals on the means whereby disputes are settled in the form of laws.

There are many variants of states, some are relaxed allowing people and entrepreneurship to prosper, others are totalitarian in charge of all the means of production. There are different degrees of domination in society, promoting freedom of speech and enterprise and total submission from the population are current examples. In most cases, the state allows the free market and in other cases it becomes the main producer, importer, and distributor of goods and services, implying a system where people must obey without complaining unless they don't care about dying young. Some states are freedom-oriented whereas others are oppressive, those who dare to oppose the state are rapidly purged by restraining their access to basic surviving goods.

The interference of the state in community and individual matters is a source of criticism. The monopoly of the power of the state can be seen in many political systems. However, people are unclear about how much intervention of the state must be allowed. Some people support a larger state, as opposed to a smaller state and the reasons can be trivial, for example, to maintain the status quo. And there are some authoritarian cases with the monopoly of power of the party-state or the strong man.

## Politics

Political ideas also help to shape the nature of political systems. Systems of government vary considerably throughout the world and are always associated with particular values or principles. Absolute monarchies are based upon deeply established religious ideas, notably the divine right of kings. Political systems in most contemporary western countries are founded upon a set of liberal-democratic principles. Western states typically respect the ideas of limited and constitutional government and also believe that government should be representative, based upon regular and competitive elections. In the same way, traditional communist political systems conformed to the principles of Marxism–Leninism. Communist states were dominated by a single party, a ruling Communist Party, whose authority rested upon Lenin's belief that the Communist Party alone represents the interests of the working class. Even the fact that the world is divided into a collection of nation-states and that government power is usually located at the national level reflects the impact of political ideas, in this case of nationalism and, more specifically, the principle of national self-determination. [Heywood 2003]

What is the first thought it comes to your mind when you hear the word "politician," the answer is always the same: dishonest, sleazy, liars. Other softer synonyms for politicians different from "liar" and "thief," are well-meaning, good one, hard-working. Canadians admire individual politicians, but they do not admire politicians as a class. What does it mean to think like a politician? Politicians learn habits of thinking, behavior, and speech that serve political purposes. The political habits are expressed by the Rule of the Political Game: [Steele 2017]

- Nothing is more important than getting elected and re-elected.
- Focus on voters' beliefs, not the facts.
- Keep everything as simple as possible.
- Keep everything as secret as possible.
- Fight for influence and status.
- Always be loyal to your party and leader.
- Always attack the other parties.
- Take credit often and avoid blame always.
- Focus on constituency work.
- Deny these are the rules.

Fundamentally, political thinking is not about good government. Good government is hard. Science is hard. Math is hard. Economics is hard. It is easier to develop a simple political response than to develop a solution-oriented response. Politics, in contrast with science or math, is quick and ruthless. In a world where perception-is-reality, there is only marketing and bludgeoning. The fact is that anecdotes are more powerful than statistics. Politicians are or tend to turn into, storytellers. This is what door-to-door campaigning gives you – an almost inexhaustible fund of stories about people in their community. [Steele 2017]

Participation in the political process is another key public good that enables citizens to contribute freely, openly, and fully in politics. This good encompasses the essential freedoms: the right to compete for office; respect and support for national and regional political institutions, like legislatures and courts; tolerance of dissent and difference; and fundamental civil and human rights.

Need for Regulations (The Public Goods Game)

A model society requires the establishment of regulations. Without some form of regulation, slackers and cheaters will crash economic systems because people don't want to feel like suckers. It isn't true that we could create a system with no regulations where everyone would contribute to the good of society, everyone would benefit, and everyone would be happy. So what about public goods, things which everyone contributes to instead of taking from? It looks like the tragedy of the commons is true. Research into human behavior shows people are not so smart when it comes to contributing to the public good. [McRaney 2011]

The public good game can be associated, among many other alternatives, with paying taxes. If everybody pays taxes, society gets the benefits of better services. However, there are always some people who don't want to contribute and the services start getting worse. The crazy thing about this game is how illogical it is to stop contributing just because someone in the group is free riding. If everyone else is still being a good citizen, everyone will still win. This game is sometimes used to illustrate how regulation is necessary to keep any sort of nonprofit public good alive. Streetlights would never get put along dark roads, and bridges would collapse if people weren't forced to pay taxes

Rules to rule by [Bueno 2011]

Professor Bueno de Mesquita has cleverly suggested some rules to attain and sustain power.

First, politics is about getting and keeping political power. It is not about the general welfare of "We, the people."

Second, political survival is best assured by depending on a few people to attain and retain office.

Third, when the small group of cronies knows that there is a large pool of people waiting on the sidelines, hoping to replace them in the queue for gorging at the public trough, then the top leadership has great discretion over how revenue is spent and how much to tax. All that tax revenue and discretion opens the door to kleptocracy from many leaders and public-spirited programs from a very few. And it means enhanced tenure in power.

Fourth, dependence on a small coalition liberates leaders to tax at high rates.

Political Survival

Professor Bueno de Mesquita has also proposed some rules for political survival. Governing suggests five basic rules leaders can use to succeed in any system. [Bueno 2011]

Rule 1: Keep the winning coalition as small as possible. A small coalition allows a leader to rely on very few people to stay in power. Fewer essentials equal more control and contribute to more discretion over expenditures.

Rule 2: Keep the nominal electorate as large as possible. Maintain a large electorate of interchangeable to easily replace any troublemakers in the coalition, influentials and essentials alike.

Rule 3: Control the flow of revenue. It's always better for a ruler to determine who eats than it is to have a larger pie which lets the people feed themselves. The most effective cash flow for leaders is one that makes lots of people poor and redistributes money to keep selected people – their supporters – wealthy.

Rule 4: Pay key supporters just enough to keep them loyal. Remember, backers would prefer to be leaders than dependent. The leader's advantage over them is knowing where the money is.

Rule 5: Don't take money out of supporter's pockets to make people's lives better. The flip side of rule 4 is not to be too cheap toward the coalition of supporters. Being good to the people at the expense of the coalition means it won't be long until some "friends" will be gunning for the leader.

What would a leader do with any money that need not go to the coalition to buy loyalty? One way is to sock it away in a secret account or lavish it on the people. Some leaders are civic-minded and spend discretionary money to help the people, but only some of them are good at it. "A politician who stays poor is poor at politics." [Bueno 2011]

The word kleptocrat means rule by theft. Zaire's Mobutu made kleptocracy famous. Small-coalition leaders have tons of money to use as they see fit. Even though they compensate their coalition of essential backers well, with so few who need to be bribed, plenty is left over. Some use their discretionary money for civic-minded purposes but an awful lot just want to sock the money away for a rainy day. [Bueno 2011]

The ultimate political skill is to get things done. Cut through the clutter. Find the right person. Say the right things. Make it happen. Try to become the go-to person to get things done. What matters is the hierarchy of influence or ability-to-make-things-happen. The longer a politician is in the business, the more pragmatic it becomes. [Steele 2017]

## The Party

It is almost impossible to win an election in a democratic country without being a party member. The advantage of being at a party is that a lot of work will be done for you. It's like buying into a franchise. There are workers, donors, and voters who will support you just because you're wearing their color. You don't have to be well-known already. There is a brand, and now you are part of it. [Steele 2017]

The disadvantage of being in a party is that you're no longer a free agent. You're part of a team, and you have to be a team player. You have to do what you're told. That's how the politician culture starts taking hold of you. The grip is tight and it starts early. [Steele 2017]

Politicians themselves buy into the importance of party loyalty. They take to heart the idea of politics as a team endeavor. They will get nowhere on their own. They are told they will not always agree with their party colleagues, but to keep the disagreement internal. [Steele 2017]

Political language demonstrates the violence in politics. Always attack the other parties. Count the number of times people hear politicians talk about politics as a fight, a battle, or a campaign. The tribal nature of party politics is reinforced by the frequent use of war metaphors. The war-like attitude is present in political parties. There is a particular danger when the politician believes the war metaphors, and treats anyone who doesn't agree with them as an enemy to be destroyed. [Steele 2017]

Politics is much more difficult than people think. Public-policy issues are many-sided. There are no easy solutions. Political thinking offers an attractive, simple alternative. Most politicians are elected because of their party and leader, not because of their merit. The party and leader have substantial power over the politician. Therefore, the politician has to protect the party and leader. Always be loyal to your party and leader. [Steele 2017]

## Leadership

Anyone who thinks leaders do what they ought to do – that is, do what is best for their nation of subjects – ought to become an academic rather than enter political life. In politics, coming to power is never about doing the right thing. It is always about doing what is expedient. [Bueno 2011]

A successful leader always puts the wants of his essential supporters before the needs of the people. Without the support of his coalition a leader is nothing and is quickly swept away by a rival. But keeping the coalition content comes at a price when the leader's control depends only on a few. The threat posed by the risk of coalition defection is the highest, although if the people take to the streets on large-scale then they may succeed in overwhelming the power of the state. Therefore, socialists and would-be revolutionaries must prevent and deal with revolutionary threads. [Bueno 2011]

We must stop thinking that leaders can lead to unilaterally. No leader is monolithic. No emperor, no king, no sheik, no tyrant, no chief executive officer (CEO), no family head, no leader whatsoever can govern alone. [Bueno 2011]

One important lesson to learn is that where politics are concerned, ideology, nationality, and culture don't matter all that much. When addressing politics, we must accustom ourselves to think and speak about the actions and interests of specific, named leaders rather than thinking and talking about fuzzy ideas like the national interest, the common good, and the general welfare. [Bueno 2011]

Politics, like all of life, is about individuals, each motivated to do what is good for them, not what is good for the others. The prime mover of interests in any state (or corporation for that matter) is the person at the top – the leader. The self-interested calculations and actions of rulers are the driving force of all politics, it constitutes how they govern. The leader has to first come to power, then stay in power, and control as much national (or corporate) revenue as possible all along the way. [Bueno 2011]

The big questions of how the world ought to be are indeed important but they should not be the main initial focus. Questions of philosophical values and metaphorical abstractions don't apply to the view of politics. The world can only be improved if first, we understand how it works and why. Working out what makes people do what they do in the realm of politics is fundamental to working out how to make it in their interest to do better things. [Bueno 2011]

For leaders, the political landscape can be broken down into three groups of people: the nominal electorate, the real electorate, and the winning coalition. A simple way to think of each of these groups is interchangeable, influential, and essentials. Any leader worth his or her salt wants as much power as he or she can get, and keep it for as long as possible. Managing the interchangeable, influential, and essentials to that end is the act, art, and science of governing. [Bueno 2011]

# Chapter 7: Economic System

Capital and politics influence each other to such an extent that their relations are hotly debated by economists, politicians and the general public alike. Ardent capitalists tend to argue that capital should be free to influence politics, but politics should not be allowed to influence capital. They argue that when governments interfere in the markets, political interests cause them to make unwise investments that result in slower growth. For example, a government may impose heavy taxation on industrialists and use the money to give lavish unemployment benefits, which are popular with voters. In the view of many business people, it would be far better if the government left the money with them. They would use it, they claim, to open new factories and hire the unemployed. [Harari 2014]

In this view, the wisest economic policy is to keep politics out of the economy, reduce taxation and government regulation to a minimum, and allow market forces free rein to take their course. The free-market doctrine is today the most common and influential variant of the capitalist creed. The most enthusiastic advocates of the free market criticize military adventures abroad with as much zeal as welfare programs at home. They offer governments the same advice that Zen masters offer initiates: just do nothing. [Harari 2014]

But in its extreme form, belief in the free market is also naïve. There simply is no such thing as a market free of all political bias. The most important economic resource is trust in the future, and this resource is constantly threatened by thieves and charlatans. Markets by themselves offer no protection against fraud, theft, and violence. It is the job of political systems to ensure trust by legislating sanctions against cheats and to establish and support police forces, courts, and jails which will enforce the law. [Harari 2014]

There is an even more fundamental reason why it's dangerous to give markets a completely free rein. What happens if the greedy entrepreneur increases his profits by paying employees less and increasing their work hours? The standard answer is that the free market would protect the employees. If our entrepreneur pays too little and demands too much, the best employees would naturally abandon him and go to work for his competitors. However, avaricious capitalists can establish monopolies or collude against their workforces. If there is a single corporation controlling all similar factories in a country, or if all factory owners conspire to reduce wages simultaneously, then the laborers are no longer able to protect themselves by switching jobs. [Harari 2014]

## Wealth Production

Economic wealth is represented by goods and services that can be perceived with our senses, some are produced with human effort or the use of machinery, they directly satisfy human desires and needs, and they have an exchange value. Nature's gifts such as fresh air, water, and land are not economic wealth, because no human being has made them. Human-made goods and services are economic wealth because goods and services can add value to our lives. Money, for example, isn't economic wealth, since it can't satisfy human desire directly, but only indirectly when we exchange it for something else. So, when we talk about wealth we need to establish how it is created, what human effort and tools are required.

The term wealth production means the process by which more wealth is created, and this includes not just making a product, but also its transportation and distribution. A computer at a nearby store is more valuable than a computer located at a distant factory where it can't yet be used. On a foundational level, wealth is created from nature, human labor, and tools. Wealth has been traditionally related to land, labor, and capital. Land refers to all gifts of nature; labor to human effort; and capital to capital goods such as raw materials, tools, and machinery.

Therefore, land refers not simply to parcels of land, but anything freely provided by nature, including the sun, air, minerals, trees, and water, and even the electromagnetic spectrum. The term land doesn't include raw materials; since raw materials have been processed, they're considered capital. For example, oil reserves still in the ground are allocated to land, while oil extracted from the ground is capital.

The term labor signifies all human exertion, both mental and physical, aimed toward the production of wealth. The term capital means all previously created wealth that's put toward the creation of new wealth. The word capital here doesn't mean money, but rather refers to capital goods: human-made objects such as tools, machines or buildings that assist in the production of new wealth. Over time, we generally produce more wealth than we consume or destroy, and so our societies have a surplus of capital goods; everywhere we look, we see factories, office buildings, computers, trucks, and railroads, all standing by and ready to assist humanity in the production of new wealth.

There are, essentially, three ways to obtain wealth. Create wealth, receive it from someone else, or take it away from someone else. In economics, the term rent-seeking signifies a person's attempt to take away wealth, which the person can accomplish by manipulating the social and political environment to redirect the flow of income. The term wealth production means the process by which more wealth is created, and this includes not just making a product, but also its transportation and distribution. A chicken at a supermarket is more valuable than a chicken located at a distant farm where it can't yet be processed or eaten.

When human beings add value to the wealth production process through their labor, that added value can be classified as a wage (for example, when a mechanic repairs a car, the car runs better and he receives an income for his labor); and when capital goods add value to the wealth production process, that added value is what economists call a capital return (for example, the value added by the mechanic's use of time-saving power tools is a return on the customer's capital because the job gets done faster and relatively cheaper for the customer).

To extract rent from society means receiving without providing a wealth of a corresponding value. This is the only other way people can make an income receiving what economists call economic rent. The problem with rent extraction is that the more rent people extract from society, the fewer resources remain to pay people for their goods and services. Because many people extract economic rent from society on an ongoing basis, the people who add value to society – employees, small business owners, independent contractors, and so forth – are left with a much smaller share of the economic pie from which to draw an income.

## Financial Flow

Money is the most important, and least understood, part of politics. Finding money to pay for public services is a real problem. Where is the money going to come from, what justifies taking it from people in the form of taxes, and what it should be spent on? Federal money, tax money, or borrowed money have to be raised for public services. [Steele 2017]

Borrowing is a wonderful thing for leaders. They get to spend the money to make their supporters happy today, and, if they are sensible, set some aside for themselves. Repaying today's loan will be another leader's problem in the future. Governments of all flavors are more profligate spenders and borrowers than the citizens they rule. [Bueno 2011]

Money issues are so difficult for honest administrators that politicians like to avoid them, or at least pretend they are much simpler than they are. They will instead try to put non-monetary issues – social or cultural – at the center of the debate. These issues involve no money but can trigger strong emotional reactions, for example, wearing a niqab or a turban. Politicians love these social hot-button issues and go back to them again and again. They are a distraction from the real issues of government. [Steele 2017]

Money was invented to facilitate commerce. Hunter-gatherers had no money. Money is one of the greatest instruments of freedom ever invented by man. It is money which in existing societies opens an astounding range of choices to the poor man – a range greater than that which not many generations ago was open only to the wealthy. [Hayek 1994]

One can fall back on barter. But barter is effective only when exchanging a limited range of products. It cannot form the basis for a complex economy. In a barter economy, every day the shoemaker and the apple grower will have to learn anew the relative prices of dozens of commodities. If ten different commodities are traded in the market, then buyers and sellers will have to know the combinations of ten elements taken two by two, representing 45 different exchange rates. And if one hundred different commodities are traded, buyers and sellers must juggle 4,950 different exchange rates! How do you figure it out? [Harari 2014]

Credit

To understand modern economic history, we need to understand just a couple of words. The words are growth and credit. For better or for worse, in hardship and prosperity, in sickness and in health, the modern economy has been growing like foam in a poured beer. A glass of beer is made of liquid and foam; together with barley they make up a beer and the taste of the beer depends on all the ingredients. In a beer, bubbles' unstoppable growth is due to nucleation. In the economy, unstoppable growth is due to the availability of credit; the economy is a mix of money, wealth, and credit.

The Scientific Revolution brought the idea of progress. It was soon translated into economic terms. This trust created credit. Credit brought real economic growth, and growth strengthened the trust in the future and opened the way for even more credit. Whoever believes in progress believes that geographical discoveries, technological inventions, and organizational developments can increase the total of human production, trade and wealth. Today, there is so much credit in the world that governments, business corporations and private individuals easily obtain large, long-term and low-interest loans that far exceed current income. [Harari 2014]

### Reinvesting

The belief in the growing global pie eventually turned revolutionary. In 1776 the Scottish economist Adam Smith made the following novel argument: when a landlord, a weaver, or a shoemaker has greater profits than he needs to maintain his own family, he uses the surplus to employ more assistants, to further increase his profits. The more profits he has, the more assistants he can employ. It follows that an increase in the profits of private entrepreneurs is the basis for the increase in collective wealth and prosperity. [Harari 2014]

This may not strike you as very original, because we all live in a capitalist world that takes Smith's argument for granted. We hear variations on this theme every day in the news. Yet Smith's claim that the selfish human urge to increase private profits is the basis for collective wealth was one of the most revolutionary ideas in human history. What Smith said is that greed is good, and that by becoming richer we benefit everybody, not just ourselves. Egoism is altruism. [Harari 2014]

Smith taught people to think about the economy as a 'win-win situation,' in which my profits are also your profits. Not only can we both enjoy a bigger slice of pie at the same time, but the increase in your slice depends upon the increase in my slice. If I am poor, you too will be poor since I cannot buy your products or services. If I am rich, you too will be enriched since you can now sell me something. Smith denied the traditional contradiction between wealth and morality and threw open the gates of heaven for the rich. The rich are accordingly the most useful and benevolent people in society because they turn the wheels of growth for everyone's advantage. [Harari 2014]

## Managing the Means of Production

Some governments are based on fantasy, they believe the production of goods and services is done magically. They believe that collectivization is the best alternative to overcome exploitation. The state is going to provide for all people's needs and people don't have to worry about wealth production. These governments forget how to maintain the services of electricity, water, propane, communications, or transportation. The fun versus effort dichotomy defines these societies (go for the fun first, latter maybe go for the effort). The elite enjoys giving parties inviting the population and promoting fairs to make people believe they are living a happy life. However, people's future is bleak, just wait a certain time and everything is going to be ruined. Services won't work, education becomes ignorance, and production stagnates.

Governments promote economic equality because of their feud against the status quo. A government which undertakes to direct economic activity will have to use its power to realize somebody's idea of distributive justice. But how can and how will it use that power? By what principles will it or ought it to be guided? What about the relative merits that will arise? Is there a scale of values? Does it justify a new hierarchical order of society to satisfy the demands for economic justice? [Hayek 1994]

The notion that 'society as a whole' can control 'its productive resources' is common in socialist writing but is patently unrealistic. The machinery of social control has never been devised. There is no conceivable way in which a citizen can control the controllers of 'his' state railway or telephone company, except so indirectly that it is in effect inoperative. What belongs nominally to everyone on paper belongs in effect to no-one in practice. Coalfields, railways, schools, and hospitals that are owned 'by the people' are in real life owned by nobody. No nominal owner can sell, hire, lend, bequeath or give them to family, friends or good causes. [Niemietz 2019]

We can also see a quasi-socialist mindset in populist rhetoric which frames practically all social conflicts as conflicts between 'the people' (also known as 'working people' or 'ordinary people') and 'the elites', or some variation thereof, such as 'the 99 percent' versus 'the 1 percent.' But the People-versus-Elites template is a very poor guide to the political conflicts we observe. This is because socialist mythology treats The People as a romanticized abstraction, which has little to do with actual people. [Niemietz 2019]

The liberation of working people from exploitation has always been a common desire of many social systems. This is another aspiration of socialists and communists that has been impossible to implement through institutional organizations. Because this goal is not reached and cannot be reached by a new directing and governing class substituting itself for the bourgeoisie, socialists use to say that it can only be 'realized by the workers themselves being master over production.' And it requires converting the means of production into the property of freely associated producers and thus the social property of people who have liberated themselves from exploitation by their master, as a fundamental step towards a broader realm of human freedom. [Niemietz 2019]

Profit versus The Common Good

The tragedy of the commons is an idea suggesting people aren't very good at sharing. It is an idea affecting collectivization policies, demonstrating how damaging such policies are. In a socialist economy, the state becomes the main employer, the main landlord, the main supplier of goods and services, the main financial intermediary, etc. What belongs nominally to everyone on paper belongs in effect to no-one in practice. Coalfields, railways, schools, and hospitals that are owned 'by the people' are in real life owned by phantoms. No nominal owner can sell, hire, lend, bequeath or give them to family, friends or good causes. Public ownership is a myth and a mirage. It is the false promise and the Achilles' heel of socialism. [Niemietz 2019]

Private versus Public Ownership

A traditional source of conflict in economic systems is found in the convenience or not of accepting private economic activity. Some governments want to keep private activity at a minimum or assign certain organizations under public state control. Non-capitalist ownership of the means of production and public ownership of large industries and corporations is a typical aspiration in socialist countries. In socialist countries the slogan is the working class owns everything, everyone works toward the same communal goal, and people work to improve the life of every other citizen.

It is conventional wisdom that nationalization brings an industry 'under democratic control' and makes it 'accountable to the public.' This follows from the argument that 'profiteering corporations' are 'ripping off the public,' and must, therefore, be nationalized to make them work for 'the common good.' They must be made accountable to the public rather than to private shareholders.[Niemietz 2019]

1. This suggests that the argument for nationalization is not economic at all, but a moralistic impulse – a knee-jerk condemnation of the profit motive.

2. The argument rests on the assumption that the public sector is driven by altruistic motives, and that therefore, whatever is done by the state is done with 'the common good' in mind. This is a quintessentially socialist assumption. It is also, to say the least, debatable.
3. There is the assumption that there must be a conflict between the aim of satisfying people's needs and the aim of earning a profit. But under conditions of voluntary exchange within the rule of law, how else can a company make a profit other than by supplying what people want, at a price they are prepared to pay? How could it be profitable to ignore people's needs?
4. There is the idea that nationalization brings an industry 'under democratic control' and makes it 'accountable to the public.' This, too, is a socialist assumption, and a very dubious one at that.

## Planned Society

One of the fundamental differences between a socialist economy and a market economy is that the former is a collective endeavor. We all know from our personal lives that, when we take part in collective endeavors, we give up some degree of personal autonomy. This is not a problem as long as we do so voluntarily. If we live on our own, we can do whatever we like at home (for example, decorate the home as we see fit, play loud music at night, etc.); if we share a home with other people, we can no longer do that. If we work on a project as part of a team, we have to act as a team player; we do not have the same flexibility that we have when we work on our own. And so on. [Niemietz 2019]

In a liberal society, communities are voluntary and self-selecting. We choose to what extent we want to take part in collective endeavors, in which areas of life, and with whom. In a socialist society, most economic life is a collective endeavor. Limitations of personal liberty are therefore inevitable, and, within the logic of the system, justifiable. Emigration restrictions are an example of this. This is why the Berlin Wall and the Iron Curtain were not a 'betrayal' of socialism, but its consistent application. [Niemietz 2019]

A market economy is a testing ground, in which different business ideas, different management styles, different organizational models and different industry structures can be tried and tested in competition with one another. In a competitive society, nobody can exercise complete power over the means of production. These societies decentralize power to reduce the possibility of concentrating too much power into a few hands. The modern movement for planning is a movement against competition as such, a new flag under which all the old enemies of competition have rallied. [Hayek 1994]

Central planning has many disadvantages regarding diversity; to manage the system, simplicity must be imposed over variety. In contrast to a competitive society, a socialist planning board would possess complete power over the decisions regarding production and distribution. A competitive society has not even a fraction of the power of a socialists planning board. It is entirely fallacious to argue that the great power exercised by a central planning board would be 'no greater than the power collectively exercised by private boards of directors.' The idea that business owners are all in cahoots with one another, and act as one, is a socialist fantasy. Business owners compete with each other – often fiercely so. This greatly limits whatever 'power' any of them may wield. [Niemietz 2019]

Planned economies typically restrict people's freedom of movement, including domestic trips. They have to, large-scale movements of people would jumble the Five-Year Plans. One cannot plan an economy when the factors of production have a will of their own and move around all the time. Planners need to be able to allocate factors of production, including labor, and those factors then have to stay where they have been allocated to. Moving residence and changing jobs have repercussions for complementary factors of production and other parts of the Five-Year Plan, and, unlike in a market economy, no price mechanism leads to automatic adjustments. Therefore, people's movements must be controlled.

Economic planning can only ever be done in a technocratic, elitist fashion, and it requires an extreme concentration of power in the hands of the state. It cannot 'empower' ordinary workers. It can only ever empower a bureaucratic elite. A minority of planners, representing the 'best minds' available, decide for the rest of the people. [Niemietz 2019]

## Commerce and Consumerism

Commerce is one of the oldest professions ever invented. Merchants, conquerors, and prophets were the first people who managed to transcend the binary evolutionary division, 'us vs them', and to foresee the potential unity of humankind. For the merchants, the entire world was a single market and all humans were potential customers. They tried to establish an economic order that would apply to all, everywhere. [Harari 2014]

The forces of supply and demand have been well known for thousands of years. Once trade connects two areas, the forces of supply and demand tend to equalize the prices of transportable goods. To understand why consider a hypothetical case. Merchants traveling between India and the Mediterranean would notice the difference in the value of gold. To make a profit, they would buy gold cheaply in India and sell it dearly in the Mediterranean. Consequently, the demand for gold in India would skyrocket, as would its value. At the same time, the Mediterranean would experience an influx of gold, whose value would consequently drop. Within a short time, the value of gold in India and the Mediterranean would be quite similar. [Harari 2014]

Commerce developed the need for buying and selling. The supreme commandment of the rich is 'Invest!' The supreme commandment of the rest of us is 'Buy!' The new ethic promises paradise on condition that the rich remain greedy and spend their time making more money, and that the masses give free rein to their cravings and passions – and buy more and more. [Harari 2014]

Societies started to grow and division of labor facilitated commerce. The rise of cities and kingdoms and the improvement in transport infrastructure brought about new opportunities for specialization. Densely populated cities provided full-time employment not just for professional shoemakers and doctors, but also for carpenters, priests, soldiers, and lawyers. An economy of favors and obligations doesn't work when large numbers of strangers try to cooperate. It's one thing to provide free assistance to a sister or a neighbor, a very different thing to take care of foreigners who might never reciprocate the favor.

Consumerism sees the consumption of ever more products and services as a positive thing. It encourages people to treat themselves, spoil themselves, and even kill themselves slowly by overconsumption. Frugality is a disease to be cured. Consumerism has worked very hard, with the help of popular psychology ('Just do it!') to convince people that indulgence is good for you, whereas frugality is self-oppression. It has succeeded. We are all good consumers. [Harari 2014]

State and Market

The Industrial Revolution gave the market immense new powers, provided the state with new means of communication and transportation, and placed at the government's disposal an army of clerks, teachers, policemen, and social workers. At first, the market and the state discovered their path blocked by traditional families and communities who had little love for outside intervention. Parents and community elders were reluctant to let the younger generation be indoctrinated by nationalist education systems, conscripted into armies or turned into a rootless urban proletariat. [Harari 2014]

Over time, states and markets used their growing power to weaken the traditional bonds of family and community. The state sent its policemen to stop family vendettas and replace them with court decisions. The market sent its hawkers to wipe out longstanding local traditions and replace them with everchanging commercial fashions. Yet this was not enough. In order really to break the power of family and community, they needed the help of a fifth column. [Harari 2014]

The state and the market approached people with an offer that could not be refused. 'Become individuals,' they said. 'Marry whomever you desire, without asking permission from your parents. Take up whatever job suits you, even if community elders frown. Live wherever you wish, even if you cannot make it every week to the family dinner. You are no longer dependent on your family or your community. We, the state and the market, will take care of you instead. We will provide food, shelter, education, health, welfare, and employment. We will provide pensions, insurance and protection.' [Harari 2014]

Socialist countries should be aware that increased wages and pensions are inflationary. In those countries wages and prices, instead of being set by the market, are established based on justice as determined by the officials in charge. If we judge market economies primarily by their shortcomings, while judging socialism primarily as an idea, and by the intentions of its proponents, then the market economy can never win.

## Industriousness and Productivity

Some approaches see living standards primarily as a result of power struggles. These approaches consider that living standards of ordinary people rise when they organize and fight for it, and stagnate or fall when they cease to organize and fight for it. In this mindset, the focus is almost exclusively on the distribution of wealth, not on its generation. If you don't have to worry about generating wealth, it is easy to claim a piece of the cake somebody else produced. Most economists, whatever their political persuasion, would argue that the main determinant of pay levels is productivity. And productivity is not the exclusive fault of the entrepreneur, it is related among other things to labor, therefore, workers. Attacking entrepreneurship instead of worker's inefficiency is not a smart strategy, actions against industries may well often be justified, but they are a sideshow, if we want to see wage increases, then we must, first and foremost, support measures that facilitate productivity growth.

The best measure for anything is progress. And there's nothing else that brings more results consistently than hard work. What's more, the action itself leads to more action and at any moment of the day, people are building momentum and making sure their journey continues. A universal law is that the more people are focused on something and take action connected to it, the more doors are open and the more life gives them chances to get closer to their vision.

Getting results makes people feel accomplished, grateful and truly satisfied with what they're doing. It makes the whole process enjoyable and they must find the strength to persevere, to take action instead of waiting for things to happen, to stop blaming others, and to take responsibility for anything they have done or not in their job.

Effective interpersonal skills are crucial for any worker. Period. If a worker wants to be effective and efficient, she needs to have good listening and communication skills to be able to develop relationships that can promote organizational objectives. Good interpersonal skills allow people to get what they want, whenever they want, wherever they need it from.

When a worker has a task to do, people want it to get done and get done well. There's a reason to delegate tasks, the job has to be completed without having to worry about it. What people don't want is having that worker ask a million questions! This is why being resourceful is one of the most important qualities of a good worker.

Two heads are better than one – it's as simple as that! A great quality of a worker is his willingness to open up and share his ideas and experiences. After all, it's our past experiences that have taught us all we know, and if workers are willing to share that knowledge then everyone is benefiting.

Most economists, whatever their political persuasion, would argue that the main determinant of pay levels is productivity. Industrial action may well often be justified, but it is a sideshow: if we want to see wage increases, then we must, first and foremost, support measures that facilitate productivity growth. Economists disagree profoundly over what those measures are, but not on the fundamental point.

Empowering the Population

For decades, and under successive governments, the language of 'empowerment' has permeated politics. It seeks to empower civil society to allow participation in the decisions that affect people's lives. Health reforms are about 'empowering' patients; education reforms are about 'empowering' parents; electoral reforms are about 'empowering' voters, and so on. If it were so easy to 'empower' people, how come that many of us do not feel all that empowered? Why is there such a widespread anti-politics mood?

Empowering people may signify, 1) to decommodify labor, and as many other domains of life as possible; 2) to reduce or eliminate workers' alienation from their labor, society, and themselves; 3) to reduce the vast social and political inequality brought about by capitalism; and 4) to diminish or destroy capital's control over politics, society, and the economy.

Empowering Workers

Enabling people to 'organize together to chart new destinations for humanity', 'empowering civil society,' and 'allowing participation in the decisions that affect people's lives' are fine aspirations, but they are just that. A democratized economy seeks to empower civil society to allow participation in the decisions that affect people's lives. The idea that a socialist system should empower ordinary working people, rather than party apparatchiks, is not remotely as original as contemporary socialists think it is. That has always been the idea. [Niemietz 2019]

For example, the Soviet government was a government that paid lip service to empower workers but then failed to do so. There are no deeper reasons for this. If a government does not empower the workers, it is because it lacks the political will to empower the workers. That is all there is to know. The solution, then, is not to give up on the idea of empowering the workers, but to elect a government which does have that political will. And from a socialist perspective, the fact that socialism has failed more than two dozen times only proves that more than two dozen governments lacked the will to empower the workers. [Niemietz 2019]

Democratizing the economy

Several slogans are describing the aspirations of social systems regarding the economy. Traditionally, the poor have no chance to become an entrepreneur, only people with enough capital enter the process of creating income. The poor can only offer labor in exchange for income. Democratizing the economy is one slogan used by politicians to convince the less favored that it is possible to take them out of the hook and start becoming entrepreneurs. In most cases, loans are offered to potential entrepreneurs without capital at very low interest to be able to start a business. The same happens to cooperatives offering loans to assemble groups of people to work in certain projects at low-interest rates. There can be many different types of entrepreneurship available to integrate less favored groups.

Popular Economic Policies

There are several policies popular with the population that is normally unjustified. For example, price controls, rent controls, and industry nationalizations enjoy widespread support, while government regulation and interference with business decisions are also very popular. Some policies can confiscate or closely regulate major industries, the means of transportation and communication, and utilities (such as electricity and oil). And part of the population applauds those measures.

All these measures have their pros and cons, not because people support them they have to be implemented unilaterally. Any economic policy has effects on the production and distribution of goods and services, it is not only the viewpoint of the consumer that has to be considered, the producer and distributor have also a say. For example, anti-house-building protesters present housing developments as activities that merely line the pockets of developers without considering the immense benefit for tenants.

# Chapter 8: Personal Influence

Humans are diverse and imperfect. Either biologically or culturally, humans are random organisms. Humans are a bunch of improvisers that keep trying new ways of understanding life, and in most cases, they fail multiple times before coming up with good solutions. Failing often makes people react defensively, avoiding to be criticized because people don't like to be held responsible. The habit of blaming people arises as a natural offshoot of our competitiveness, and we may respond aggressively to criticism but also with an excuse, an apology, or an act of repentance.

No doubt, in certain circumstances, people come to put a greater emphasis on what distinguishes them from their neighbors than on what they share; no doubt the idea of human life as a single narrative, to be understood as whole in itself, comes to the fore in some epochs and not in others; no doubt the art of some cultures celebrates individuals and their way of "standing out" from the community, while the art of other cultures looks on this posture with indifference or hostility. [Scruton 2017]

Everything around people says something about their personality. As humans, people have many similarities and at the same time many differences. Cultivating an incomparable self either through consumption or creation is not something people take lightly. People are characterized by diversity, therefore, everybody is different. The nerve system is fundamental to define people's reflexes and capacity of endurance. If variation in mental and athletic ability is influenced to a moderate degree by heredity, as the evidence suggests, we should expect individuals of truly extraordinary capacity to emerge unexpectedly in otherwise undistinguished families, and then fail to transmit these qualities to their children. [Wilson 1978]

<u>Expectations</u>

The expectation is a nasty beast. Expectation, as it turns out, is just as important as raw sensation. The buildup to experience can completely change how we interpret the information. Political experts get mislead when the environment is manipulated; their objectivity and powers of analysis get mislead. True objectivity is pretty much considered to be impossible according to psychology. Memories, emotions, conditioning taint every new experience. Some expectations come from within and some come from without. The experience at the end of many political changes is less important, as long as it is not total crap. The experience will match up with people's expectations. People's expectations are the horse, and their experience is the cart. They get this backward all the time because people are not so smart.

People have expectations on the performance of the state, they believe there is going to be a transformation of society thanks to a new government or new laws and regulations. People get frustrated once governments are not able to perform. At the same time, there is the perspective of the state regarding the population. The state is expecting also very much from them. Sometimes, the state expects many sacrifices or more productivity from the population and they are not prepared for the task.

Egocentricity

Humans are primarily egocentrics and they have no choice. Humans tend to see things according to their viewpoint at first and then, after some reflection, they may consider the point of view of others. To survive in life, people must struggle and must do the effort of living; first, by their effort and next sharing efforts with others. Even though egocentric is related to egotism, it is the inexorable condition of living with themselves that makes humans revolve around their ego.

Egotism and egoism are related, even though they are not the same, the former describes people who are full of themselves and don't care about others whilst the latter considers that self-interest is the actual motive of all conscious action. Egoism is a doctrine that establishes individual self-interest as the actual motive of all conscious actions. Egoism is also an excessive concern for oneself with or without exaggerated feelings of self-importance. Egotism includes the practice of talking about oneself too much. Both terms describe a conscious decision-making process compared to egocentrics which is an innate characteristic.

Some political systems aim at a new human being without egoism and ready to collaborate. Human nature makes people a certain way instead of another and it is impossible to change human beings. The eternal objective of transforming humans into perfect beings is unattainable. The most we can do is to understand diversity and act in consequence.

Emotions

The world is full of interactions between humans, they respond to others with emotions that lie beyond the repertory of other animals: indignation, resentment, envy, admiration, commitment, and praise – all of which involve the thought of others as accountable subjects, with rights and duties and a self-conscious vision of their future and their past. Only responsible beings can feel these emotions, and in feeling them, they situate themselves in some way outside the natural order, standing back from it in judgment. [Scruton 2017]

Emotions such as resentment, guilt, gratitude, and anger are not human versions of responses that we might observe in other animals but ways in which the demand for accountability, which arises spontaneously between creatures who can know themselves as "I," translates into the language of feelings. [Scruton 2017]

Humans feel sometimes an unpleasant, often strong emotion caused by anticipation or awareness of danger. Fear involves some other emotions such as anxiety, dread or fearfulness that in some situations can develop into terror. Governments can exploit these weaknesses to make people more submissive in front of the injustices created by the state.

Most of the time, societies are not capable of solving the problems of their citizens and they are prone to strong feelings of annoyance, displeasure, and hostility. When people think that the government has behaved in an unfair, cruel, or unacceptable way, they may shout with anger and frustration. Anger is an intense emotional state, it involves a strong, uncomfortable and hostile response to a provocation, hurt, or threat. Citizens require complaint channels to resolve their disputes and when governments devise the correct institutions to solve the problems, citizens can refrain from frustration.

It seems that today everybody has a grievance, the unemployed steelworker, the low-wage fast-food employee, the student up to her ears in debt, the businessperson who feels harassed by government regulations, the veteran waiting too long for a doctor's appointment. Obviously, personal gripes – legitimate or not – have been part of the human condition. The concern is that now there is a lack of effective mechanisms for assuaging anger. People live in media and information bubbles that reinforce their grievances instead of looking at the problems from many sides. This creates the opportunity for demagogues who know how to bring people together in opposition to everyone else. [Albright 2018]

Some governments search to shape the minds of citizens with propaganda to bring about emotions that prepare them for action. People are called to sacrifice for the revolution, unite for a better tomorrow, and labor harder for the good of the whole society. Some leaders drew on the literary, religious, and artistic traditions that bound people together to exploit their anger to avoid ancient injustices.

## Non-violent Strategies

There are positive strategies to avoid violence, for example, "If our first response to injury is not violence but blame, the other is allowed to make amends. Violence is forestalled or postponed, and a process can then begin – the process that is well described in the Roman Catholic theology of repentance – whereby guilty parties are first marginalized and then, through atonement and contrition, reincluded, their fault duly forgiven. It is obvious that communities that can resolve their conflicts in this way have a competitive advantage over those whose only response to injury is violence." [Scruton 2017]

To avoid deaths during the war, some non-violent strategies are preferred, "The habit of capitulation rather than fighting to the end over territory and mates likewise has a life-preserving and therefore general preserving function." Having the opportunity to express your thoughts is also a source of promoting peace, "When you rightly accuse me of injuring you, I may look for excuses, and there is an elaborate dialogue here through which we express our intuitions concerning the avoidable and the unavoidable." [Scruton 2017]

Expressing guilt is another strategy to prevent additional violence, "Guilt feelings may be more or less strong, some people are experts at entertaining them, and they prompt the great yearning which engages with our most urgent loves and fears in this world: the yearning for redemption, for the blessing that relieves us of our guilt. Glimpses of this blessing are afforded by such liminal experiences as falling in love, recovering from illness, becoming a parent, and encountering in awe the sublime works of nature." [Scruton 2017]

The path of reconciliation is preferable to the eternal pursuit of conflict. Good and evil, sacred and profane, redemption, purity, and sacrifice all then make sense to us, and we are along a path of reconciliation, both to the people around us and to our destiny as dying things. Even for those who do not consider the dogmas of religion to be true, the religious posture, and the rituals that express it provides another kind of support to the moral life. Religion, on this understanding, is a dedication of one's being." [Scruton 2017]

Happiness
There are many interpretations of happiness, starting at the individual level up to the whole population. Humans are the main recipients of happiness, they are the ones looking for explanations. The consequences of people's actions stretch infinitely outward in both space and time. The best of intentions can lead to the worst of results. And values are many and in tension with each other. What place should people accord to beauty, grace, and dignity – or do these all creep into their deliberations as parts of human happiness? ... what happiness consists of, by what scale it should be measured, or what human beings gain from their aesthetic and spiritual values? [Scruton 2017]

Philosophers, priests, and poets have brooded over the nature of happiness for millennia, and many have concluded that social, ethical and spiritual factors have as great an impact on our happiness as material conditions. Happiness is a sense of well-being, joy, or contentment. When people are enjoying life, feel successful, or safe, or lucky, they feel happy. Whenever doing something causes happiness, people usually want to do more of it. No one has ever complained about feeling too much happiness.

In recent decades, psychologists and biologists have taken up the challenge of studying scientifically what makes people happy. Is it money, family, genetics or perhaps virtue? The first step is to define what is to be measured. The generally accepted definition of happiness is 'subjective well-being'. Happiness, according to this view, is something people feel inside, a sense of either immediate pleasure or long-term contentment with the way their life is going. [Harari 2014]

One interesting conclusion of published psychological research is that money does indeed bring happiness. But only up to a point, and beyond that, it has little significance. Another interesting finding is that illness decreases happiness in the short term, but is a source of long-term distress only if a person's condition is constantly deteriorating or if the disease involves ongoing and debilitating pain.

Family and community seem to have more impact on people's happiness than money and health. People with strong families who live in tight-knit and supportive communities are significantly happier than people whose families are dysfunctional and who have never found (or never sought) a community to be part of. Marriage is particularly important. But the most important finding of all is that happiness does not depend on objective conditions of either wealth, health or even community. Rather, it depends on the correlation between objective conditions and subjective expectations. [Harari 2014]

But are people happier? Did the wealth humankind accumulated over the last five centuries translate into new-found contentment? Did the discovery of inexhaustible energy resources open before us inexhaustible stores of bliss? Going further back, have the seventy or so turbulent millennia since the Cognitive Revolution made the world a better place to live? Was the late Neil Armstrong, whose footprint remains intact on the windless moon, happier than the nameless hunter-gatherer who 30,000 years ago left her handprint on a wall in the Chauvet Cave? If not, what was the point of developing agriculture, cities, writing, coinage, empires, science and industry? [Harari 2014]

Responsibility

The feature of responsibility is another characteristic related to humans. We hold each other accountable for what we do, and as a result, we understand the world in ways that have no parallel in the lives of other species. Our world, unlike the environment of an animal, contains rights, deserts, and duties; it is a world of self-conscious subjects, in which events are divided into the free and the unfree, those that have reasons and those that are merely caused, those that stem from a rational subject and those that erupt into the stream of objects with no conscious design. [Scruton 2017]

It is interesting to recognize that people would like to do whatever they want without any interference. People do not like to be accountable for what they do. Maturity makes people understand that anything they do is observed by others and there are consequences for their decisions. Immature people always complain about this constant interference in their own affairs. Society should prepare people to adapt to possible interference and help regulate misbehavior towards better comprehension and empathy.

Obligations and Choices

For humans, who enter a world marked by the joys and sufferings of those who are making room for us, who enjoy protection in our early years and opportunities in our maturity, the field of obligation is wider than the field of choice. We are bound by ties that we never chose, and our world contains values and challenges that intrude from beyond the comfortable arena of our agreements. In the attempt to encompass these values and challenges, human beings have developed concepts that have little or no place in liberal theories of the social contract – concepts of the sacred and the sublime, of evil and redemption, that suggest a completely different orientation to the world than that assumed by modern moral philosophy. [Scruton 2017]

Filial obligations provide a clear example. I did not consent to be born from and raised by my mom. I have not bound myself to her by a contract, and there is no knowing in advance what my obligation to her at any point might be or what might fulfill it. The Confucian philosophy places enormous weight on obligations of this kind – obligations of li – and regards a person's virtue measured almost entirely on the scale of piety. The ability to recognize and act upon unchosen obligations indicates a character more deeply imbued with a trustworthy feeling than the ability to make deals and bide by them – such is the thought. [Scruton 2017]

When the fault is ours we blame ourselves, and good people blame themselves more severely than others would. We recognize obligations to those that depend on us and on whom we depend, and we exist at the center of the sphere of accountability, which stretches out from us with dwindling force across the world of other people. [Scruton 2017]

It would be fair to say that the main task of political conservatism was to put obligations of piety back where they belong, at the center of the picture. And they were right to undertake this task. One thing that is unacceptable in the political philosophies that compete for our endorsement today is their failure to recognize that most of what we are and owe has been acquired without our own consent to it. In Hegel's Philosophy of Right, the family is defined as a sphere of pious obligations, and civil society, as a sphere of free choice and contract; the destiny of political order and the destiny of the family are connected. Families and the relationships embraced by them are nonaccidental features of interpersonal life, just like the experiences of pollution and violation. [Scruton 2017]

Virtues

Ancient thinkers distinguished four cardinal virtues – courage, prudence, temperance, and justice – and vice was its opposite. Virtues are dispositions that we praise, and their absence is an object of shame. It is through virtue that our actions and emotions remain centered in the self, and vice means the decentering of action and emotion so that the I and its undertakings no longer have a place in determining what one feels and does. Vice is a loss of self-control and the vicious person is the one on whom we cannot rely on matters of obligation and commitment. [Scruton 2017]

Virtues are human characteristics that require constant support. Aristotle's virtue consisted of the ability to pursue what reason recommends, despite the motives that strive against it. Virtue consists of the ability to take full responsibility for one's acts. Intentions, and avowals, in the face of all motives for renouncing or denouncing them we are human beings, with animal fears and appetites, and not transcendental subjects, motivated by reason alone. [Scruton 2017]

The virtues of Anglo-Saxons are independence and self-reliance, individual initiative and local responsibility, the successful reliance on voluntary activity, noninterference with one's neighbor and tolerance of the different and queer, respect for custom and tradition, and a healthy suspicion of power and authority. [Hayek 1994]

Nobility is related to virtue, even though it was associated with a social class during the Middle Ages. Today, nobility should be associated with the characteristics of people who have high morals and ideals, and who are always honest and charitable. Nietzsche was one who used the term most frequently to emphasize high personal qualities. Pursuing nobility means developing the courage to push yourself beyond anywhere you expected to be. It is anything but rest, peace, and complacency. It is an aggressive drive into enemy territory, welcoming every painful injury as a friend, as an encouragement to further growth. [Huenemann 2009]

<u>Altruism</u>

Generosity without hope of reciprocation is the rarest and most cherished of human behaviors, subtle and difficult to define, distributed in a highly selective pattern, surrounded by ritual and circumstance, and honored by medallions and emotional orations. We sanctify true altruism to reward it and thus to make it less than true, and by that means to promote its recurrence in others. Conscious altruism is a transcendental quality that distinguishes human beings from animals.

There are two forms of cooperative behavior: "hard-core" and "soft-core" altruism. An irrational and unilaterally altruistic impulse directed at others is hard-core, serving primarily the closest relatives. Soft-core altruism, in contrast, is ultimately selfish, it expects reciprocation from society for itself or its closest relatives. [Wilson 1978]

Tolerance

The largest sources of discrimination in humanity came from religious misguidance and political wrongdoing. Many battles have been fought in the name of God or the homeland. Tolerance was not the supreme criterion to avoid bloodshed. Uncomprehending is a normal attitude in humans. Human nature makes us potentially intolerant. It is difficult to get rid of that characteristic. Some say education should help to combat these defects but most of the time we have to accept imperfections. [Adler 1992]

Tolerance is the ability or willingness to accept something that we do not necessarily agree with, in particular, the expression of opinions or behaviors that collides with our own. Human beings have been persistent on discrimination and bigotry; the unjust or prejudicial treatment of different categories of people or things, especially on the grounds of race, age, sex, or ideology, and the intolerance toward those who hold different opinions from ourselves.

Forgiveness

Forgiveness means to stop blaming or being angry with someone for something that person has done, or not punishing him for something. It does not mean forgetting, nor does it means condoning or excusing offenses. Forgiveness cannot be offered arbitrarily and to all comers – so offered it becomes a kind of indifference, a refusal to recognize the distinction between right and wrong. Forgiveness is only sincerely offered by a person who is aware of having been wronged, to another who is aware of having committed a wrong. [Scruton 2017]

Animals use to have a better approach to forgiveness. Most of the time they just want to stay alive and avoid trouble. Humans are more resentful, they do not forget and keep fighting back for long periods.

Morality

Morality is concerned with our duties, but our duties all reduce, in the need, to one, which is the duty to do good – in other words, to obey those "optimistic" principles that promise the best outcome in the long run. The good person is the one who strives for the best outcome in all the moral dilemmas that he or she confronts. If, as suggested, morality is rooted in the practice of accountability between self-conscious agents, this is exactly what we should expect. The impartial other sets the standard that we all must meet. [Scruton 2017]

Persons are moral beings, conscious of right and wrong, who judge their fellows and who are judged in their turn. They are primarily individuals, and any account of the moral life must begin from the apparent tension that exists between our nature as free individuals and our membership in the communities in which our fulfillment depends. [Scruton 2017]

The abstract liberal concept of persons as centers of free choice, whose will is sovereign and whose rights determine our duties toward them, delivers only a part of moral thinking. Persons can be polluted, desecrated, defiled. As a self-conscious subject, a person has a point of view on the world. The world seems a certain way to them, and this "seeming" defines their unique perspective. [Scruton 2017]

## Human Rights

Those who build a universal political doctrine on the foundations of human rights require a theory that tells them which rights belong to our nature – our nature as persons – and which are the product of convention. That theory will be a theory of the person. Marxists who found their critique of bourgeois society on the idea of exploitation and the dignity of labor rely on the view that there is a fulfilled and free relation between people, which the capitalist system suppresses. Theists see the goal of human life as the knowledge and love of a personal God, whose presence is revealed in the natural order. Left-liberals see political order as a mechanism for reconciling individual freedom with social justice. In every area of political conflict today we find the concept of the person at the center of the dispute yet created as a mere abstraction, with little or no attention to its social and historical context. [Scruton 2017]

It is easy to accept that Hammurabi's Code was a myth, but we do not want to hear that human rights are also a myth. If people realize that human rights exist only in the imagination, isn't there a danger that our society will collapse? Voltaire said about God that 'there is no God, but don't tell that to my servant, lest he murders me at night.' Hammurabi would have said the same about his principle of hierarchy, and Thomas Jefferson about human rights. Homo sapiens have no natural rights, just as spiders, hyenas, and chimpanzees have no natural rights. [Harari 2014]

Human rights have been defined to protect citizens, they are not an instrument of the state. Humans rights should be independent of political systems. Liberty, equality before the law, and private property are just a few examples of rights that are not available in socialist countries. The objective is to define universal human rights that must be implemented in

any political system. There are civil, political, economic, social, cultural and collective rights.
- Civil rights (to life, liberty, and security)
- Political rights (protection by the law and equality before the law)
- Economic rights (to work, to own property and equal pay)
- Social rights (education, consenting marriage)
- Cultural rights (participation in the community)
- Collective rights (self-determination)

## Chapter 9: Social Influence

Human behavior is first and foremost a kind of "doing" or "acting" according to specific interests or motivators. Individuals do what they do because of either implicit or explicit ethical or practical (including economic cost-benefit) analyses to produce certain outcomes. When we try to understand people's behavior and explain why they do what they do, what framework do we use? One alternative is to use a framework of motivators, actions, personal and social influences and the justifications supporting these elements. [Boloix 2019b]

Human behavior is directed by interests, instincts or motivators to start actions or work efforts to produce change or satisfaction. As persons, we have specific characteristics originated initially by genetics and improved by our interaction with the environment during our lifespan. The social environment influences our actions and might impact others or define how the actions themselves might be shaped by social factors. Finally, there is the explanatory system that people use to make sense of the world around them and legitimize what they are doing and why.

Regarding motivators, the most common, intuitive approach to establish the motivators of human behavior is the "belief-desire-needs" trilogy. That is, people in everyday situations use beliefs, desires, intuitions, and needs to explain why they do what they do. Evolution has primed us to value certain states of affairs (e.g., safety, territory, food, sex, higher social status) over others. And, of course, our learning history directly shapes our motivational value system.

Regarding doing or acting, work efforts for survival, which involve several possible considerations, include among others, productive, spiritual, and recreational activities. Specific outcomes are guided by expected time and effort, reward objectives, opportunity analysis, costs, risks, and so forth.

There are personal influences, specific to each person, because people differ in terms of talents, temperaments, and dispositions, much of which are strongly influenced by genetics and adaptation. For example, extroverted people find stimulating social situations more rewarding than introverted people. Extroverted people may find autonomous activities arduous compared to introverted people that prefer isolation.

"Justification" is a broad concept that refers to both the systematic structure and the legitimizing function of verbal communication (including reading and writing). Justification can be thought of as anything that involves questions and answers which lead to claims about what is and what ought to be. Arguments, reasons for and against things, rationalizations, laws, and even scientific truth claims, all are "justifications." Justifications abound, why are we motivated? Why do we do what we do? What influence has the person or society?

Knowledge

Human's most important information that needs to be conveyed is about other humans, and not only about the rest of the world. Homo sapiens are social animals, cooperation is key for survival and capacity of reproduction. Human language evolved as a way of gossiping and personal exchange. It was not enough for individual men and women to know the whereabouts of lions and bison. It was much more important for them to know who in their band hated whom, who was sleeping with whom, who was honest, and who was a cheat. [Harari 2014]

When people try to communicate something complex and having vast knowledge of a subject that others don't, it is going to be difficult to get it across the gulf between one brain and the other. The explanation process may become thorny, but don't take it out on the others. Just because those persons can't see inside others' minds doesn't mean they are not smart enough. People don't suddenly become telepathic when they are angry, anxious or alarmed. Keep calm and carry on. Try to do your best and explain slowly your point of view. [McRaney 2011]

Knowledge is important when talking about political systems, they differ in their approach to knowledge. Capitalism and socialism are two extremes of knowledge. Capitalism is primarily competition, socialism is primarily collaboration. It is a common misunderstanding that the main role of competition is to act as an incentive, we work harder when we are under competitive pressure than we do when we can take our current position for granted; there is a by-product in the process: knowledge. But this incentive was never the main issue, socialist economies had other, less benign, ways of spurring people on. What they lacked, however, was the knowledge-creating capacity of competition. This is the main role of competition in economic life, knowledge. Socialist economies deprive themselves of the vast amount of knowledge created by competition. To a lesser extent, so do market economies that hinder the competitive process, for example, by erecting barriers to market entry. [Niemietz 2019]

When particularly complex societies began to appear in the wake of the Agricultural Revolution, a completely new type of information became vital – numbers. Foragers were never obliged to handle large amounts of mathematical data. No forager needed to remember, say, the number of fruit on each tree in the forest. So human brains did not adapt to storing and processing numbers. Yet in order to maintain a large kingdom, mathematical data was vital. It was never enough to legislate laws and tell stories about guardian gods. One also had to collect taxes. In order to tax hundreds of thousands of people, it was imperative to collect data about people's incomes and possessions; data about payments made; data about arrears, debts, and fines; data about discounts and exemptions. [Harari 2014]

Education and Knowledge

Education requires effort, teachers and students have to be prepared for the task, one group possessing the experience of knowledge and the other the thirst for knowledge. Each animal species is "prepared" to learn certain stimuli, barred from learning others, and neutral with respect to still others. The learning potential of each species appears to be fully programmed by the structure of its brain, the sequence of the release of its hormones, and ultimately, its genes. We like to think that given enough time and will power we can learn anything. We have to concede that there are sharp limits in quantity and complexity to what can be mastered even by geniuses and that everyone acquires certain mental skills far more easily than others. [Wilson 1978]

Education, as a means for getting ahead in life, is a big deal for any country's citizenry. To be objective, people need education and exposure to different environments and conditions. When facing a new problem, people look for similar experiences stored in their memory and through reasoning, they come up with possible solutions. Deepening on the subject, people are capable of designing better solutions.

Equality

There are political ideologies that advocate for an egalitarian redistribution of wealth and power in society through 'democratic' ownership and distribution of society's means of production (or means of making money). This means, in the simplest of terms, making more efforts to balance the scales between the rich and the poor. Since all people have broadly similar needs, distributing wealth on the basis of need-satisfaction has clearly egalitarian implications. For example, 'Cooperation' sounds very altruistic, but it is not always voluntary and seldom egalitarian. Most human cooperation networks have been geared toward oppression and exploitation. The family unit - according to an overwhelming majority of historians - was the only instance of an egalitarian society in human history and we know how authoritarian a family may become.

According to biology, humans were not created, they have evolved. And they certainly did not evolve to be 'equal.' The idea of equality is inextricably intertwined with the idea of creation. The Americans got the idea of equality from Christianity, which argues that every person has a divinely created soul and that all souls are equal before God. However, if we do not believe in the Christian myths about God, creation, and souls, what does it mean that all people are 'equal'? Evolution is based on differences, not on equality. Every person carries a somewhat different genetic code and is exposed from birth to different environmental influences. This leads to the development of different qualities that carry with them different chances of survival. 'Created equal' should, therefore, be translated into 'evolved differently'. [Harari 2014]

What kind of equality are we talking about? A fair approach would be equality equivalent to opportunity. Everybody having equal opportunities to demonstrate their capacities and those more capable would get the chance to excel and keep ahead. Are men equal to women or blacks equal to whites? Physically they are different, there is no choice, blacks have pigmentation that whites don't; women and men differ on gender. However, having equal opportunities according to skills is an excellent equality proposition. The same analysis applies to other contexts either physical or mental: skilled and unskilled, good and evil, smart and dumb, and so on. Sociopolitical systems must be precise on what equality means.

<u>Social Justice and Liberty</u>

Justice denotes a particular kind of moral judgment, in particular one about the distribution of rewards and punishment. Justice is about giving each person what he or she is 'due.' Social justice refers to the distribution of material rewards and benefits in society, such as wages, profits, housing, medical care, welfare benefits, and so on.

Social justice and liberty are at the heart of the arguments for a just society. Both are important ingredients for a well balanced society. Up to now, the inconvenience is how to please both at the same time. Some turn towards socialism, which emphasizes social help, and others prefer liberty which appreciates entrepreneurship. It is evident that the solution requires taking both arguments into consideration and designing the appropriate apparatus of government to control its implementation. For example, capitalist approaches facilitating social programs and socialist's approaches allowing some form of economic and social freedoms.

There is a relationship between the concepts of morality, politics, and philosophy that must be taken into consideration when defining social justice. Current political philosophy explores the virtues of a benevolent state and usually makes social justice, sometimes liberty, into the overarching aim of government. The critical instruments of social coordination are the system of rights and duties (morality), the virtues that motivate us to obey it, and the political backing that makes obedience possible and which coordinates our many and diverse interests. [Scruton 2017]

Liberty is a valued principle for humans, it stands for something greater than just the right to act however we choose; it includes, among other things, the absence of a despotic government. Free speech, free assembly, and free enterprise are some of the most looked after values. Freedom also stands for securing to everyone an equal opportunity for life, liberty, and the pursuit of happiness. Humans deserve freedom, although with some limitations, regarding coexistence with other fellow humans. Individual autonomy and respect for human rights are the root conceptions of the moral order, with the state conceived either as an instrument for safeguarding autonomy or – given a larger role – as an instrument for rectifying disadvantages in the name of "social justice."

Community

At its heart, a society possesses a unifying vision of human beings as social creatures, capable of overcoming social and economic problems by drawing upon the power of the community rather than simply individual effort. This is a collectivist vision because it stresses the capacity of human beings for collective action, their willingness and ability to pursue goals by working together, as opposed to striving for personal self-interest. Human beings are, therefore, 'comrades,' 'brothers' or 'sisters,' tied to one another by the bonds of common humanity. However, most of the time, self-interest produces an indirect benefit to society and should not be discouraged.

Socialists are far less willing than either liberals or conservatives to believe that human nature is unchanging and fixed at birth. Rather they believe that human nature is 'plastic', molded by the experiences and circumstances of social life. In the long-standing philosophical debate about whether 'nurture' or 'nature' determines human behavior, socialists resolutely side with nurture. However, it is clear that nature and nurture are distributed at least half and half.

Before birth, while in the womb, individuals acquire a set of natural capacities, different from other individuals. After birth, individuals are subjected to experiences that have some influence on his or her personality. Many human skills and attributes are learned from society, the language we speak is one of them. Whereas liberals draw a clear distinction between the 'individual' and 'society,' socialists believe that the individual is inseparable from society. Human beings are willing to be self-sufficient or self-contained; they can be separated or atomized 'individuals,' related to the social groups to which they belong.

Collectivism is, broadly, the belief that collective human endeavor is of greater practical and moral value than individual self-striving. It thus reflects the idea that human nature has a social core, and implies that social groups, whether 'classes,' 'nations,' 'races' or whatever, are meaningful political entities. It is preferable to pursue a balance of collectivism and individualism than just lean towards only one of them.

Diversity

In Twilight of the Idols (Morality as Anti-nature), Nietzsche expresses clearly the principle of diversity in humans: "Finally, let's consider how naïve it is, in general, to say, 'Human beings should be such and such!' Reality shows us a captivating treasury of types, the exuberance of an evanescent play and alteration of forms. And some pathetic bystander of a moralist says to all this, 'No! Human beings should be different'? ... He even knows how human beings should be, this sanctimonious sniveler; he paints himself on the wall and pronounces, 'ecce homo!' ..." [Nietzsche 1998]

Humans have so many characteristics that their combinations can produce infinite types of variants. Taking a detailed look at the many attempts to describe some part of what is distinctive of the human condition, let us present the following sample – the use of language (Chomsky, Bennet), second-order desires (Frankfurt), second-order intentions (Grice), convention (Lewis), freedom (Kant, Sartre), self-consciousness (Kant, Fichte, Hegel), laughing and crying (Plessner), the capacity for cultural learning (Tomasello) – you will be surely persuaded that each is tracing some part of a single holistic accomplishment. [Scruton 2017]

One characteristic that distinguishes humans is that we understand things differently. We never agree on many things. Each experience has many interpretations and therefore no two people will draw the same conclusion from the same event. This accounts for the fact that we do not always learn from our experiences. Older is not always wiser! A senior citizen that never tried to improve during his life is not a good example to follow. Some seniors citizens repeat the same mistakes over and over, how are they going to help new generations? To give advice, we need privileged active minds that look always for better approaches to human behavior. It has been demonstrated that our pattern of behavior does not usually change as a result of experiences.[Adler 1992]

Obedience

Obedience is one important topic for any society. However, the obedient individuals are rendered unfit for life because their habits of slavish obedience have left them incapable of any independent action or thought. This submissive tendency developed as obedient children may evolve into adults that submit to any authoritative commands. [Adler 1992]

It is a pity that there are so many obedient people in the world. Sometimes, obedience is required but other times disobedience at the right time makes a difference. When a law is wrong, it must be changed, it is not acceptable to punish people under the umbrella of an insensible law.

The problem with obedience is mostly related to uncontested obedience. Any citizen should comply with the law if the law is just. However, it is the responsibility of citizens to contest unjust laws. It is in this regard that conflict arises, people bypassing the laws instead of fighting to abolish them. The first responsible entity regarding unjust laws is the state. The state is always slow to get rid of unjust laws, making citizens uncomfortable and anxious. There is a lack of appropriate communication channels, and it is not convenient to test the patience of citizens.

Respect and Dignity

Respect is the adequate regard for the feelings, wishes, rights, or traditions of others. People are becoming more and more self-centered and unsympathetic to those around them. As a result, they have little or no regard for other people's rights and feelings. Many people act without politeness, thoughtfulness, and civility. Disrespectful behavior is on the rise and people who have earned great achievements are no longer treated with the respect they deserve. Governments who treat people disrespectfully make the world a lot less peaceful. Treating people miserably is the source of unhappiness for many of them. "Life is too short to waste our time on people who don't respect, appreciate, and value us."

Dignity is the sense people have of their importance and value, and it is related to other people's respect for you. Dignity is our inherent value and worth as human beings; respect, on the other hand, is earned through one's actions. The glue that holds human relationships together is the mutual desire to be seen, heard, listened to, and treated fairly; it is also related to being recognized, understood, and to feel safe in the world. We all know the gut feeling that results from being mistreated or neglected – it is up to each one to honor other people's dignity, in the process, they strengthen their own.

Reasoning

One important human characteristic, which is related to the possibility of justifying results, is the capacity to reason. Without reasoning, humans cannot get along. To improve human relations, some principles of reasoning are required. Those principles establish the required balance between individuality and collectivity. The following principles seem to be accepted by those who lay down their weapons and reason toward solutions instead: [Scruton 2017]

1. Considerations that justify or impugn one person will, in identical circumstances, justify or impugn another.
2. Rights are to be respected.
3. Obligations are to be fulfilled.
4. Agreements are to be honored.
5. Disputes are to be settled by negotiation, not by force.
6. Those who do not respect the rights of others forfeit the rights of their own.

Unlike Kant, Aristotle did not recognize reason as a metaphysically distinct motive; but he did think that the disposition to follow what reason commands is a real motive, one that depends on cultivating good habits and one that puts the agent in the very position that Kant sees as central to the moral life: the position of honoring obligations, despite the passions that oppose them. [Scruton 2017]

The peculiar force of morality and the sense of duty set us outside and against the order of nature. We are law-governed creatures, and even when we defy the law, we act on the assumption that we are subject to nonnegotiable demands – reasons that have the power to silence countervailing considerations, however closely they represent our empirical interests. [Scruton 2017]

When faced with a policy issue, a normal thought process should go something like this: [Steele 2017]
- Define the problem you are trying to solve.
- Identify the causes of the problem.
- Develop policy options to resolve the causes.
- Select the best policy option.
- Decide on an implementation and communication plan.
- Implement and communicate.

Negotiation

Negotiation is a popular term these days but most people have difficulties accepting other's opinions and reaching consensus. Frequently people prefer confrontation and isolation instead of negotiation. Humans need to follow some principles to live in a society and they should be known by everybody. However, most people are aware of those recommendations but they do not follow them.

Negotiation is an art, it requires intelligence, empathy, justice, and resolution. Negotiation requires an open mind ready to produce acceptable alternatives. Negotiation also needs creativity, obtuse minds are the worst participants in negotiation. Good negotiation requires that you first be creative about how to serve each side's interests, and only then get down to the business of choosing options. [Steele 2017]

Negotiation requires morality. The fundamental intuition is that morality exists in part because it enables us to live on negotiated terms with others. We can do this because we act for reasons and respond to reasons too. When we incur the displeasure of those around us, we attempt to justify our actions, and it is part of our accountability that we should reach for principles that others too can accept and which are perforce impartial, universal, and lawlike. [Scruton 2017]

Politicians are frequently involved in a negotiation because they are running a business, and the business they're in is called re-election. You need to think of your interaction with politicians as a business negotiation. People are negotiating the scarce allocation of public resources and the allocation of the politician's interest and energy. [Steele 2017]

'The Getting to Yes' method is built on four basic ideas: [Steele 2017]
- Separate the people from the problem;
- Focus on interests, not positions;
- Invent options for mutual gain;
- Insist on using objective criteria.

Good negotiation requires that people understand the other side's position. The ability to see the situation as the other side sees it as part of the solution. Those that only see their side are going to have a hard time during a negotiation. Good negotiation requires that people focus on the needs, desires, concerns, and fears of each side. These are their interests, and they are not the same as the other side's position, which is how they want their interests to be served. Positions come and go; interests are steady or at least evolve very slowly. Good negotiations focus on interests. [Steele 2017]

# Chapter 10: Ideological Sphere

Humans have always looked for a justification of their actions and a way to do it is through the invention of an ideology. Ideologies combining theories of history regarding class conflict, economics involving the labor theory of value, and justice implying empowerment of the proletariat, and egalitarian redistribution of wealth and power in a society were the drivers to build social systems as the ultimate, legitimizing goal. Additionally, some ideologies promoted participation in an international movement to make the struggle feasible with the support of other partisans around the globe.

Throughout history, leaders have used – or in some cases invented – ideologies to legitimize their power. At its best, ideology is a coherent set of ideas about how to understand the world, what constitutes a good life, and how we should relate to one another through the government. At its worst, ideology is like a short circuit in the politician's brain. No matter what you say, they can't take in anything that clashes with their ideology. Ideology is a political philosophy. Don't waste your time on an ideologue because there is literally nothing you can say that will change its mind. [Steele 2017]

Among the meanings that have been attached to ideology the following is a sample: [Heywood 2003]
- A political belief system.
- An action-oriented set of political ideas.
- The ideas of the ruling class.
- The world-view of a particular social class or social group.
- Political ideas that embody or articulate class or social interests.
- Ideas that propagate false consciousness among the exploited or oppressed.
- Ideas situating the individual within a social context and generating a sense of collective belonging.
- An officially sanctioned set of ideas used to legitimize a political system or regime.
- An all-embracing political doctrine that claims a monopoly of truth.
- An abstract and highly systematic set of political ideals.

The ideas of the ruling class are in every epoch the ruling ideas, i.e., the class which is the ruling material force of society is at the same time the ruling intellectual force. The class which has the means of material production at its disposal, has control at the same time over the means of mental production, so that thereby, generally speaking, the ideas of those who lack the means of mental production are subject to it. [Heywood 2003]

Appeals to ideological principles and rights are generally a cover. We must be suspicious of some idealistic motives. There is always some principled way to defend any position, especially one's own interests. Both freedom and stability are principled positions (the good reason) selectively asserted depending upon how we like the leader (the real reason). In devising fixes to the world's ills, the essential first step is to understand what the protagonists want and how different policies and changes will affect their welfare. A reformer who takes what people say at face value will quickly find their reforms at a dead end. [Bueno 2011]

Ideological Criteria

An ideology suggests criteria by which people act, and this criterion takes the form of an obligation – not an entitlement, and it is related to the language of duties rather than the language of rights. Ideologies are about judging politics in terms of what or whom a fundamental debt is owed. In older times, the debt was owed to a god or a king, but now debts are owed elsewhere. Environmentalism suggests that we owe a debt to the earth. Nationalism suggests that we owe a debt to the nation. Feminism suggests that we owe a debt to women. An ideology is a view about what ought to be thought, said and done about politics in terms of some criteria, including to what or whom a fundamental debt is owed. Additionally, in modern politics, there is doubt about to what or whom debts are owed.

Major ideologies suppose that the debt is owed to the self, implying human nature considerations, and this suggests that the self is difficult to characterize. However, each ideology characterizes the self in a different way; the individual, the society, the poor, the nation. Most ideologies form successive elaborations from a common initial criterion, what is intrinsically necessary (the self), adding other justifications on top of it, such as, what is necessary to support that intrinsic necessity (a system of standards, rules, and laws), and what is contingent (everything else, including all other beliefs, practices, and institutions).

Each ideology takes order seriously and it must be enforced through conviction, laws or force. Each ideology is critical of other orders in relation to which it posits itself as having a superior ideal and being enlightened and critical to justify its hegemony. An order is founded upon 'three principles, first, the principle of freedom for all members of a society (as humans); second, the principle of the dependence of everyone upon a single common legislation (as subjects); and third, the principle of legal equality for everyone (as citizens).' Each self exists in relation to other selves in terms of right, where 'right is the sum total of those conditions within which the will of one person can be reconciled with the will of another in accordance with a universal law of freedom.'

Order and Stability

Social order arose out of the shared beliefs, values, norms, and practices of groups of people. A sense of social connection – what is called solidarity – emerged between and among people and helped to bring them together into a collective. It is through the culture shared by a group, community, or society that order is attained. To bound society together, it is necessary for each other to fulfill different roles and functions. It is through our interactions with institutions, such as the state, media, education, law enforcement, and the people around us that we participate in the maintenance of rules and norms and behavior that enable the smooth functioning of society.

Social order must acknowledge that it is the product of multiple and sometimes contradictory processes. Social order is a necessary feature of any society and it is deeply important for building a sense of belonging and connection with others. A "stable" society is one where widespread and continued lawlessness, violence, rioting, and so on, don't occur, or occur sporadically and locally. When order and stability are required, a high degree of energy must be poured into the system. In human societies, the order requires the pervasive threat of violence and punishment. Societies have to put in a great deal of effort and expenditure to preserve order and to keep it stable.

Some ideologies consider the importance of history to maintain the status quo. These ideologies propose that people have to see themselves as involved in 'a partnership not only between those who are living, but between those who are living, those who are dead, and those who are to be born.' This may imply that people should be inclined to hold onto what they have rather than seeking what they do not have, 'to prefer the familiar to the unknown, the actual to the possible, the limited to the unbounded, the near to the distant, the convenient to the perfect.' These ideologies argue that there is no obligation to change the world because human imperfection, on the one hand, and unforeseen consequences, on the other, make it impossible to know that any change will be for the better. People need their prejudices and the traditions which are the embodiment of those prejudices.

Ideology explains why liberals are concerned with law, why socialists are concerned with the economy, society and power, and why conservatives are concerned with tradition, history, and religion to maintain the status quo. Conservatives look backward, not forward, and so look to the very traditions which liberalism and socialists put into question. This is why they are less securely secular than liberals or socialists. Even if a conservative is not religious, he tends to respect religion. Unlike the liberal or the socialist, who attempts to liberate man from tradition, the conservative seeks no liberation from tradition. The conservative, in general, distrusts argument because argument simplifies what should not be simplified. This is why the conservative argument usually takes the form of negation or reaction. Its criterion is the complete, even if contradictory, one, that people owe a debt to the self as constituted by its existence not only in society but also in history.

Political Action

An ideology is represented by a set of ideas that provides the basis for organized political action, whether this is intended to preserve, modify or overthrow the existing system of power. Ideologies offer an account of the existing order, usually in the form of a 'current world-view;' present a model of the desired future, a vision of the 'model society;' and explain how political change can and should be brought about, in other words, how to transit from the existing order to the 'desired future.' [Heywood 2003]

## Current World-view

Ideas and ideologies influence political life in a number of ways. In the first place, they provide a perspective through which the world is understood and explained. People do not see the world as it is, but only as they expect it to be; in other words, they see it through a veil of ingrained beliefs, opinions, and assumptions. Whether consciously or unconsciously, everyone subscribes to a set of political beliefs and values that guide their behavior and influence their conduct. Political ideas and ideologies thus set goals that inspire political activity. In this respect, politicians are subject to two very different influences. Without a doubt, all politicians want power. This forces them to be pragmatic, to adopt those policies and ideas that are electorally popular or win favor with powerful groups such as business or the army. However, politicians seldom seek power simply for its own sake. They also possess beliefs, values, and convictions about what to do with power when it is achieved.

To understand the current society or world situation, ideologies have to demonstrate an understanding of the processes through which the modern world came into existence. The process of modernization in the world had social, political, and cultural dimensions. Socially, it was linked to the emergence of increasingly market-oriented and capitalist economies, dominated by new social classes, the middle class, and the working class. Politically, it involved the replacement of monarchical absolutism by the advance of constitutional and, in due course, democratic government. Culturally, it took the form of the spread of Enlightenment ideas and views, which challenged traditional beliefs in religion, politics, and learning in general, based upon a commitment to the principles of reason and progress. The 'core' political ideologies, the ones out of which later ideologies emerged or developed in opposition to – liberalism, conservatism, and socialism – reflected contrasting responses to the process of modernization. [Heywood 2003]

While modern societies were structured by industrialization and class solidarity, postmodern societies are increasingly fragmented and pluralistic 'information societies' in which individuals are transformed from producers to consumers, and individualism replaces class, religious, and ethnic loyalties. Post-modernity, sometimes portrayed as late modernity, has both thrown up new ideological movements and transformed established ones. The former tendency has been reflected in the growing importance of so-called 'lifestyle' and 'identity' issues, linked to the rise of post-material sensibilities and the declining ability of a class to generate a meaningful sense of social identity. This has been evident since the 1960s in the growth of new social movements – the peace movement, the women's movement, the gay movement, the green movement and so on – and in the emergence of new ideological traditions, notably radical feminism, radical fundamentalism, and ecologism. [Heywood 2003]

## Proposed Model Society

To understand how to define a model society, let us take three important issues, namely, emancipation, equality, and religion to identify the influence of ideologies. On emancipation, liberalism is a search for emancipation from the unenlightened liberties justified by tradition to individual liberty, which is justified by the secular criterion of the self. Socialism is emancipation from individual liberty towards social cooperation. And conservatism is the emancipation in terms of the recognition of the incomplete nature of any abstract or unhistorical liberty.

On equality, liberalism is wholly for equality, but only equality of the self in relation to all other-selves in terms of a shared structure of law. Socialism seeks equality that does not offer the same to every self but offers the same to the social self. It is unclear whether socialism is about equality as such, instead of overcoming inequalities according to phrases like, 'From each according to his abilities, to each according to his needs.' And if there is any enthusiasm for equality in conservatism at all, as more than a concession to secular society, it is in the sense that we are all equal before God.

On religion, liberalism separates 'church' and 'state' by locating all matters of religion in privacy, so leaving the secular state dominant in public. Socialism alleges that the separation is an error, which leaves the self in thrall to religion, so it refuses the separation and instead suggests that church and state together have to be transformed. And conservatism alleges that religion is what it is, in its publicity and its authority, so it should neither be displaced nor replaced.

## Transition to the Desired Future

Humans want to improve the world but they must first understand how. What are the world forces into play? What are the motivations of people? What are the objectives of humankind? It is not acceptable to make people miserable in the name of an absurd idea. Humans need to understand human nature and diversity. Humans are imperfect and society must consider that. Societies are imagined by humans, therefore, let us come up with realistic solutions to real problems.

To improve the world, all of us must first suspend faith in conventional wisdom. Let logic and evidence be the guide and our eyes will be opened to the reasons why the world works the way it does.

Knowing how and why things are as they are is a first, crucial step toward learning how to make a better world. [Bueno 2011]

The world has many deficiencies, there are too many difficulties: how to make a living, how to be happy, how to be successful, how to attain justice, are just some examples of shortcomings humans endure during their life. We all know how injustices in every realm of human life proliferate. However, some people still believe it is possible to improve the world and live in a 'Just World' such that they can live happily and secure forever.

Making the world better is a difficult task. If it were not, then it would already have been done. The misery in which so many people live would already have been overcome. The enrichment of CEOs while their stockholders lose their shirts would be a thing of the past. However, the inherent problem with change is that improving the life for one group generally means making at least some other persons worse off. New leaders of the latter group will raise if change really will solve the people's problems. [Bueno 2011]

The 'means' politicians should use to achieve ideological ends, or the 'roads to a new ideology' have conflicting opinions. This concern with means follows from the fact that some ideologies have always had an antagonistic character, they are forces for change to modify the status quo, they involve the transformation of the capitalist or colonial societies in which they emerged. The 'road' that some ideologies have adopted is not merely a matter of strategic significance, they determine the character of the idealistic movement and influence the form of what eventually would be achieved. In other words, means and ends within ideologies are often interconnected.

Revolutionary Path

Some ideologies could only be attained by the revolutionary overthrow of the existing political system, and accept that violence would be an inevitable feature of such a revolution. Marx and Engels envisaged a 'proletarian revolution,' in which the class-conscious working masses would rise up to overthrow capitalism. The first successful socialist revolution did not, however, take place until 1917, when a dedicated and disciplined group of revolutionaries, led by Lenin and the Bolsheviks, seized power in Russia in what was more a coup d'état than a popular insurrection. In many ways, the Bolshevik Revolution served as a model for subsequent generations of socialist revolutionaries.

Although some ideologies, such as socialism, often supported the idea of revolution, as the nineteenth century progressed enthusiasm for popular revolt waned, at least in the advanced capitalist states of western and central Europe. Capitalism itself had matured and by the late nineteenth century, the urban working class had lost its revolutionary character and had been integrated into society.

There are some cases of governments created after a coup d'etat. The military intervenes by force to avoid the disastrous consequences of a power void. Some other times, the military is appointed as provisional juntas that remain in power indefinitely due to an ungovernable situation. Some regions of the globe are prone to military intervention according to their history. Latin America is one of the hottest places on the planet prone to undemocratic governments.

A unifying set of political ideas and values can develop naturally within a society. However, it can also be enforced from above in an attempt to manufacture obedience and thereby operates as a form of social control. The values of elite groups such as political and military leaders, government officials, landowners or industrialists may diverge significantly from those of the masses. Ruling elites may use political ideas to contain opposition and restrict debate through a process of ideological manipulation. [Heywood 2003]

Evolutionary Path

Even though it is a good idea to struggle for a 'Just World,' at the same time we must understand that it is impossible to attain perfection. People must accept world deficiencies but push for a better human future. It is preferable an imperfect solution that works than an unattainable fantasy. People should never let the quest for perfection block the way to lesser improvement. Utopian dreams of a perfect world are just that: Utopia. Pursuing the perfect world for everyone is a waste of time and an excuse for not doing the hard work of making the world better for many. [Bueno 2011]

Wages and living standards started to rise, partly as a result of colonial expansion into Africa and Asia after 1875. The working class had also begun to develop a range of institutions – working men's clubs, trade unions, political parties and so on – which both protected their interests and nurtured a sense of security and belonging within industrial society. Furthermore, the gradual advance of political democracy led to the extension of the franchise (the right to vote) to the working classes. By the end of the First World War, a large majority of the western states had introduced universal manhood suffrage, with a growing number extending voting rights also to women. The combined effect of these factors was to shift the attention of socialists away from violent insurrection and to persuade them that there was an alternative evolutionary, 'democratic' or 'parliamentary' road to socialism. [Heywood 2003]

Their optimism was founded on a number of assumptions. First, the progressive extension of participation would eventually lead to the establishment of universal adult suffrage and therefore of political equality. Second, political equality would, in practice, work in the interests of the majority, that is, those who decide the outcome of elections. Socialists thus believed that political democracy would invest power in the hands of the working class, easily the most numerous class in any industrial society. Third, socialism was thought to be the natural 'home' of the working class. As capitalism was seen as a system of class exploitation, oppressed workers would naturally be drawn to socialist parties, which offered them the prospect of social justice and emancipation. The electoral success of socialist parties would, therefore, be guaranteed by the numerical strength of the working class. Fourth, once in power, socialist parties would be able to carry out a fundamental transformation of society through a process of social reform. In this way political democracy not only opened up the possibility of achieving socialism peacefully, it made this process inevitable. The achievement of political equality had to be speedily followed by the establishment of social equality.

Furthermore, is the working-class socialist at heart? Is socialism genuinely in the interests of the working class? Socialist parties have been forced to acknowledge the ability of capitalism to 'deliver the goods', especially during the 'long boom' of the post-1945 period, which brought growing affluence to all classes in western societies. During the 1950s socialist parties, once committed to fundamental change, revised their policies in an attempt to appeal to an increasingly affluent working class. A similar process took place in the 1980s and 1990s, as socialist parties struggled to come to terms with changes in the class structure of capitalism as well as the pressures generated by economic globalization. In effect, socialism came to be associated with attempts to make the market economy work, rather than with the attempt to reengineer the social structure of capitalism.

Can socialist parties, even if elected to power democratically, carry out socialist reforms? Socialist parties have formed single-party governments in a number of western countries, including France, Sweden, Spain, the UK, Australia, and New Zealand. Once elected, however, they have been confronted with entrenched interests in both the state and society. As early as 1902, Karl Kautsky pointed out that 'the capitalist class rules but it does not govern, it contents itself with ruling the government'. Elected governments operate within a 'state system' – the administration, courts, police, and military – whose personnel are not elected and come from similar social backgrounds to business people. These groups reflect a class bias and are capable of blocking or at least diluting, radical socialist policies. Moreover, elected governments, of whatever ideological inclination, must respect the power of big business, which is the major employer and investor in the economy as well as the wealthiest contributor to party funds. In other words, although democratic socialist parties may succeed in forming elected governments, there is the danger that they will merely win office without necessarily acquiring power.

# Chapter 11: Pragmatic Sphere

The pragmatic sphere represents the decisions governments make to administer society most realistically. These practical decisions are not part of the ideological sphere and come about forced, most of the time, by simplifying criteria under pressing circumstances. Experience tells us that some pragmatic decisions should not be taken but, communist, socialist, and fascist governments don't care about results. For example, the only lesson from the Gulags is that we should not build Gulags, from the show trials we should not have show trials, from the Berlin Wall we should not build walls in Berlin or Mexico, and so on. Anything else would be caveman-like grunting. [Niemietz 2019]

Many regimes don't recognize their ideology is responsible for their disastrous performance. Every failure or atrocity is the result of the wrong men in power (Stalin, Mao Zedong, Pol Pot, Chavez, and Maduro), or originated by the global economic crisis (depression, inflation, oil prices), or not a failure at all, only a success that has been misrepresented by critics (e.g., the Yugoslav "miracle," high literacy rates in Cuba and Nicaragua). Those regimes have decided to follow the wrong path, the pragmatic path, and they did it on purpose, they knew what they were doing. [Fleming 2008]

## Learning from the Masters

The herd mentality is powerful in international affairs. Leaders around the globe observe, learn from, and mimic one another. They see where their peers are heading, what they can get away with, and how they can augment and perpetuate their power. They walk in one another footsteps, as Hitler did with Mussolini – and today the herd is moving in a fascist direction. With all their differences, there are also links connecting figures like Maduro, Erdogan, Putin, Orban, Duterte, and Kim Jong-un. Each has tried to nudge followers away from the consensus of support for democratic norms that required decades of struggle and sacrifice to build. These willful men see access to a high office not as a temporary privilege but as a means of imposing their desires for as long as they can. They display no interest in cooperation outside the specific groups they support to speak for and represent. They all claim for themselves the mantle of "strong leader," they all say they speak for "the people," and they look to one another for help in further enlarging their ranks. [Albright 2018]

The leader understands how weak people are and that knowledge is used to stay in power for the rest of his life. The leader learns from the masters, his ambition makes him benefit from other leaders; how Stalin stayed in power indefinitely, Hitler was so popular, Castro and Chavez were in power until their deaths, and Kim Il Sung created a dynasty.

The leader gets information or finds out advisers to teach him how to proceed under difficult circumstances. The leader learns from the experience of the regimes of the Soviet Union, China, and Cuba. Usually, the leader has charisma, he comes from the poor and makes believe he understands people's demands. The leader has, most of the time, some skills, such as clear thoughts, interpersonal relations, easy speech, empathy, and so on. Some leaders can be ignorant but they are not dumb.

The Nazis' main theme was that only Hitler could unite a Germany that under parliamentary democracy had become deeply divided and split into competing interest groups. In 1930 18.3 percent of the electorate (6.5 million) voted for the Nazis; in July 1932 this increased to 37.3 percent (13.7 million). Young voters contributed to the Nazi successes; Hitler's pledges to create work made the Nazis attractive to unemployed first-time voters. Hitler had no intention of expropriating private industry as long as it was useful to him. Big business remained a partner of the Nazi regime, but it was a partnership that could be terminated by the Nazi Party in the event of a clash of interests.

Cult of Personality

The cult of personality is a strategy utilized by the leader in charge. Human nature makes people believe in the benefactor that is capable of providing for the population; people love to have somebody to help them direct their lives towards the best possible path. In the same way, people adore God, they want to adore a charismatic leader; people leave the responsibility of government to the leader so that they can do their life without getting into the trouble of administering society.

Personality cult is typical of dictatorial regimes. All authoritarian regimes venerate one leader, it is probably a cult taken from religious creeds. Even atheists have a bias toward individual leadership. Leaders cannot be blinded by greatness. Insane leaders must be identified as soon as possible, they make irreparable mistakes against humanity. Leaders should be servants of the people, they should not take the role of masters.

## Controlling the Population

To stay in power, governments must gain the consent of the population. They manipulate the needs of the population on their benefit to stay longer in power. For those purposes, they define practical strategies outside the ideological sphere forcing the population to obey unjust rules. Unfortunately for ordinary people, the first activity in any totalitarian's survival guide is about controlling the population. It might be assumed this means violent repression – torturing and killing people – but there are other, more subtle, forms of repression that limit the population's ability to mobilize against the government.

Some mechanisms are economic, like taking charge of food production or distribution; price controls; and currency exchange control. There are plenty of pragmatic strategies to follow, use of force, the rigging of elections, violating the constitution, using the rule by law instead of the rule of law. Creating inflationary situations, making life difficult for the population, providing poor basic services, such as power, water, garbage, and so on, are other mechanisms to keep an obedient population.

What matters to governments is making sure that no matter what, enough people will still support the regime, and those people can be depended upon to make sure it stays in power. Keeping the right people happy is the key to success, some follow the populist route (Mao Zedong, Fidel Castro, Hugo Chavez) and win the support of the lower strata of society, while others keep the elites living high off the hog (Mubarak, Maduro).

Totalitarians use some simple tools to control the population. First of all, they understand the theory of evolution to attain their objectives and know quite well that there are some instinctive behaviors still affected by what went on several thousand years ago. One of those instincts say that common people bond and adapt to powerful leaders. In Human evolution, the people who bonded with the leader survived. Therefore, today, people still bond with the leader to maintain a certain status. Next, they understand the human tendency of lest effort and lest suffering. In reality, people prefer dictatorships if the alternative is chaos.

People use to agree with wrongful states because the explanation looks attractive, "We are going to be all equals!" "Private property would disappear," "We are going to be poor no more." In most cases, people accept manipulation to survive, they have no choice, they are incapable of making a living. There are many cases of injustices accepted by the people on the hope of living better in the future, for example, violation of the constitution or imprisoning political dissidents. There are other situations where people disagree with the explanations and are willing to protest but in the end obey the orders of the state. There is a tendency in humans to yield and accept injustices regardless of reasons.

Use Politics of Distraction

To keep power, some regimes must distract the population towards subjects unrelated to their performance. Because these regimes don't solve the problems of society, they prefer to hide their vulnerabilities blaming others of the reasons for their failure. In many cases, they blame the opposition or they blame the imperial powers.

Another source of distraction is to keep the financial system under stress by applying regulations to the flow of capital or the free currency exchange rates. In this type of regime, problems with health care, water, propane distribution, electricity, and garbage services worsen living conditions and the population is engaged in a continual distraction losing time protesting and asking for the services.

Controlling the Elites

To stay in power, governments must gain the consent of the population, but primarily of the elites. Ideologically, equality should be against the existence of elites but practically, inequality succeeds. The elites are the ones who can jeopardize the control of power, therefore, the leadership must pay attention to them. In some societies, the elite gets used to a good life, they are the ones enjoying life. They have good jobs full time, they find good food, they get good services, they can travel and spend money as they wish. The people on the street are the ones always suffering, they cannot make ends meet.

One of the worst situations is the way the elite in these countries is blackmailed through corruption channels. Entrepreneurs and politicians get used to large amounts of income that allows them to get nice cars or own big houses. The elite doesn't want to lose these benefits, they become anchored and find it difficult to move back down later when things come to normal. So the elites try to embrace power as much as they can.

Of course, totalitarian leaders can use sticks as well as carrots. Sometimes, the dominating party allocates public housing, food packages, and other services. When neighborhoods fail to deliver the expected votes at election time, they find their provisions of housing, food, and services cut off. [Bueno 2011]

An effective policy for the masses doesn't necessarily produce loyalty among essentials, and it's darn expensive to boot. Hungry people are not likely to have the energy to overthrow the leader, so don't worry about them. Disappointed coalition members, in contrast, can defect, leaving the leader in deep trouble. [Bueno 2011]

Happy, well-cared-for people are unlikely to revolt. Keep them fat and happy and the masses are unlikely to rise against the leader. It seems equally true, however, that sick, starving, ignorant people are unlikely to revolt. Who makes the revolution? It is the great in-between; those who are neither in misery nor coddled. [Bueno 2011]

Controlling the Information and the Press

One of the first actions of any aspiring dictator should be to control the free flow of information because it plugs a potential channel of criticism. In recent years, regulating the Internet has become a normal practice to penalize dissidence.

Turn the media into a propaganda machine for your regime like Hitler, Stalin, Castro, and Chavez did and Erdogan and Maduro do today. The leaders of Myanmar were able to shut down media outlets completely. Other leaders may be somewhat more restrained, but if they have enough powers, they can rig an election or do away with meddlesome journalists (like Vladimir Putin's Russia or Maduro's Venezuela) or, if money is no object, build their own media empire.

Use Blackmail and Coercion

Governments know that people prefer to live in peace, therefore, most people decide to obey and avoid fighting. In a totalitarian society, muzzling the media is one of the most effective controllers: a 2007 poll of more than 11,000 people in 14 countries, on behalf of the BBC, found that 40 percent of respondents across countries from India to Finland thought social harmony was more important than press freedom.

This explains the nostalgia for rulers like Stalin and Mao, who were mass murderers but who provided social order. One retired middle-ranking official in Beijing told the Asia Times: "I earned less than 100 yuan a month in Mao's time. I could barely save each month but I never worried about anything. My work unit would take care of everything for me: housing, medical care, and my children's education, though there were no luxuries…"

Profiting from Idiosyncrasy

Idiosyncrasy is a term that can be used in several contexts, primarily personal and national. It defines the peculiarity of people, it also defines the peculiarity of nations, what institutions matter, what policies are convenient, and so on.

Understanding the patterns of relationships (social relations) between individuals who share a common culture and institutions and the stratification or dominance patterns in subgroups makes governments profit on their benefit. For example, knowing people's sense of humor despite difficult situations help regimes to stay in power longer. Knowing people's tolerance helps regimes promote unacceptable policies because they know people are not going to react.

Idiosyncrasy affects several policies at different levels and governments profit of that knowledge. Wage-bargaining institutions, monetary authorities (including central banks), distributive policies, tax regimes, political ideologies, and patterns of party-political competition constitute the focus of concern for macro-analysis. Social capital, interpersonal trust, popular values, and the economics of the family lie at the micro-layer.

## Mishandling Wealth

Corruption is a beautiful structure in a political system that depends on very few people. On the one hand, by allowing the elites to be corrupt induce them to be loyal because they are getting rich. And if they should be suspected of not being loyal... then you accuse them of corruption. Corrupt politicians are attractive to would-be supporters, and politicians eager for power find it easiest to attract corrupt people to their cause. Leaders want to stay in power and must take whatever actions are needed to do so. Successful leaders are not above repression, suppression, oppression, or even killing their rivals, real and imagined. Anyone unwilling to undertake the dirty work that so many leaders are called on to do should not pursue becoming a leader. Certainly, anyone reluctant to be a brute will not last long if everyone knows he is unprepared to engage in this vicious behavior, essential to political survival. [Bueno 2011]

Profiting of naturals resources is a common behavior of wrongful regimes. It is easier to establish and maintain a political system in a country with vast amounts of natural resources, for example, oil, than in a country that counts on people's work effort. If the government has access to money that isn't generated in the economy, it can give the populace free or subsidized things to keep them quiet and happy.

Doing what is best for the people can be bad for staying in power. The logic of political survival teaches us that leaders, whether they rule countries, companies, or committees, first and foremost want to get and keep power. Second, they want to exercise as much control over the expenditure of revenues as they possibly can. Leaders must rivet their attention on building and maintaining a coalition loyal enough that the ruler can beat back any rivals. Leaders reward their essential backers before they reward the people in general. [Bueno 2011]

Successful leaders must place the urge to do good deeds a distant third behind their political survival and their degree of discretionary control. Private goods are the benefits that most help rulers keep coalition loyalty. It is only the private gains that separate the essential backers from the masses. [Bueno 2011]

When a system is structured around corruption, everyone who matters, leaders and backers alike, are tarred by that corruption. They would not be where they were if they had not had their hand in the till at some point. Increasing sentences simply provides leaders with an additional tool with which to enforce discipline. It is all too common for reformers and whistle-blowers to be prosecuted for one reason or another. [Bueno 2011]

More than a trillion dollars is spent annually on bribes worldwide, presumably with most of it going to government officials. With so much money on the line, it is no wonder that we are witnessing an era of major backtracking on the anti-corruption drive. The fate of the few anti-corruption commissions that have had courageous leadership is embattlement or death. [Bueno 2011]

Money to Buy Consciences

"Knowing where the money is" is particularly important in autocracies – and particularly difficult in socialism. Such systems are shrouded in secrecy. Supporters must be paid but there are no accurate accounts detailing stock and flows of wealth. Of course, this lack of transparency is by design. Secrecy ensures that everyone gets the deal they can negotiate, not knowing how much it might cost to replace them. [Bueno 2011]

"Misuse" of government money is what keeps leaders in power for long time. "Misuse" has many meanings, including buying consciences.

For example, allowing public employees to increase their income by charging for free services. This is not unique to socialist regimes, governments or continents. It applies to all organizations, especially when they rely on a small group of essentials. Private rewards work well in small-coalition regimes looking benign and even praiseworthy such as sports organizations. [Bueno 2011]

To keep backers happy a leader needs money. Leaders are kings in oil-rich countries where income is huge. Anyone aspiring to rule must first ask how much can he extract from his country and his constituents – whether they are citizens of a nation or shareholders in a corporation. This extraction can take many forms – oil income, personal income taxes, property taxes, duties on imports, licenses, and government fees. [Bueno 2011]

Explaining the calculus of politics, another step is to figure out how much money a leader can keep and how much be spent on the coalition and the public if the incumbent is to stay in power. [Bueno 2011]

Survival Guide

The government's survival guide seems to imply that staying in power is not so difficult. Monitor and control the population, pay off a small number of influential people and use elections to demonstrate its power. And to some extent that's true. Once a government has ruled for a few years and mastered these levers of power, it becomes very difficult to dislodge.

Moreover, there are very strong disincentives for those governments to choose to stand down:

Losing power will open up an entirely unpredictable situation in which their rivals will be able to enact revenge. Since 1960 in Africa, more than a third of African presidents who lost power were either jailed, exiled or killed. Chavez lost power only when he died; Maduro is following his steps and probably would end two meters down the ground before quitting office. In general, some governments cling on to the bitter end. Castros in Cuba are remaining in power until their death.

The key to regime survival is "coup-proofing." First, consolidate an inner core bound to the regime by "family, ethnic, religious, ideological or corrupt loyalties" – in essence, a mafia, with Goodfellas in various guises protecting the regime's backbone. Second, create a parallel military devoted to regime protection, like Iran's Revolutionary Guard Corps, which does the Supreme Leader's bidding while the remnants of the shah's

Army stand by or the Special Action Force (FAES), created by Maduro to suppress the opposition in Venezuela. Third, maintain multiple secret police, security, and espionage services that spend much of their time keeping each other in check. But keep in mind, coup-proofing isn't cheap. The region's big oil producers can usually afford it, especially when crude prices are as high as they used to be. Regimes without substantial oil reserves tend to rely on foreign patrons.

In Venezuela, Chavez's political heirs, a large number of military officers and other relatives and members of the ruling oligarchy are the components of the real power. Of course, Maduro, his wife, Cilia Flores, and many of his relatives and associates are part of that oligarchy. In this elite, there are different "families," "cartels," and groups that compete for influence on government decisions, for political appointments, and the control of illicit markets – ranging from human and drug trafficking, to money laundering.

## Using Terror

Ideologically, there is no doctrine overtly aiming at terror activities, it is a practical decision to follow the belligerent approach; fascism is the only system that accepts violence and we already know it has no ideology. In ancient societies, aggressiveness had to be restrained and forms of overt dominance replaced by complex social skills. Young males would find it profitable to fit into the group by controlling their sexuality and aggression and awaiting their turn at leadership. The dominant male of these societies possessed a mosaic of qualities that reflect the necessities of compromise, "Controlled, cunning, cooperative, attractive to the ladies, good with the children, relaxed, tough, eloquent, skillful, knowledgeable and proficient in self-defense and hunting." [Wilson 1978]

Human beings are strongly predisposed to respond with unreasoning hatred to external threats and to escalate their hostility sufficiently to overwhelm the source of the threat by a respectably wide margin of safety. Our brains are programmed to partition other people into friends and aliens. We tend to fear deeply the actions of strangers and to solve the conflict by aggression. These learning rules are most likely to have evolved during the past hundreds of thousands of years of human evolution and have conferred a biological advantage on those who conformed to them with the greatest fidelity. [Wilson 1978]

Primitive men divided the world into two parts, the near environment of homes, local villages, kin, and friends, and the more distant universe of neighboring villages, intertribal allies, and enemies. There is an elemental topography to distinguish between enemies who can be attacked and killed and friends who cannot. [Wilson 1978]

Some can imagine ancient hunter-gatherer societies as peaceful paradises and argue that war and violence began only with the Agricultural Revolution when people started to accumulate private property. Others maintain that the world of the ancient foragers was exceptionally cruel and violent. Which better represents the world of the ancient foragers? The answer is neither, just as foragers exhibited a wide array of religions and social structures, so, too, did they probably demonstrate a variety of violent rates. While some areas and some periods may have enjoyed peace and tranquility, others were riven by ferocious conflicts. [Harari 2014]

How the cultural traditions of warfare have evolved within the abilities of human beings to survive and reproduce? Are they independent? Or are they related to the genetic fitness of human beings? Or they evolved by a process of group selection that favored the self-sacrificing tendencies of some warriors. [Wilson 1978]

The particular forms of organized violence are not inherited. No genes differentiate the practice of platform torture from pole and stake torture, headhunting from cannibalism, the duel of champions from genocide. Culture gives a particular form to the aggression and all members of society practice it uniformly. [Wilson 1978]

Creating Fear

Creating a culture of fear is also a strong strategy for some regimes. Violence, fear, and punishment are always present in socialist societies. Public employees are manipulated to comply strictly with the mandates of the government, including administrative measures to penalize the opposition. The regime enforces, through fear, the sense of loyalty towards the leader. The military, the secret police, and the administrators are the mechanisms of punishment. These regimes are characterized by big military support and a strong army using the most recent technology.

Are human beings innately aggressive? The answer to it is yes. This is a question that raises emotions in political ideologies of all stripes. Throughout history, warfare, representing only the most organized technique of aggression, has been endemic to every form of society, from hunter-gatherer bands to industrial states. [Wilson 1978]

Virtually all societies have invented elaborate sanctions against rape, extortion, and murder while regulating daily commerce through complex customs and laws designed to minimize conflict. Human beings have a marked hereditary predisposition to aggressive behavior. Human beings share a general instinct for aggressive behavior with other animal species. [Wilson 1978]

Aggression is an ill-defined array of different responses with separate controls in the nervous system. Several categories can be identified: the defense and conquest of territory, the assertion of dominance within well-organized groups, sexual aggression, acts of hostility by which weaning is terminated, aggression against prey, defensive counterattacks against predators, and moralistic and disciplinary aggression used to enforce the rules of society. [Wilson 1978]

## Security Forces

Some regimes use security forces to maintain order in the country. These forces are well trained and equipped to disperse any manifestation of dissidence. Instead of protecting dissidents in the street to guarantee their human rights, security forces arrest, beat, and even kill demonstrators. The objective is to show what the regime is capable of doing to stay in power. Many people have died in the streets on the hands of security forces.

### Controlling the Secret Police

Some regimes use to develop their secret police to decide independently the path to follow against dissidence. The regime decides who is a suspect from the pool of opposing politicians, first, and from opposing citizens, second. The secret police is an organization that follows directly the orders of the leadership without additional control.

The interrogation methods used by the state police are elaborations and refinements of current police practice. The principles and practices used by the state police involve the identification of suspects, the accumulation of evidence, the carrying out of the arrest, detention, interrogation, trial, and punishment. The "confessions" obtained by the state police are readily understandable as results of the police control pressure utilized.

### Using The Military

The military behaves similarly to any political pyramid. At the top, you have the chief commander, who is presumably a key supporter of the regime, and who is being kept happy by the state. The chief commander is then appointing and keeping happy the top officers he needs to keep the army under control (typically with help from the regime's coffers or corruption channels). These top officers will dispense and acquire whatever influence they need to keep their subordinates under control, and so on.

The army, with the chief commander in the lead, is not likely to abandon the current regime unless a new regime is likely to improve their welfare. At which point they might throw their weight behind a revolution. It is important to note that populist uprisings are typically seen as the people rising against the establishment, this is not completely true. What happens is that a new regime is moving to push the old regime out, probably having swayed some key supporters. It's just a better public image to let the people (aka the angry mob) do the dirty work for you.

Some regimes cannot survive for long without disarming the people and buttering up the military. Former dictators such as Pervez Musharraf of Pakistan, Mobutu Sese Seko of the Congo, and Idi Amin of Uganda were high-ranked army officers who co-opted the military to overthrow democracies in favor of dictatorships. Most recently, Chavez and Maduro co-opted the military to retain power indefinitely, instigating the use of force to curb public protest.

## Wrongful Approaches

Socialism and communism have serious theoretical flaws. What belongs nominally to everyone on paper belongs in effect to no-one in practice. Gold mines, oil fields, telephone, and vegetable oil companies that are owned 'by the people' are in real life owned by nobody. Public ownership is a myth and a mirage. Any company owned by the people becomes unproductive and destined for extinction.

<u>Stay Eternally in Power</u>

A severe criticism against some regimes is the tendency to perpetuate its power forever. Once unscrupulous leaders take power, they assume they are destined to stay in power until their death and some cases creating a patriarchal society. In most cases, countries that took that path feel they should not lose the opportunity to build a dynasty. Leaders in power know that if they lose it, that opportunity will not come back.

According to socialists, all social conflicts are conflicts between 'the people' (also known as 'working people' or 'ordinary people') and 'the elites', or some variation thereof, such as 'the 99 percent' versus 'the 1 percent.' But the People-versus-Elites template is a very poor guide to the political conflicts we observe. This is because socialist mythology treats The People as a romanticized abstraction, which has little to do with actual people.

In capitalism, sometimes the problems of the world seem beyond our capacity to solve. Yet there is no mystery about how to eradicate much of the world's poverty and oppression. Give people the right to say what they want; to write what they want; and to share ideas about what they want, and you are bound to be looking at people whose persons and property are secure and whose lives are content. Some regimes succeed economically without freedoms but eventually return to liberal societies.

When the state is run by leaders with totalitarian approaches, the people must obey but the people are convinced of their non-viability. Sooner or later those regimes yield to more democratic rulers. Economic successes in Singapore and parts of China prove that it is possible to have a good material life with limited freedom, but these are exceptions and not the rule. [Bueno 2011]

Some governments interpret clearly how the fight for power must proceed. "Focus on voters' beliefs, not the facts," or "perception is reality," is at the heart of all the dark political arts. People vote based on what they believe to be true, not what is true. In other words: facts don't matter. The biggest lesson of politics is the easiest route to election and re-election is to manage voters' beliefs. It's so much easier than the hard slog of researching the facts, developing good policy that respects those facts, and building support for that policy. [Steele 2017]

Declaring War to Neighbors

It is common for bad regimes to start feuds against their neighbors. It is another way of distracting the population from their real problems. Sometimes war represents a way of unifying the country against external enemies. Wars congregate different forces into a coalition against external enemies capable of confusing internal enemies. The regime makes people believe it is looking for peace and that only as a last resort it has entered the war.

The practice of war is a straightforward example of a hypertrophied biological predisposition. Primitive men cleaved their universe into friends and enemies and responded with quick, deep emotions to even the mildest threats emanating from outside the arbitrary boundary. War was adopted as an instrument of the policy of the new societies, and those that employed it best became – tragically – the most successful. [Wilson 1978]

## Rule by Law

Another important consideration is how the law is enforced in these regimes. Rule of law and rule by law are different concepts. The rule of law refers to a state of constitutionalism where the law (nor parliament) is supreme and where all government's power is subject to the law. Rule by law means the opposite. It refers to a police state in which the government invokes the law (indeed creates law) to "justify" excessive use of government force. During a period of tyranny, leaders need to be visionaries, with prophetic voices, who can rise above the present crisis and take a principled stand against the rule by law.

The rule of law refers to a state of constitutionalism where the law (nor parliament) is supreme and where all government's power is subject to the law. It is the antithesis of authoritarianism, and it provides that individuals' rights may only be interfered with to the extent authorized by law. [Freeth 2011]

Rule by law means the opposite. It refers to a police state in which the government invokes the law (indeed creates law) to "justify" excessive use of government force. Detention without trial laws is a common example of these. When a country is under rule by law dictatorship is complete. [Freeth 2011]

The rule of law is preserved in democracies while the rule by law is implemented in tyranny. Socialism and communism use the rule by law to twist the rules using their immense power seized over the kidnapping of all the institutions.

The case of Venezuela is the most recent collapse of a regime calling itself absurd socialist. Using existent democracies' facade, the crooked regime makes people believe in the rule of law but instead imposes the rule by law, forcing its ideas using the existent institutions such as the Supreme Court.

## Identify Enemies

Identifying enemies is another strategy very common in many regimes. This strategy demonstrates an image of power, constantly challenging the adversary. However, the enemy is not only from outside, but the internal challenge of power also becomes a trauma for the leader. The party members and the population daring to go against the leader are going to suffer the most. Lucky opponents can leave the country, but in most cases, they are imprisoned or killed.

# Know Thyself Ideologically — germinal Boloix

Totalitarians are defined by singular rule, including military juntas or any form of oligarchies. They must be formed by abusing the rule of law and using the rule by law instead. Lastly, totalitarians must wield absolute power. This is effected by command of a nation's military, political, and oil, agricultural or industrial capabilities.

The four main causes of totalitarians' rise are oriented to the control of the population, identification of the enemies and control of the production networks in the country. First, a sizeable portion of the state's population must be disenfranchised to form the bulk of their support. Second, the regime always finds an enemy within the state to blame for the state's problems. Third, they will find an enemy outside of the state to manipulate as a threat to the state. Lastly, for the regime to rise to the political body of the state, they must have become unable or unwilling to attend to the needs of the population.

Unemployment, or underemployment, is one of the greatest factors in disenfranchising the population. When people are unable to have the dignity of work that produces tangible benefits they lose confidence in the government. Historically this was done by driving people off of common lands, but with the advent of the Industrial Revolution, it has involved controlling the means of production.

Some regimes use perceived internal enemies to bolster their cause. Minority groups bear the brunt of the trouble for this perception. By pointing out an internal enemy, these regimes can turn the people against his political opposition. Those that support the opposition are therefore cast as enemies of the state.

Just as important as internal enemies, external enemies form a necessary part of some regime's oratory. After they take power, they use the external enemy to unite the people behind a cause. Whether that cause is preemptively attacking, defending, or even just organizing is dependent on the specifics of the situation.

The last, and one of the most important, factors that lead to the rise of wrong regimes is a broken political system. Corruption, control, and impotence lead to the stagnation of laws and the inability to act. Political bodies that no longer serve the function of operating the government for the benefit of the people under it quickly become the focus of socialists.

Get rid of your political enemies or, more cleverly, embrace them in the hope that the bear hug will neutralize them. Zimbabwe's former dictator Mugabe abandoned the unpopular practice of murdering political rivals and instead bribed them, with political office, for their support. Venezuela's socialists Chavez and Maduro have bribed opposition leaders to retain power. Idi Amin, who came to power in Uganda after a military coup, stuck with the murderous route: during his eight years at the top, he is estimated to have killed between 80,000 and 300,000 people. His victims included cabinet ministers, judicial figures, bankers, intellectuals, journalists, and a former prime minister. At the lower end of the scale, that's a murder rate of 27 executions a day.

Spying and Gossip

Governments spying citizens are well-known activities. Traditionally, governments have people spying on possible dissidents. With the advent of technology, people got spied through communication channels such as telephones, and computers. More recently, some countries, such as China, have started to spy on their citizens using cameras located all around the cities. The citizens can get a good score that allows access to faster internet service or visas to travel overseas or a bad score and the police show up at their door. While this Orwellian technology may improve 'public safety,' it poses a chilling new threat to civil liberties in oppressive societies.

To identify the enemies of the Cuban Revolution, gossip became an arm of state power. The organization of party cells, selection of party members, and all promotions and dismissals had to be cleared through the powerful Organization Secretary Anibal Escalante. [Bethell 1993]

In Cuba, the Committees for Defense of the Revolution (CDR) are social organizations that keep a vigilant eye on potential 'counterrevolutionaries' and are, in effect, a network of government informers. They reflected Castro's hard-line view that 'To be a traitor to the revolution is to be a traitor to the country.' [Brown 2009]

Using Political Sectarianism

People who supported referendums against Chávez's and Maduro's presidencies have been fired from government jobs. A government program that distributes food and basic goods at government-capped prices has been credibly accused of discriminating against government critics.

In April 2018, President Maduro said he would "give a prize" to Venezuelans who voted for him in the May elections and presented their "carnet of the Fatherland," a government-issued ID required for accessing housing, pensions, certain medical procedures, and boxes of food subject to government-set prices. During the presidential campaign, participants who attended government rallies got bags of food.

Suppress Protests

Some regimes have to crush the opposition because they know the population is not satisfied with their performance. Repression is a way to neutralize dissidence and send the message that the regime is in power and don't admit disturbances. Dissatisfaction with government performance is an entirely different matter in democracies than it is in dictatorships. In a democracy, protest is relatively cheap and easy. People have the freedom and, indeed, the right to assemble. They also have easy means through which to coordinate and organize. In dictatorship, although the people desire change, they cannot act upon these wants. [Bueno 2011]

In a democracy, protest is about alerting leaders to the fact that the people are unhappy, and that, if changes in policy are not made, they'll throw the rascals out. Yet in a dictatorship, a protest has a deeper purpose: to bring down the very institutions of government and change the way the people are governed. [Bueno 2011]

Among the politically most active sections of society, socialist – or at least anti-capitalist – ideas have long been predominant, and highly fashionable. For example, all high-profile protest movements in recent decades – be it anti-austerity, Occupy or anti-globalization – were explicitly anti-capitalist. We are so used to the idea that protest must be left-wing and anti-capitalist that the idea of a protest against government largesse feels jarring. [Niemietz 2019]

# Chapter 12: Societal Evaluation Framework

Aznavour proposes to abandon his land without remorse. He does not explain why he wants to leave in a hurry, forgetting his past.

>Je fuirai, laissant là mon passé
>Sans aucun remords
>Sans bagage et le coeur libéré
>En chantant très fort

The English translation would look like:

>I would fly away, leaving there my past
>Without any remorse,
>Without any baggage and my heart liberated
>in singing . . . just belting out!

In political terms, people don't care to abandon a sociopolitical system that has given some acceptable results (capitalism-democracy) and accept a non-viable approach just because it looks fair and against the status quo (socialism). What happens later, after you leave, is not portrayed in the song, suffering and injustices would become the norm later on.

An evaluation framework is proposed to structure the features of each characteristic of the societal dimension:

- Political System
- Economic System
- Personal Influence
- Social Influence
- Ideological Sphere
- Pragmatical Sphere

## Political System

The political system describes how the political power is organized, how democracy is being implemented, what is the importance of elections to assure a proper political representation, what is the importance of the state, how realistic are the aspirations, what political institutions are defined to implement the aspirations suggested by the political ideology, how politics are handled, what is the importance of the party, and what is the influence of the leadership in political decisions.

The first defining feature of a political system is the organization of the political power. Important political institutions, including the state, the party, the leadership, and other institutions are structured to keep control of the governmental apparatus.

The second feature is the understanding of the national idiosyncrasy. What are the particular characteristics of the country that define the requirements of institutions.

The third feature refers to what institutions are developed to implement the ideology. How are political aspirations fulfilled through institutions. How are the institutions evaluated to determine their performance and continuity.

The fourth defining feature defines how democracy is implemented in the social system. Most governments use democracy to assign capable representatives to fundamental institutions but democracy is much more than that. Democracy involves primarily independent institutional control.

The fifth feature is related to the importance of elections in the social system. How elections are organized, how different flows of opinion are allowed to participate, and how the validity of the elections is evaluated.

The sixth defining feature regards the importance of the control of the state. How the social contract is implemented, surrendering total control to the state, conditional acceptance or letting the people be the rulers. Determining the state's purpose, methods, and sovereignty, as well as the acceptable degree of state interference .

The seventh feature regards the handling of politics. What is the understanding of the political responsibility, what groups are benefiting from the political exercise, and how successful are the strategies of political survival.

The eighth feature is related to the importance of the party. What are the principles that define the participation of members in the party and what sectors come to dominate policy decision making. How open minded is the participation of the members of the party.

The ninth feature is related to the importance of leadership in decision making. What is the structure of the institutional channels of decision making and what is the influence of the leadership on decision making.

## Economic System

The economic systems describes the use of resources to generate wealth, how the management of money is administered, the management of the means of production, how the economy is planned, how work and compensation are administered, how workers are empowered, how the economy is democratized, what popular economic measures are implemented, and how commerce and consumerism are implemented.

The first defining feature of the economic system is its capacity of producing wealth. How wealth is produced, how natural resources are considered, how labor is managed.

The second feature is related to the understanding of money's origin, production, and distribution. What is the importance of money, what are the stages of money production and distribution.

The third defining feature is how the means of production are managed. It is capitalist or non-capitalist ownership and whether private property is allowed.

Linked to this feature is the fourth one, how the economy is planned. Is there a dominance of a command economy or a market economy. How precise are the plans, how equitable is the distribution of resources.

The fifth feature is how providing work and compensation to the population is managed and under what criteria. How work is distributed, how wages are defined, and so on.

The sixth feature is the issue of worker's empowerment. Are there considerations of worker empowerment or different classes are predominant.

The seventh feature regards how the issue of democratizing the economy is handled. Are there some efforts to democratize the economy, does people get the possibility of contributing.

The eighth feature is what type of popular economic measures are implemented. For example, price controls, rent controls, industry nationalizations, and so on.

The ninth feature refers to the way commerce and consumerism are implemented. What is the importance of commerce in the society and what is the culture of consumerism in the population.

## Personal Influence

The personal influence characteristic regards several aspects relating people and their relations to society, what are the expectations of the state, how is people's happiness interpreted, what is the responsibility of people in society, what kind of altruistic behavior is expected, what is the degree of tolerance expected, what are the virtues of people and how are they enforced, what are the expectations of people about the state, how people's emotions are handled by the state, what complaint channels are available to express people's emotions, what kind of non-violent mechanisms are available to express dissatisfaction, and how human rights are respected by the state.

The first defining feature of the personal influence system regards what expectations has the society regarding human beings. Is the society expecting humans without egoism and ready to collaborate.

The second feature is the interpretation of people's happiness. Is happiness something coming from the inside of people or there is some collective style of happiness being proposed.

The third feature is the degree of responsibility accorded to each human being. How is responsibility handled in the society, are people expected to be responsible for their activities and how responsibility is enforced.

The fourth feature determines how much altruistic behavior is expected from the population. Is altruism an spontaneous characteristic or is forced by the state.

The fifth feature is the establishment of the degree of tolerance expected from the population. How tolerant are people, how is tolerance being enforced.

The sixth defining feature regards how the virtues of the people are promoted and respected. What are the virtues of the people and how they are enforced.

The seventh defining feature is related to the expectations of the population on the performance of the state. What is the people expecting from the state, what happens if people don't get what they expect.

The eighth feature regards how people's emotions are encouraged by the state and how the state manipulates people's emotions.

The ninth feature presents how people manage their emotions within the social system. What complain channels are available to alleviate powerful emotions of discomfort.

The tenth feature regards what type of non-violent strategies are used to let the population express their difficulties. Are institutional channels established to solve disagreements.

The eleventh feature is related to how human rights are handled by the social system. How are human right enforced in the society. What people can do when their human rights are disrespected.

## Social Influence

The social influence characteristic analyses the problems of living in a society. Governments have been ultimately responsible for maintaining the security and economic welfare of their citizens, as well as the protection of human rights and the environment within their borders. Issues regarding the right behavior of the population, how important is knowledge and education, how is class struggle handled, what are the criteria of equality, how justice is implemented, how living in community is achieved, how diversity is administered, how obedience is maintained, how respect and dignity are considered, what type of mechanisms are available for reasoning about problems, and what kind of facilities are available to negotiate difficult situations.

The first defining feature of social influence regards how governments maintain the security and economic welfare of their citizens, the protection of human rights and the environment.

The second feature is related to the expected behavior of the population. What are the motivators, personal or social influences for actions, and the justifications.

The third feature is the understanding of social idiosyncrasy. How people relate, how people are used to live, how people organize, how institutions take in consideration the particularities of the population.

The fourth feature is the importance of knowledge and education. What is the compromise of society to encourage knowledge and education. What is the interest in the search for knowledge. What is the educational model for knowledge transformation.

The fifth feature is how class struggle is handled in society, what are the perspectives of imposing a classless society.

The sixth feature regards how equality and egalitarianism are treated in the social system. Are there considerations about egalitarianism and how it is implemented. What type of equality are we talking about, how that equality is manifested and enforced.

The seventh feature is related to how justice and liberty are implemented. How benefits and rewards are distributed, how justice and liberty become complementary or divergent.

The eighth feature regards how is living in community implemented. How people contribute in communal activities. What is the balance between individuality and collectivity.

The ninth feature regards the management of diversity in the society. Is diversity well accepted in the society or there are discrimination issues.

The tenth feature is related to the implementation of obedience. What measures are available to guarantee obedience from the population. How disobedience is managed.

The eleventh feature regards how respect and dignity are encouraged. How people are respected in the society, how people dignify themselves in society.

The twelfth feature is related to the opportunity for reasoning in the society. When facing difficult situations, is the society capable of establishing reasoning mechanisms to make everybody aware and informed to be able to produce alternatives to solve the problems.

The thirteenth feature is related with the possibility of negotiating difficult situations encountered in society. How is negotiation established to understand different viewpoints and come up with solutions that satisfy the different participants without overpowering some against others.

## Ideological Sphere

The ideological sphere characteristic includes considerations about the fundamental debt owed, the maintenance of the social order, the importance of history in the definition of the ideology, the understanding of the current world-view, the definition of the model society according to the ideology, the establishment of the stages to attain the model society from the current one, is the ideology a goal to be attain as specified, and is there an objective of establishing the ideology internationally following an international organization.

The first defining feature of the ideological sphere is the establishment of who is the recipient of the fundamental debt that justifies any actions. Examples are individuals, society, the poor , the nation.

The second feature is the degree of importance of maintaining order and stability in the society. How society encourages people to comply with the established order, what efforts are required to maintain a stable order.

The third feature indicates the importance of history in the decisions regarding ideology. How important is history to define ideological statements, how important is tradition.

The fourth feature demonstrates the understanding of the current world-view. How deep is the degree of understanding of the world we live in, what are the advantages and disadvantages of the current state of affairs.

The fifth feature indicates the characteristics of the model society. What are the characteristics of the proposed society, what is new, what is feasible, what is the same.

The sixth feature establishes the transit to a desired future. What is the plan to transition from the current society to the new society. What are the expected difficulties, what would be the benefits, what the advantage and disadvantages are.

The seventh feature is the declared aim of building a social system as the ultimate, legitimizing goal. How important is the ideology, how flexible, how the resulting society is going to be evaluated.

The eighth defining feature is the existence of, and the sense of belonging to, an international social system movement. Is there an interest in pledging to convert other parts of the world, are there international organizations already promoting the ideology.

## Pragmatical Sphere

The pragmatical sphere characteristic include aspects such as use of politics of distraction, understanding of people and nation's idiosyncrasy, using knowledge about natural resources, mismanagement of financial resources, establishment of regime survival institutions, use of terror to maintain a submissive population, use of security forces to stay in power, constant violation of laws and the constitution, importance of staying eternally in power, and treatment of the political enemies.

The first feature of the pragmatical sphere is how to distract the population from the miserable reality when things are not going well. Regimes utilize politics of distraction, controlling the press, and so on.

The second feature is the understanding of the idiosyncrasy of the nation and the population. Regimes learn to exploit the intrinsic characteristics of nations and people to keep them submissive.

The third feature is the understanding of the physical characteristics of the country. For example, what kind of natural resources are available, how can they be exploit for the benefit of the regime.

The fourth feature is the possibility of financial resources mismanagement. Commonly, regimes become corrupt, profiting the institutional disorder they help to establish.

The fifth feature is related to the establishment of structures for regime survival. Regimes design special structures to maintain power, some involve relatives in power positions or identifying partisans to manage important institutions. The establishment of special forces is also a common approach.

The sixth feature involves how the use of terror is implemented. The regime utilizes terror to maintain the population submissive, special forces are always spying to determine who is plotting against.

The seventh feature is the utilization of security forces to repress the dissidence. Some regimes use special forces to combat any danger against the status quo.

The eighth feature is related to the constant violation of the laws and the constitution. Partisans in key institutions define the next changes to the constitution or the law to avoid penalties.

The ninth feature involves the importance of staying eternally in power. Most regimes work to stay eternally in power, they know it is not possible to relinquish power or else they can be indicted.

The tenth feature is how the enemies of the regime are treated and whether political dissidents are incarcerated. Political opposition is severely persecuted, the regime cannot afford constant criticism and decides to punish dissidents.

The eleventh feature is related to the management of protests. Are protests allowed, are there measures taken to overcome the causes of the protest, how protests are suppressed by the government.

# Chapter 13: Globalization Dimension

Globalization is the word used to describe the growing interdependence of the world's economies, politics, cultures, and populations, brought about by cross-border trade in goods and services, technology, and flows of investment, people, and information. Globalization can be a hard sell to the public because the benefits are widely distributed and not as easily understood, compared with the personal costs to very specific companies or workers.

"Globalization" can mean many things. To some, it means equal integration of individual societies into worldwide political, economic and cultural processes. To others, it means accentuated uneven economic development, accompanied by cultural imperialism, which merely exaggerates the political dependence of "peripheral" on "core" societies. For still others, globalization is shorthand for the social and cultural changes that follow when societies become linked with and, in an escalating way, dependent upon the world capitalist market. The idea that underlies these multiple meanings of globalization is the radical intensification of worldwide social relations and the lifting of social activities out of local and national conditions.

The globalization dimension includes political, social, economic, and environmental considerations worldwide and its relation to the study at hand; the historical evolution of those factors; and the expectations for the future. The global environment includes such factors as economic and political interactions, social and cultural influences, and specific historical conditions (e.g. revolutionary movements, military involvement in politics, the consequences of World War II, the possession of colonies).

How should we approach the study of world affairs? How is the world best understood? World affairs have traditionally been understood based on an international paradigm. In this view, states (often understood as 'nations', hence 'international') are taken to be the essential building blocks of world politics, meaning that world affairs boil down, essentially, to the relations between states.

Globalization is a slippery and elusive concept. The major theme in globalization is the emergence of a 'borderless world', the tendency of traditional political borders, based on national and state boundaries, to become permeable. Globalization thus reconfigures social space in that territory matters less because an increasing range of connections has a 'transworld' or 'transborder' character. Obvious examples of this include the greater ease with which transnational corporations can relocate production and investment, the fact that financial markets react almost immediately to economic events anywhere in the world, and the emergence of so-called global goods, such as Coca-Cola, McDonald's beefburgers, Nike running shoes, and Starbucks coffee houses, that are available almost worldwide. [Heywood 2003]

Origins of Globalization

The Peace Treaties of Westphalia and Osnabruck (1648) established the legal basis of modern statehood and by implication the fundamental rules or constitution of modern world politics. In the course of the subsequent four centuries, it has formed the normative structure or constitution of the modern world order.

The Westphalia settlement agreed that states enjoy sovereign jurisdiction, in the sense that they have independent control over what happens within their territory (all other institutions and groups, spiritual and temporal, are therefore subordinate to the state). Also, relations between and among states are structured by the acceptance of the sovereign independence of all states (thus implying that states are legally equal).

But it was only in the twentieth century, as global empires collapsed, that sovereign statehood and with it, national self-determination finally acquired the status of universal organizing principles of world order. Constitutions are important because they establish the location of political authority within a polity and the rules which inform the exercise and limits of political power. It welded together the idea of territoriality with the notion of legitimate sovereign rule.

There are three main classifications of globalization: economic, political, and social.

Globalization of the Economy

The Globalization of the Economy has been the main driver of change but also the Globalization of Politics, of Culture and Law define the future of the world. The globalized world sweeps away regulation and undermines local and national politics, just as the consolidation of the nation-state swept away local economies, dialects, cultures, and political forms. Globalization creates new markets and wealth, even as it causes widespread suffering, disorder, and unrest. It is both a source of repression and a catalyst for global movements of social justice and emancipation.

Economics of globalization refers to the interconnectedness of economies through trade and the exchange of resources. Automation is delivering advances in productivity and profits at the expense of increased job insecurity. For emerging markets, lower wages reduce the incentive to automate. That doesn't mean the risk of disruption is low. Automation is rapidly approaching the level at which a substantial share of low value-added work can be done by machines, undermining the low-cost advantage of developing markets.

Globalization encourages each country to specialize in what it produces best using the least amount of resources, known as comparative advantage. This concept makes production more efficient, promotes economic growth, and lowers prices of goods and services, making them more affordable especially for lower-income households.

The traditional drivers of development are the labor force, investment availability, and productivity of enterprising. The big disruptive forces are populism, protectionism, automation, digitization, and climate change. Disruptive forces are sweeping the global economy. Populist regimes are throwing out the policy rulebook. Protectionism is deadening the trade flows that drove China's rise. Automation and the digital economy are booming economic factors for some, eroding old sources of advantage for others. The threat of climate change looms.

Done right, digitization holds out the promise of higher productivity, with the potential for low- and middle-income economies to leapfrog along the development process. In China, for example, e-commerce is creating new opportunities for entrepreneurs and consumers in support of economic rebalancing. Done wrong, the digital divide will exacerbate income polarization in high-income economies, and make it harder for the rest to tap the mainstream of global opportunity.

The origins of many of the changes sweeping the global economy can be traced to two sources: trade and technology. Trade is a driver of prosperity, it has been like that for centuries. Trade without agreement on the rules of the game, and compensation for losers, has resulted in a protectionist backlash that is anything but successful. The technology incorporates new ways of doing things productively.

Twenty years ago, China's economy was a tenth of the size of the United States. In 2019, it is two-thirds as big. In 2039, on the current trajectory, it will be more than 10% bigger. India will have leapfrogged Japan and Germany to claim the No. 3 spot in the global rankings. Vietnam will be closing in on the top 20.

Consider China's development process. With the global economy acting more as a drag on growth than a boon to it, China may confront the risk that it has overplayed its hand. Heavy reliance on short-term stimulus measures is increasingly inconsistent with pursuing the longer-term reforms that it needs, and its geopolitical ambitions and regional economic and financial commitments are becoming costlier. Among other challenges, the change in the Chinese economy, becoming a more services-oriented economy, means it is unlikely to grow as strongly in the future.

The US is entering a tense and divisive election year. Germany, Italy, and Spain are amid difficult political transitions. The EU has to deal with Brexit and other regional divisions. And China's government is trying to consolidate power in the face of slowing growth and continuing protests in Hong Kong. The main worry – one that too few market participants have spotted – is that over the next five years, global economic and market conditions may need to deteriorate nearer to crisis levels before national, regional, and multilateral political systems muster an adequate response.

Effectively, therefore, no national economy operates in isolation, which means national economies influence each other. This is evidenced by the global recession from 2007 onward. Economic globalization also means that there is a two-way structure for technologies and resources. For example, countries like the USA will sell their technologies to countries, which lack these, and natural resources from developing countries are sold to the developed countries that need them.

Economists look at the effects of globalization across the entire economy to weigh the pros vs. cons. Since the overall payoff is so much greater than the costs to individual workers or groups who have lost out, nearly all economists support having an open global market versus closing it off.

A perennial challenge facing all of the world's countries, regardless of their level of economic development, is achieving financial stability, economic growth, and higher living standards. Many different paths can be taken to achieve these objectives, and every country's path will be different given the distinctive nature of national economies and political systems.

International Trade

International trade gives rise to a world economy, in which supply and demand, and therefore prices, both affect and are affected by global events. A product that is sold to the global market is called export, and a product that is bought from the global market is an import. Imports and exports are accounted for in a country's current account in the balance of payments. A core element of globalization is the expansion of world trade through the elimination or reduction of trade barriers, such as import tariffs. Greater imports offer consumers a wider variety of goods at lower prices while providing strong incentives for domestic industries to remain competitive. Exports, often a source of economic growth for developing nations, stimulate job creation as industries sell beyond their borders.

Political change in Asia, for example, could increase the cost of labor, thereby increasing the manufacturing costs for an American sneaker company based in Malaysia, which would then increase the price charged at your local mall. A decrease in the cost of labor, on the other hand, would likely result in you having to pay less for your new shoes.

More generally, trade enhances national competitiveness by driving workers to focus on those vocations where they, and their country, have a competitive advantage. Trade promotes economic resilience and flexibility, as higher imports help to offset adverse domestic supply shocks. Greater openness can also stimulate foreign investment, which would be a source of employment for the local workforce and could bring along new technologies—thus promoting higher productivity.

Restricting international trade – that is, engaging in protectionism – generates adverse consequences for a country that undertakes such a policy. For example, tariffs raise the prices of imported goods, harming consumers, many of which may be poor. Protectionism also tends to reward concentrated, well-organized and politically-connected groups, at the expense of those whose interests may be more diffuse (such as consumers). It also reduces the variety of goods available and generates inefficiency by reducing competition and encouraging resources to flow into protected sectors.

Global trade allows wealthy countries to use their resources – whether labor, technology or capital – more efficiently. Because countries are endowed with different assets and natural resources (land, labor, capital, and technology), some countries may produce the same goods more efficiently and therefore sell it more cheaply than other countries. If a country cannot efficiently produce an item, it can obtain it by trading with another country that can. This is known as specialization in international trade.

## Political Globalization

Political globalization refers to the amount of political cooperation that exists between different countries. This ties in with the belief that "umbrella" global organizations are better placed than individual states to prevent conflict. The League of Nations established after WW1 was certainly one of the pioneers in this. Since then, global organizations such as the World Trade Organization (WTO), United Nations (UN), and more regional organizations such as the EU have helped to increase the degree of political globalization.

Global politics thus takes place not just at a global level, but at and, crucially, across, all levels – worldwide, regional, national, sub-national and so on. Global means worldwide, having planetary (not merely regional or national) significance. The globe is, in effect, the world. Global politics, in this sense, refers to politics conducted at a global rather than a national or regional level.

Transnational corporations (TNCs), non-governmental organizations (NGOs), and a host of other non-state bodies have come to exert influence. In different ways and to different degrees, groups and organizations ranging from al-Qaeda, the anti-capitalist movement, and Greenpeace to Google, General Motors and the Papacy contribute to shaping world politics.

Traditionally politics has been undertaken within national political systems. National governments have been ultimately responsible for maintaining the security and economic welfare of their citizens, as well as the protection of human rights and the environment within their borders. With global ecological changes, an ever more integrated global economy, and other global trends, political activity increasingly takes place at the global level.

Under globalization, politics can take place above the state through political integration schemes such as the European Union and intergovernmental organizations such as the International Monetary Fund, the World Bank and the World Trade Organization. Political activity can also transcend national borders through global movements and NGOs. Civil society organizations act globally by forming alliances with organizations in other countries, using global communications systems, and lobbying international organizations and other actors directly, instead of working through their national governments.

## Global Security and Terrorism

The idea of global justice is a belief in universal moral values, applying to all people in the world regardless of nationality and citizenship. The most influential example of universal values is the doctrine of international human rights.

Security is the deepest and most abiding issue in politics. At its heart is the question: how can people live a decent and worthwhile existence, free from threats, intimidation, and violence? Security is a particularly pressing issue in international politics because, while the domestic realm is usually ordered and stable under the existence of a sovereign state, the international realm is anarchical and therefore threatening and unstable.

Terrorism is a form of political violence that achieves its objectives through a climate of fear and apprehension. As such, it uses violence in a very particular way, not primarily to bring about death and destruction but to create unease and anxiety about possible future acts of death and destruction. Terrorism shares more features related to guerrilla warfare. Both compensate for an enemy's greater technological, economic, and conventional military strength.

Liberal-democratic societies may be uniquely vulnerable to the threat of terrorism because they protect individual rights and freedoms and

state security has been strengthened by extending the legal powers of government

For example, states have reasserted control over global financial flows; immigration arrangements have been made more rigorous, especially during high-alert periods; the surveillance and control of domestic populations, but particularly of members of 'extremist' groups or terrorist sympathizers, has been significantly tightened; and, in many cases, the power to detain terrorist suspects has been strengthened.

Force-based or repressive counter-terrorism has, in recent years, been particularly associated with the 'war on terror'. Military responses to terrorism have been based on two complementary strategies. In the first, attempts have been made to deny terrorists the support or 'sponsorship' of regimes that had formerly given them succor.

## Populism

A populist is "a believer in the rights, wisdom, or virtues of the common people" according to the Merriam-Webster dictionary. Common people are the majority, and having the majority on one's side is a pretty good strategy for winning elections. Politicians use to speak for the common people, most political movements of appreciable size are populist to one degree or another, but that doesn't make them fascist, or even intolerant. The problem is when populism involves the willingness to do whatever is necessary – including the use of force and trampling on the rights of others – to achieve victory and command obedience.

Another interpretation establishes populist rulers as those who advocate for the common people against corrupt elites, common-sense solutions versus complex policies, and national unity over international engagement. Following that definition, 43% of GDP in G-20 economies is now under the control of populist rulers, up from 8% in 2016.

On the evidence so far, populist rulers are better at identifying problems than they are at finding solutions. The result, in various experiments, has been protectionism, opposition to immigration, unfunded tax giveaways, attacks on central bank independence and head-spinning policy uncertainty.

Populist rulers differ. Some people even question the value of the term as a catch-all category but practice says otherwise. A family of factors contributes to their rise. High inequality, low social mobility and high unemployment triggered by recession or financial crisis are common denominators. Other factors – rising immigration, imports displacing domestic manufacturing, high crime rates, and weak political institutions – are frequent contributors.

Social Globalization

Social globalization refers to the sharing of ideas and information between and through different countries. In today's world, the Internet and social media are at the heart of this evolutionary process. Good examples of social globalization could include internationally popular films, books, and TV series. The Harry Potter/ Twilight films and other books that have been successful all over the world, making the characters featured globally recognizable. However, this cultural flow tends to flow from the center (i.e. from developed countries such as the USA) to less developed countries. Social globalization is often criticized for eroding cultural differences.

The broad reach of globalization easily extends to daily choices of personal, economic, and political life. For example, greater access to modern technologies in the world of health care could make the difference between life and death. In the world of communications, it would facilitate commerce and education, and allow access to independent media. Globalization can also create a framework for cooperation among nations on a range of non-economic issues that have cross-border implications, such as immigration, the environment, and legal issues. At the same time, the influx of foreign goods, services, and capital into a country can create incentives and demands for strengthening the education system, as a country's citizens recognize the competitive challenge before them.

Globalization often appears to be a force of nature, a phenomenon without bounds or alternatives. But peoples' movements have shown that it is neither unalterable nor inevitable. Citizens all over the world – ordinary people from the global North and South – can work together to shape alternate futures, to build a globalization of cooperation, solidarity, and respect for our common planetary environment.

Global Environment

Extreme weather events could lead to disruption of economic activity and could inflict long-lasting damage on capital and land. Global climate change is becoming a systemic risk and inward-looking leaders are ill-placed to confront it. Uncertainty about climate risks and the impact of mitigation measures creates a disincentive for businesses to invest. The lack of direction on climate policy is holding back business investment. Higher temperatures reduce labor productivity. The need for climate adaptation diverts resources away from more productive uses.

In many countries, it is investment and trade that has been at the center of weakening economic performance. It implies governments must act quickly. "Without a clear sense of direction on carbon prices, standards and regulation, and without the necessary public investment, businesses will put off investment decisions, with dire consequences for growth and employment," entrepreneurs are going to delay their decisions.

Although there is not a recession being forecast, it is decidedly a downbeat possibility. Climate change is perhaps the most striking example of recession peril. The consequence is that temperatures 1°C above pre-industrial levels are already evident. As temperatures continue to move higher, the economic impacts will be wide-ranging. Extreme weather events, from floods in Thailand to category-five storms battering the U.S., are wreaking havoc on housing, infrastructure and supply chains. Insurance losses have risen fivefold since the 1980s.

And while the transition to a low-carbon economy brings new opportunities, a trade-off between emissions and growth may be tough to avoid. They could also lead to what it is called disorderly migration flows. Insufficient policy action could increase the frequency of such perturbing events. There is a long term challenge for governments in addressing these issues, but there is already an impact on business investment.

There are calls for action from governments to address challenges, some of which have both long term and more immediate consequences. More clarity on climate policy - and also on digitization - would trigger a marked acceleration of investment by business. It suggests the creation of national funds to make public investments in several key areas.

<u>Global Expectations</u>

There is the hope of a global growth pickup, trade tensions have lessened and central banks have reaffirmed they will maintain ultra-low interest rates and continue to provide ample liquidity. Financial volatility is subdued, and there are reasonable expectations of solid investor returns across many asset classes. Many countries are facing structural uncertainties that could have far-reaching, systemic implications for markets and the global economy. For example, over the next five years, the EU will seek to establish a new working relationship with the UK, while also dealing with the harmful social and political effects of slow, insufficiently inclusive growth.

Moreover, in the years ahead, the US, having notably outperformed many other economies, will decide whether to continue disengaging from the rest of the world – a process that is at odds with its historic position at the center of the global economy. Most important, in the next five years, China and the US, the world's two largest national economies, will have to navigate an increasingly narrow path as they try to secure their interests while avoiding an outright confrontation. Bad outcomes are not inevitable (at least not yet). They could still be averted through the sustained implementation of policies to promote stronger, more inclusive growth; restore genuine financial stability; and usher in a fairer, more credible (while still free) system of international trade, investment, and policy coordination.

The path to prosperity followed by such success stories as Korea and Japan is increasingly hard to follow. From Beijing to Brasilia, getting the right mix of smart investment, skilled workforce, innovation capacity, and effective governance in place is already tough to do. Combating disruptive forces – which, from protectionism to climate change, threaten an outsize impact on low- and middle-income economies – adds to the challenge. Catching up is getting harder to do. Low and middle-income economies are, in general, poorly positioned to adapt to coming disruptions. Without an early and ambitious response forged at a national and international level, the number moving from low- to middle-income, and then on to high-income status—already limited—could dwindle further.

# Chapter 14: Sociopolitical Summary

The following paragraphs present a summary of the features associated with each of the sociopolitical systems. Know Thyself Ideologically is the objective of a personal sociopolitical understanding.

The sociopolitical systems considered are:
- Communism
- Socialism
- Anarchism
- Absurd Socialism - 21st Century Socialism
- Social Democracy
- Liberalism
- Conservatism
- Capital Democracy
- Fascism

## Political System

### THE STATE

The conception of the state varies from no state at all (Anarchism) to moderate states that follow the laws (Liberalism, Conservatism, Capital Democracy) or interventionist states (Social Democracy) or totalitarian states (Socialism, Communism) and dictatorial states without scruples (Absurd Socialism, Fascism).

### AUTHORITY

The notion of authority varies from a rejection of authority (Anarchism) to moderate authority complying with the law (Liberalism, Conservatism, Capital Democracy, Social Democracy) or using authority to force people to comply with authority (Socialism, Communism) and totalitarian authority supported by charismatic leaders (Absurd Socialism, Fascism).

### LEADERSHIP

The subject of leadership varies from a distributed view (Anarchism) to constitutional and hierarchical leadership (Liberalism, Capital Democracy, Conservatism, Social Democracy) or totalitarian leadership (Socialism, Communism) and charismatic or supreme commander leadership (Absurd Socialism, Fascism).

### DEMOCRACY
The notion of democracy varies from decentralized (Anarchism) to parliamentary (Liberalism, Capital Democracy, Conservatism, Social Democracy) to radical democracy (Socialism, Communism) and democracy of the charismatic or supreme commander (Absurd Socialism, Fascism).

### CONSTITUTIONALISM
The use of constitutional ideas varies from encouraging distributed constitutions (Anarchism) to respecting a centralized constitution (Liberalism, Capital Democracy, Conservatism, Social Democracy) and disrespect the constitution (Socialism, Communism, Absurd Socialism, Fascism).

### THE PARTY
The participation of the party goes from rejection of the unique party concept (Anarchism) to multiparty participation (Liberalism, Conservatism, Capital Democracy, Social Democracy) to the participation of the exclusive dominant party (Socialism, Communism, Absurd Socialism, Fascism).

## Economic System

### PRIVATE versus PUBLIC PROPERTY
The notion of private and public property varies from a mix of acceptance for both public and private property (Anarchism, Liberalism, Conservatism, Social Democracy, Fascism) to a preference for the private property (Capital Democracy) to a preference for the public property (Socialism, Communism, Absurd Socialism).

### WORKERS and ENTREPRENEURS
The emphasis to prefer workers over entrepreneurs varies from bias toward workers (Anarchism, Social Democracy, Socialism, Communism) to a balance between workers and employers (Liberalism, Conservatism, Social Democracy, Fascism) to a preference for entrepreneurs (Capital Democracy).

### COMMON GOOD versus PROFIT
The search for the common good or profit varies from favoring both approaches at various levels (Anarchism, Liberalism, Conservatism, Social Democracy) or pursuing only the common good (Socialism, Communism) or pursuing only profit (Capital Democracy) or pursuing the good of the nation, race or the poor (Fascism, Absurd Socialism)

WELFARE ORIENTATION
Governments vary on their promotion of welfare benefits from those that consider welfare a social right (Socialism, Communism, Social Democracy, Absurd Socialism) to consider welfare a complement to productive life (Liberalism, Conservatism, Capital Democracy, Anarchism) and those that consider the welfare of the nation, class or race (Fascism).

COMMAND PLANNING
The orientation to command planning is stronger in totalitarian regimes (Communism, Socialism, Fascism, Absurd Socialism) and gets transformed into strategic planning in liberal economies (Liberalism, Conservatism, Capital Democracy, Social Democracy) and distributed towards the affected (Anarchism).

PRICE CONTROL
Regarding price controls, governments vary from interventionists (Socialism, Communism, Absurd Socialism, Fascism) to relatively free supply and demand (Liberalism, Capital Democracy, Conservatism, Social Democracy) to letting the affected decide (Anarchism).

## Personal Influence

INDIVIDUALITY versus COLLECTIVITY
The duality between individuality and collectivity gets manifested by governments pushing the collective approach (Socialism, Communism, Absurd Socialism, Social Democracy) to those that are biased towards the individual (Anarchism, Liberalism, Capital Democracy) to those that see the individual just as a collaborator to the good of the nation (Conservatism, Fascism).

COOPERATION
Regarding cooperation, governments consider the free initiative of the individual to cooperate (Anarchism, Liberalism, Capital Democracy) to those forcing the individual to participate (Socialism, Communism, Social Democracy, Absurd Socialism) to those defining the importance of collectivity for historical reasons or the national interest (Conservatism, Fascism).

HUMAN'S NURTURE versus NATURE
The controversy between the influence of nature and nurture has been around for many years varying from those considering nature a stronger motivator than nurture (Liberalism, Conservatism, Capital Democracy, Fascism) to those considering nurture stronger (Socialism, Communism,

Social Democracy, Absurd Socialism) and those been neutral on the subject (Anarchism).

### EQUALITY

On the issue of equality, governments vary from those favoring social equality including equality of outcome (Socialism, Communism, Social Democracy) to those favoring equality of opportunity (Liberalism, Capital Democracy) to political equality (Anarchism) to hierarchical or unequal equality (Conservatism, Fascism) to equality of wealth (Absurd Socialism).

### FREEDOM

Freedom is a strong human need and governments have differing views, some limiting the freedom of individuals (Socialism, Communism, Absurd Socialism) others considering freedom the supreme value at various levels (Anarchism, Liberalism, Social Democracy) others having a biased view on freedom (Capital Democracy, Conservatism) and others considering freedom a complete submission to the leader (Fascism).

## Social Influence

### SOCIETY

The view on society varies among governments. In one extreme, the individual is the one defining society (Liberalism) or the individual being naturally social (Anarchism) or the individual contingent on society (Socialism, Communism, Absurd Socialism, Social Democracy) or the society existing on its own or the leader (Conservatism, Fascism) or society defined for commercial purposes (Capital Democracy).

### SOCIAL JUSTICE

The way rewards are distributed defines how governments define social justice. Some distribute rewards based on needs (Socialism, Communism, Social Democracy) others distribute rewards based on merits (Anarchism, Liberalism, Capital Democracy, Conservatism) others distribute rewards based on class or race (Absurd Socialism, Fascism).

### CONFORMING and OBEYING

On the issue of conforming and obeying, most governments coincide on having an obeying population (Capital Democracy, Conservatism, Social Democracy, Socialism, Communism, Absurd Socialism) others to obey only just laws defined in the social contract (Liberalism) others to reject injustices (Anarchism) and others to conform to the leader (Fascism).

## LEADERS and FOLLOWERS
The notion of leadership places governments at various levels, from those considering absence of leadership or coming from below (Anarchism, Liberalism) to those imposing leadership collectively (Socialism, Communism, Social Democracy) to those considering leadership from above and hierarchical (Capital Democracy, Conservatism) and those favoring leadership from charismatic and gifted individuals (Absurd Socialism, Fascism).

## CLASS STRUGGLE
The idea of class conflict identifies governments as being promoters of conflict at different levels (Socialism, Communism, Social Democracy) or accepting classes as natural or created circumstances (Liberalism, Capital Democracy, Conservatism) or helping the individual overcome oppression (Anarchism) or promoting the difference between the masses and the charismatic leader (Fascism, Absurd Socialism).

# Ideological Sphere

## IDEOLOGY
Regarding ideologies, governments vary from those being pragmatic at different levels (Capital Democracy, Conservatism, Absurd Socialism, Fascism) or those proposing fantasies without support (Socialism, Communism) or those promoting a Utopia (Anarchism) or those balancing reality and fantasy with scientific support (Liberalism, Social Democracy)

## ASPIRATIONS versus INSTITUTIONS
Regarding aspirations and institutions, governments differ on the institutional support given to ideological aspirations. Some are experts manifesting aspirations without feasibility analysis or institutional support (Socialism, Communism) others develop institutions specifically to support some aspirations (Liberalism, Capital Democracy, Conservatism, Fascism) others believe consensual support defines aspirations and institutions (Anarchism) others are incapable of defining aspirations or building useful institutions (Absurd Socialism) and others try to support some aspirations with possibly useful institutions (Social Democracy).

## FUNDAMENTAL DEBT
The fundamental debt defines the recipients of the effort of living in a society. Governments vary on the emphasis towards the recipients, some favor the individual, including the entrepreneur and traditions (Anarchism, Liberalism, Capital Democracy, Conservatism) others favors the debt being owed to the collectivity (Socialism, Communism) others propose a

balance towards individuals and collectivity (Social Democracy) and others have a constrained view oriented to a particular poor class or the supreme leader (Absurd Socialism, Fascism).

CURRENT WORLD-VIEW

Governments vary on their understanding of the current world-view. Some consider the world is wrong and propose a complete overhaul (Socialism, Communism) others consider the world with some defects that can be overcome (Liberals, Social Democrats) others have a biased understanding (Anarchism, Capital Democracy, Conservatism) others don't understand the world they live (Absurd Socialism) and others understand the world through the looking glass of the supreme leader (Fascism)

TRANSITION TO THE NEW SOCIETY

Governments vary in the proposed way to generate a new society. Some favor a revolution (Anarchism) others favor a slow but solid transition (Liberalism, Social Democracy) others consider transition unnecessary (Conservatism) others consider transition to be harsh and immediate (Socialism, Communism) others consider transition to be improvised and according to the leader (Absurd Socialism, Fascism) others based on entrepreneurship (Capital Democracy).

IDEOLOGY versus IMPROVISATION

Regarding the strength of the ideology, governments use to follow some ideologies but results always differ with expectations. Some know they are Utopia (Anarchism) others believe they have a solid ideology but never succeed (Socialism, Communism) others follow more practical ideologies with less improvisation (Liberalism, Social Democracy, Capital Democracy, Conservatism) others have no ideology at all (Fascism, Absurd Socialism).

## Pragmatical Sphere

PROPAGANDA

Regarding propaganda, governments use to promote their ideologies and political positions using various mechanisms. Some consider individuals free to decide the use of propaganda (Anarchism) others use it to convince supporters through reasoning (Liberalism, Capital Democracy, Conservatism, Social Democracy) others use propaganda to maintain a submissive population (Socialism, Communism, Absurd Socialism, Fascism).

### INDOCTRINATION

Indoctrination is related to education but serves the desires of the government. Some dislike indoctrination and lean towards open mind education (Anarchism, Liberalism, Capital Democracy, Conservatism, Social Democracy) others use indoctrination profusely to avoid opposition (Socialism, Communism, Absurd Socialism, Fascism).

### CONTROLLING THE PRESS

Controlling the press or the media, in general, is a way of maintaining an ignorant population (Socialism, Communism, Absurd Socialism) others support the free press at different levels (Anarchism, Liberalism, Capital Democracy, Conservatism) others look for a balance between free and public press (Social Democracy) and others use the press to praise the leader (Fascism).

### THE ENEMIES

The treatment of the enemies of differentiates governments. Some treat the opposition badly (Communism, Socialism, Absurd Socialism, Fascism) others avoid the term enemies preferring to use misbehavior or disobeying the laws (Anarchism, Liberalism, Capital Democracy, Conservatism) and others try to convince the opposition to accept the status quo (Social Democracy).

### CORRUPTION

Corruption is a widespread policy used to buy consciences. Governments use corruption for several purposes. Some penalize corruption according to laws (Liberals, Capital Democrats, Conservatives, Social Democracy) others penalize some types of corruption excepting buying consciences (Socialism, Absurd Socialism, Communism, Fascism) and others consider corruption an unnatural propensity (Anarchism).

### DISTRACT THE POPULATION

Governments use to distract the population to forget their miserable situation. Some use to make life harsh instead through bad services and creating shortages (Socialism, Communism, Absurd Socialism) others let people distract themselves not interfering (Anarchism, Liberalism) others distract the population through different means such as tradition, enterprising, leadership (Conservatism, Capital Democracy, Fascism) and others balance distraction with occupation (Social Democracy).

### USE OF TERROR

The use of terror has been common practice on tyrannical governments implementing state policies (Socialism, Communism,

Absurd Socialism, Fascism) others avoid the use of terror encouraging several values such as traditions, enterprising, the laws (Conservatism, Capital Democracy, Liberalism, Social Democracy) and others may not consider terror as an alternative (Anarchism).

CONTROL THE JUDICIAL SYSTEM

Governments use to control the judicial system to stay in power eternally and maintain their ideology in power (Socialism, Communism, Absurd Socialism, Fascism) others leave an independent judicial system following the laws or traditions or commerce (Liberalism, Capital Democracy, Conservatism, Social Democracy) and others favor a judicial system that is distributed to serve the affected population (Anarchism).

## Chapter 15: Absurd Socialism in Venezuela

Venezuela is a small country in South America that followed one of the worst interpretations of socialism, known as Absurd Socialism, taking experiences in Nazi Germany, the Soviets, China's Mao, North Korea, Zimbabwe, and Cuba. In Venezuela, absurd socialism took power using the democratic institutions in the same way Hitler and Mussolini did in the twentieth century. Absurd socialism is a misinterpretation of communism, socialism, fascism, and anarchism that imposes the worst practices in a society. Hugo Chavez reflected the same image Hitler and Mussolini portrayed in Europe during the twentieth century.

When Chavez was elected, there was not a clear blueprint explaining what his intentions were. Time passed by and changes to the constitution took place. The constitution was the best in the world according to the leader but immediately it started to be violated by his government. Nobody complained, and those who did were not taken into consideration or purged. The population accepted the expropriations, the injustices, the declining economic situation, the lack of services, the punishment of the opposition, the difficulty to get food and medicines, and a long list of disasters.

Absurd Socialism has been applied in a few countries, including Venezuela. There are others, such as Nicaragua and Bolivia that have applied equivalent measures but are not yet in the auto-destruction stage. Mexico, which may follow a similar paths to destruction, using the excuse of socialism to impose an authoritarian regime, has more limitations due to its closeness to the U.S. These countries use a common pattern that first benefits from democracy, then makes people believe there is some improvement, and at the end justify a tyrant in the name of social justice. Absurd Socialism should be eradicated as an alternate sociopolitical system.

Absurd Socialism is just a variant of socialism and communism that incorporates the worst aspects of anarchism and fascism. Absurd Socialism countries are characterized by strong states governed in some cases by the party in power and most cases, pleasing the desires of the Strong Man in charge. Absurd Socialist's states are ruled in a tyrannical way, spreading fear among the population. Hundreds of thousands of people have been sacrificed in the name of the stability of the regime.

Absurd Socialism benefits from a democratic infrastructure to take power. Once there, it suffices to change the constitution, control the institutions, gain the consent of the population and put the military and secret police in charge of the nation.

## Venezuela's Geopolitical Dimension

Absurd Socialism, as well as communism, socialism, and fascism, promotes a strictly regulated society. The control over the population is so strong that the state decides how people think, where they work, as well as what they eat, and how long they sleep. In this type of regime, the population is subject to fear and anxiety, making them obedient towards the state. Party members, partisans, and their accomplices are constantly supervising the population to establish how submissive people are; therefore, those that do not fit the standards are purged.

Absurd Socialism regimes believe they are capable of controlling the lives of every single individual. Its command economy is made to plan the twenty-four hours' lives of each citizen during a day: eight hours of work, eight hours or more of indoctrination, and eight hours or less of sleep.

## Venezuela's History

Venezuela was discovered by Christopher Columbus on his third journey to the Indies in 1498. Venezuela occupies an area of 912,050 square kilometers (352,143 square miles) and is surrounded by the Caribbean Sea and the Atlantic Ocean on the north; on the east by the disputed territory of English Guyana; on the south by Brazil; on the west by Colombia.

Three main ethnic groups make up the Venezuelan population: European, African, and Indigenous peoples. Despite the historical and cultural differences that have traditionally separated these groups, Venezuela is not a country of racial rivalry. The country can be considered a rarity in terms of racial integration; however, there are few pockets of regions that are inhabited by predominantly Indigenous or African descendants. The *mestizo* population, a mix of all the races, amounts to 67 percent, the whites to 21 percent, the blacks to 10 percent, and the Indigenous to 2 percent.

Major social and economic divisions were predominant in Venezuela during the colonial times. Education was primarily Catholic and only available to a small minority, which was basically comprised of Europeans and their descendants, typically known as Mantuanos.

### Venezuela's Geography

Venezuela's topography can be divided into three broad elevated divisions: the lowland plains, which rise from sea level to about 1,650 feet (500 meters), the mountains, which reach elevations of some 16,400 feet (5,000 meters), and the interior forested uplands, with scattered peaks above 6,550 feet (2,000 meters).

In the 20th century, Venezuela was transformed from a relatively poor agrarian society to a rapidly urbanizing one, a condition made possible by exploiting huge petroleum reserves.

### The Beginnings: Military Path

Simón Bolívar (1783-1830), better known as "The Liberator," (because of his leading role in the independence of Venezuela, Colombia, Ecuador, Peru, and Bolivia) was a strong believer in philosophical principles such as the rights of the individual, the ideals of justice and freedom for all, and promoted education of the masses as a means to achieve democracy and self-realization.

In 1806 Francisco de Miranda – who had earlier fought under George Washington against the British, served as a general in the French Revolution, and fought with the French against Prussia and Russia – tried unsuccessfully to land on the Venezuelan coast with a group of mercenaries whom he had recruited in New York City. Revolutionary leaders recalled him to Gran Colombia four years later to take charge of a junta, which drafted a constitution and established an independent nation. In the ensuing war with royalist forces, however, Miranda signed an armistice with Spain.

Early in 1813, the revolutionary junta appointed Simon Bolivar commander of the Venezuelan forces. Bolivar, a wealthy Mantuano landowner born in Caracas in 1783, had many reverses in his war against the Spanish. His forces were opposed by large royalist armies including a cavalry unit of llaneros (cowboys of the plains frontier), who were under the command of José Tomás Boves. In 1815 the Spanish general Pablo Morillo landed with an expeditionary force that spearheaded the reconquest of much of New Granada. Morillo administered the region in a heavy-handed fashion, however, and many of the Mantuano elites who had initially supported him soon conspired for his defeat.

By July 1814 Bolívar had once more lost Caracas. He marched instead to Bogotá, which he succeeded in recapturing from the Spanish. He made this capital city his base for a while, but soon the Spanish recover it yet again. Bolívar fled into exile, in Jamaica and Haiti. But by the end of 1817, he was back in Venezuela, building up a new army in an inaccessible region on the Orinoco river.

Instead of heading towards Caracas, the capital, he would strike at the capital city of New Granada by a route which was considered impossible - along the waterlogged plain of the Orinoco and then over the Andes for a surprise attack on Bogotá. They descended from the high passes upon an unsuspecting enemy. In an engagement at Boyacá, on 7 August 1819, the Spanish army surrendered. Three days later Bolívar entered Bogotá. On December 17 the Republica de Colombia was proclaimed. It covered the entire region of modern Colombia, Ecuador, and Venezuela.

As yet the republic was little more than a notion, Venezuela and Ecuador were still securely in Spanish hands. But the Liberator soon changed the distribution of forces. The Republic of Gran Colombia, with its capital at Bogotá, was proclaimed on December 17, 1819, with Bolívar as president. And in Ecuador on 24 May 1822 Bolívar's favorite general, the young Antonio José de Sucre won a victory at Pichincha and brought the patriots into Quito.

Bolívar left Santander in charge of Gran Colombia and headed south to meet up with Sucre. On July 26-27, Bolivar met with Jose de San Martin, liberator of Argentina, in Guayaquil. It was decided there that Bolívar would lead the charge into Peru, the last royalist stronghold on the continent. On August 6, 1824, Bolivar and Sucre defeated the Spanish at the Battle of Junin. On December 9, Sucre dealt the royalists another harsh blow at the Battle of Ayacucho, basically destroying the last royalist army in Peru. The following year Bolívar's army marched south to liberate Peru, and in 1825 it freed Upper Peru (Bolivia) from Spanish rule. The next year, also on August 6, the Congress of Upper Peru created the nation of Bolivia, naming it after Bolivar and confirming him as president.

In Venezuela on 24 June 1821, he won the battle at Carabobo, reinforced by llanero cavalry under General Jose Antonio Paez, defeated the main royalist army at the Battle of Carabobo, which yielded to him once again his native city of Caracas. The last of the royalist forces surrendered at Puerto Cabello on October 9, 1823.

Bolívar had driven the Spanish out of northern and western South America and now ruled over the present-day nations of Bolivia, Peru, Ecuador, Colombia, Venezuela, and Panama. It was his dream to unite them all, creating one unified nation. It was not to be. The first of the military dictators was General Jose Antonio Paez, who gave the country better government than it would see again for nearly a century. Bolivar had left Paez in charge of the Backed by their armies, a series of warlord-like caudillos (leaders) assumed power, which they exercised for their benefit rather than for that of the nation. armed forces of Venezuela and he soon took full control of the country.

After the destruction of the colonial system, Venezuela passed through an era of government-by-force that lasted more than a century, until the death of Juan Vicente Gomez in 1935.

Contemporary Tendencies

Those who control Venezuela are the military, the Cubans, the drug traffickers, and Hugo Chavez's political heirs. Those four groups effectively function as criminal cartels, and have co-opted the armed forces into their service; this is how every day we may see men in uniform willing to massacre their people to keep Venezuela's criminal oligarchy in power.

The most important component of this oligarchy is the Cuban regime. In 2014 Moises Naim wrote: "Venezuelan aid is indispensable to prevent the Cuban economy from collapsing. Having a government in Caracas that maintains such aid is a vital objective of the Cuban State. And Cuba has accumulated decades of experience, knowledge, and contacts that allow it to operate internationally with great efficacy and, when necessary, in an almost invisible way."

The drug traffickers, whose power is also a constraint on Maduro's survival, are the ones controlling the country. Venezuela is one of the main drug routes to the U.S. and Europe. This status is worth billions of dollars, and the country is home to a vast network of people and organizations that control the illicit trade and the enormous amount of money it generates. According to U.S. officials, one such person is Vice President Tareck El Aissami, and so are a large number of military officers and other relatives and members of the ruling oligarchy. The smuggling and selling of food, medicines, and all kinds of products are just a few of the many other corrupt activities that enrich the Maduro oligarchy as well as the Cubans, the military, and their civilian accomplices.

Characteristics of Absurd Socialism

The three pillars sustaining an absurd socialist regime are legitimation, repression, and cooptation. The three are mutually dependent, as long as they remain in balance, they ensure that rulers can maintain their grip on power.

The factor that has the greatest influence on whether a socialist leader or an undemocratic regime can hold on to power is legitimation. In a genuine democracy, all governments are legitimated by the fact of having been elected by the people. In socialism, the ruler must create his form of legitimation.

One way of doing so is to appeal to nationalist instincts, like the former Serbian leader Slobodan Milosevic; or to evoke an ideology, such as Communism. This was the method exploited by the Cambodian dictator Pol Pot. In Cuba, Fidel Castro has done both, he played the nationalist card concerning Cuba's "evil neighbor," the United States, and at the same time pledged his people to Communism. In Venezuela, Hugo Chavez always blamed the 'Empire' of the United States of plotting against his regime, and also pledged his people to Socialism (Absurd Socialism).

Another way to legitimize is by offering economic prosperity. This promise has enabled the Chinese Communist Party to abandon its ideology without fear of popular protest. The world has seen for itself how well this strategy has worked. China has improved thanks to capitalistic policies, not thanks to communism. However, in China, many people believe differently about the idea of democracy and a multi-party system in their country. "That would destabilize everything here," people replied. "No, we'll stick with the Communist Party: then we'll be well-off, too." Venezuela utilized the oil revenue to subsidize the poor and was doing good while oil prices were high but forgot to incentivize productivity by dislodging entrepreneurs; the country is living the worst relatively pacific collapse in human history.

Repression – suppressing all divergent opinions – is a stronger instrument. There is a difference between 'harsh' and 'soft' repression. Russia provides an example of 'soft' repression. From time to time it cracks down openly on demonstrators and members of the opposition, but most repression remains hidden. "Undesirable journalists get hit with a flood of libel actions, or the tax authorities go after critics of the regime," "Mr. Putin goes about it very cleverly."

For socialists, 'harsh' measures, such as imprisonment and torture, or the abduction and murder of opponents of the regime, are a double-edged sword. They make the oppressed more fearful and more compliant, but they can also spur on the opposition. If such crimes are publicly known, they can call the socialist's claim to power into question. 'Soft' measures, on the other hand – target changes in tax legislation, or freezing bank accounts, for example – are easier to implement and less likely to attract attention. The media seldom reports on them, so their potential for causing outrage is small and they provide the opposition with little in the way of ammunition.

Cooptation means incorporating people by securing their participation. They are allowed to be part of the system and benefit from it. This creates a degree of solidarity with the socialist elite and reinforces its claim to power.

The main characteristics of Absurd Socialism transferred from socialists and communists regimes include:
- Cult of Personality
- The Elite Amassing Wealth
- Building a Corrupt System
- Controlling Democratic Institutions
- Using the Rule By Law instead of The Rule of Law
- Learning from the Masters
- Stay Eternally in Power
- Use Politics of Distraction
- A Dictatorship Oriented Socialism
- Gaining Consent from the Population
- Controlling the Elites
- Using Propaganda
- Indoctrination
- Using the Carrot and the Stick
- Become Producers and Distributors of Good and Services
- Use Blackmail and Coercion
- Controlling Information
- Use of Violence
- Using Repression
- Creating a Culture of Fear
- Creating Terror
- Use Torture and Murder
- Creating a Common Enemy
- Crushing the Internal and External Enemy
- Using Political Sectarianism
- Spying on people

- Controlling the Secret Police
- Controlling the Press
- Controlling the Army
- Using Military Path to Stay in Power
- Declaring War to Neighbors to Hide their Ineptitude

## Absurd Socialism's Societal Dimension
### Political System

The first defining feature of an absurd socialism's political system is the monopoly of power of the state; the party has a reduced role as in socialism. The state becomes the most important institution, in charge of defining the rest of the activities of the society, absurd socialism promotes a stronger state. There are other important institutions within a socialist state, among them, the party, government ministries, the military, and the security police. All institutions are overseen by the organs of the executive power of the state, primarily the charismatic leader, which has a higher authority than any other body.

According to absurd socialists, total government control is necessary to transform society; the state becomes the producer and distributor of goods and people work to improve the life of every other citizen. Ideally, people would not need to earn a salary under total state control, the state manages the natural resources and is going to provide for the people independently of their contribution to the wellness of society.

The second feature is the understanding of national idiosyncrasy. Understanding people's motivation and the country's traditions are fundamental for absurd socialists, the objective is to take power and stay forever. How informal are people, how prone to corruption, how easy they sell their consciences, are important considerations for absurd socialists.

The third feature refers to institutional characteristics to implement the ideology. Absurd socialism presents primarily a set of aspirations without feasibility analysis and institutional structure. However, it adapts over time and proposes institutions to materialize its ideology; for example, collectivization and public ownership of the means of production evolved lately towards private and free-market ventures. The problem is that each change in the initial approaches represents hundred of thousands of people dead, exiled or ostracized. Absurd socialists introduce several institutional characteristics to attain their ideology. Through their charismatic leadership, absurd socialists implement policies to attain their objectives. Absurd socialism is oriented to serve the poor independently of harming everybody in the long run. The institutions are oriented to serve exclusively the poor, the rest of the population has to simulate being poor to receive benefits.

The fourth defining feature defines the concept of 'authoritarian democracy' in the absurd socialist system. In absurd socialism, democracy is used basically to elect some representatives of the state to control the population. Absurd socialism allows discussion of issues at low ranks until alternatives have been identified, the charismatic leader analyzes the situation and reaches a decision, thereafter the decision has to be implemented in the whole society, independently of how successful it is.

Every attempt to impose absurd socialism ends in authoritarian policies. Absurd socialists insist on unpopular measures to maintain some level of justice, their ideas are put into practice only by a strong dictatorial government. To them, absurd socialism meant an attempt to 'terminate the revolution' by a deliberate reorganization of society on hierarchical lines and by the imposition of a coercive 'spiritual power.'

The fifth feature is related to the importance of elections in the absurd socialist system. They do have elections, however, the elections are not oriented to introduce democracy in the country, they are used to assign certain cadres into positions to control the population. Elections are used to demonstrate who has the power and scare the opposition.

The sixth defining feature regards the importance of the control of the state. In absurd socialism, the state is the supreme leader. The rulers make people believe they are participating but it is the state and the strong man who decides. The social contract is implemented surrendering total control to the state. The state is interfering in all the decisions of society.

The seventh feature regards the handling of politics. Absurd socialism builds a complex apparatus where an elite composed by partisans, family members, the military, and the special forces become the masters of society. The elite controls all the institutions of the state, there are no independent institutions. Political survival is guaranteed by buying political consciences.

The eighth feature is related to the importance of the party. In absurd socialism, the party has a second rank. There are discussions and recommendations from the party but decisions are taken elsewhere.

The ninth feature is related to the importance of leadership in decision making. Absurd socialists give a lot of importance to a charismatic leader and a supporting elite. Experience shows that when high-rank leaders are changed, a classical example is Gorbachev during Perestroika, novel policies are implemented to transform the society toward better approaches; however, absurd socialism keeps the same elite in charge over the years sharing different political positions.

## Economic System

The first defining feature of the absurd socialist economic system is its incapacity of producing wealth. Absurd socialists are relatively indolent and get to the extreme to make people forcibly contribute to their cause. Absurd socialists are not efficient in producing different quotas. There is no place for invention or innovation in an absurd socialist society, individual inventive is crushed.

The second feature is related to the understanding of money's origin, production, and distribution. Absurd socialists tend to disdain the importance of money, making people believe money is not necessary. However, in practice, absurd socialists have to consider money and understand its usefulness. To buy consciences, absurd socialists use money or other goods and services to maintain the opposition silent.

The third defining feature is how the means of production are managed. Absurd socialism is an ideology without ideology. In theory, all property is publicly owned and the working class owns everything and everyone works toward the same communal goal. The means of production such as factories, farms, land, trade, construction, mines, and means of transport and communication, are under state ownership and control. However, the reality is more complex. The regime wants to eliminate capitalism but at the same time knows it cannot live without it. The rich benefits of the disorder becoming richer. Private property is still possible but propaganda maintains the view to crush it.

Linked to this feature is the fourth one, the dominance of a public economy, as distinct from a market economy. The utilization of national resources and the production and distribution of consumer goods is done through the state. In other words, the work of effecting a balance between demand and supply of goods is not left to the Mechanism of Prices, the state intervenes in those decisions. A minority of planners, representing the 'best minds' available, decide for the rest of the population and the plans never work.

The fifth feature regards collectivization. Socialism is seen as an economic model, usually linked to some form of collectivization and planning. Collectivism is a belief that human ends are best achieved through collaborative or collective effort, highlighting the importance of social groups.

Collectivization in socialism represents the abolition of private property and the establishment of a comprehensive system of common or public ownership, usually through the mechanisms of the state. Socialism usually took the form of state collectivization, modeled upon the Soviet Union during the Stalinist period. Economic Stalinism, therefore, took the form of state collectivization or 'state socialism.' The inevitable results of collectivization are shortages of vital goods and the need to queue for the bare necessities of life. The virtues of the market, on the other hand, are that it acts as the central nervous system of the economy, reconciling the supply of goods and services with the demand for them; absurd socialism does not benefit from any of those advantages.

The sixth feature of an absurd socialist economic system is the fact that the state is responsible to provide work and compensation according to the availability of every worker. Each individual is paid compensation according to criteria established by the state, this eliminates unfair gaps in incomes. Revenue, interest, and private profit cannot be eliminated, there is no distribution of wealth on a just and fair basis. The perspective of the state regarding the expected effort of the population implies many sacrifices and hardships.

The seventh feature is the issue of worker empowerment. Absurd socialists have aspirations of empowering the workers, and they have done so with the industries unfairly taken from honest entrepreneurs. However, those industries have been bankrupt after a few months. Absurd socialists make workers believe they are empowered but the power still rests in the state, a small leadership that decides for them.

The eighth feature regards the issue of democratizing the economy. Absurd socialists use to talk about democratizing the economy but the state is the one who decides everything, the entrepreneurs are marginalized.

The ninth feature is the implementation of popular economic measures. Absurd socialists use price controls, rent controls, industry nationalizations, and government regulation and interference with all economic activities. Absurd socialists confiscate and closely regulate major industries, the means of transportation and communication, and utilities (such as telephone, propane, water, electricity, and oil).

In absurd socialism, wages, and prices, instead of being set by the market, are established based on justice as determined by the officials in charge of making such decisions. The way absurd socialists act, control prices, establish minimum wages and eliminate the free enterprise, demonstrates their incapacity to solve economic and social problems.

The tenth feature refers to the way commerce and consumerism are treated in an absurd socialist society. The state defines the needs of people and defines the organizational structures regarding what the consumption of the population must be. Governments are faced with many economic problems, their basic promises of increased wages and pensions are inflationary, a continuous rise in prices and wages and a corresponding decrease in the value of money.

Current absurd socialist governments have not even solved simple problems of food production and distribution. Even with the capability of increasing food imports, the problems persist, famine and death are the new real actors of absurd socialist systems.

## Personal Influence

The first feature of the personal influence regards what expectations the society has regarding human beings. The society is expecting humans without egoism and ready to collaborate. Absurd socialism requires a new human being and it is impossible to change human beings. Societies must be organized according to known human nature characteristics and not according to invented standards that follow a fantasy.

The second feature is the interpretation of people's happiness. Happiness in absurd socialism is not something people feel inside, a sense of either immediate pleasure or long-term contentment with the way their life is going. It is instead an abstract view of collective happiness was the state decides when and how the individual must feel happy.

The third feature of a socialist personal influence system is the responsibility accorded to each human being. The state holds each person accountable for what they do, and as a result, it establishes penalties according to the non-contribution to the collectivity. The field of obligation is wider than the field of choice in absurd socialism. People are bound by ties that they never chose, and the state imposes values and challenges that intrude from beyond the comfortable arena of people's agreements.

The fourth feature of socialism imposes altruistic behavior to the population, "hard-core" and "soft-core" altruism. An irrational and unilaterally altruistic impulse directed at others is hard-core, serving primarily to the collectivity. Soft-core altruism, in contrast, which is ultimately selfish and expects reciprocation from society for itself or its closest relatives is not welcomed in absurd socialism.

The fifth feature is the tolerance expected in socialism from the population. It is the ability or willingness of people to accept the commands of the state that they do not necessarily agree with, in particular, the imposition of opinions or behaviors that collides with their own.

The sixth defining feature regards how the virtues of people are handled living in a socialist country. Most natural virtues have to concede in front of the state, independence, individuality and voluntary activities are not in the manual of the good absurd socialist. The population must accept the oppressive view of the state on many subjects.

The seventh defining feature is related to the expectations of the population on the performance of the state. The population is expecting a better life for all but the absurd socialist system does not deliver. After twenty years in power without solving the problems, absurd socialists expect the population accepting twenty years more.

The eighth feature regards how people's emotions are handled by the state. Absurd socialism manages people's emotions pretty well, it identifies those historical events that make people angry against the opposition or some developed countries.

The ninth feature presents how people manage their emotions within the social system. People in absurd socialism are not allowed to express their emotions freely, the state is always going to oppress any resentment against its policies.

The tenth feature regards the recommendation to use non-violent strategies to convince the population. Absurd socialists are not the most patient rulers, they are ready to dishonor this aspiration using violent strategies and forcing the population to follow the charismatic leader-defined policies.

The eleventh feature is related to how humans rights are handled by the absurd socialist state. It is well known that absurd socialists have difficulties with human rights, liberty, equality before the law, and private property. These are just a few examples of rights that are not available in absurd socialist countries.

## Social Influence

The first feature of social influence in the social system characteristic regards how absurd socialism handles security issues. Its emphasis is the protection of the elite in power, the population does not count. There are at least 25 thousand violent deaths in the country every year and the government is incapable of improving the situation.

The second feature is related to the expected behavior of the population. Absurd socialism's unique motivator is to make everybody as poor as anybody else. People must obey the laws imposed by the state, and people's actions are defined by the state. The justification is to have a just society where all are equal.

The third feature is the understanding of social idiosyncrasy. Absurd socialism imposes a new national idiosyncrasy different from what people are used to. Absurd socialism organizes the lives of citizens to perpetuate in power. Institutions are copied from other socialist countries, e.g., Russia, China, or Cuba. Absurd socialism cannot devise institutions according to the needs of the country.

The fourth feature is the position of the state regarding knowledge and education. Absurd socialists are characterized by a lack of interest in the constant search for knowledge and improvement. Because of its intrinsic complexes, an absurd socialist industry tends to stagnate by utilizing the same technology over and over again. The search for innovation is erased from the mind of bureaucrats, creating a stagnant atmosphere. In absurd socialism, education is important only up to a certain level. Elementary education is important for them and it is tied with the propaganda of the regime. University education is acceptable in areas outside political or social studies. Pure science and mathematics are welcomed but philosophy, sociology, and political sciences are not.

The fifth feature is the idea of eliminating class struggle by imposing a classless society. Absurd socialism is characterized by promoting a classless society to attain equality and communal living. People live miserable lives in absurd socialism, worse than in any other poor countries of the world.

The sixth feature regards how equality and egalitarianism are treated. Socialism is characterized by a belief in social equality, or equality of outcome instead of equality of production. Social equality upholds justice or fairness, it underpins community and cooperation, and it supports need-satisfaction as the basis for human fulfillment and self-realization.

The seventh feature is related to justice and liberty. In absurd socialism, social justice is the idea of a morally defensible distribution of benefits or rewards in society. What, for example, should be the balance between public and private ownership within a mixed economy – which industries should be nationalized and which left in private hands? Other principles of social justice include charity and cooperation and specifically prohibits usury or profiteering. It treats social justice as a commitment to greater equality and reflects values such as caring and compassion.

The eighth feature regards living in a community. In absurd socialism, human beings are social creatures, capable of overcoming social and economic problems by drawing upon the power of the community rather than simply individual effort. Absurd socialists have developed Utopian visions of a better society in which human beings can achieve genuine emancipation and fulfillment as members of a community.

Absurd socialists believe that competition pits one individual against another, encouraging each of them to deny or ignore their social nature rather than embrace it. As a result, competition fosters only a limited range of social attributes and, instead, promotes selfishness and aggression. Cooperation, however, makes moral and economic sense. Individuals who work together rather than against each other will develop bonds of sympathy, caring, and affection. Furthermore, the energies of the community rather than those of the single individual can be harnessed

The ninth feature regards the management of diversity. Absurd socialism does not address diversity, the search for unattainable equality disturbs those who are different. In socialism, everybody is the same, a misinterpretation of equality makes people miserable.

The tenth feature is related to obedience. Absurd socialism expects total obedience from its citizens. The unjust laws have been established to be obeyed not to be contested.

The eleventh feature regards to respect and dignity. Absurd socialism is oppressive, forcing everybody through the same conditions and pattern of behavior. There is no much respect for human beings and people feel an unworthy treatment.

The twelfth feature is related to reasoning. In an absurd socialist system, reasoning is biased, human relations are superseded by collective considerations letting the individual perish under the pressure of the state.

The thirteenth feature is related to the possibility of negotiation. Because in an absurd socialist system decisions are made from above, those on top of the hierarchy do not focus on the needs, desires, concerns, and fears of the population. Negotiations are not characteristics of absurd socialism.

## Ideological Sphere

The first defining feature of the socialist ideological sphere is the establishment of who is the recipient of a fundamental debt that justifies any actions. In the case of absurd socialism, the fundamental debt is owed to the collective self. Usually, it has been associated with the proletariat and the peasantry. It copies political ideas from communism and socialism that articulate class or social interests, a set of ideas that propagate false consciousness among the exploited or oppressed, and ideas situating the individual within a social context and generating a sense of collective belonging that do not solve the problems.

The second feature is the importance of maintaining order and stability. Absurd socialism has been characterized as a strong government that imposes order by force. The population is forced to follow its unique doctrine, authoritarianism is the norm and obedience is obligatory. Many people have suffered jail sentences equivalent to the Gulags and other forms of isolation time and concentration camps.

The third feature indicates the importance of history in the decisions regarding ideology. Absurd socialism uses experiences from other regimes to consolidate its doctrine. Absurd socialism is inspired by Marxism which promotes historical materialism.

The fourth feature demonstrates the understanding of the current world-view. Absurd socialists are not characterized by a good understanding of the world. Their analysis is biased favoring only the poor point of view.

The fifth feature indicates the characteristics of the model society. Absurd socialists consider humanity dependent on an abstract collective class that dehumanizes the population. Absurd socialists have taken ideas from communism, socialism, anarchism, and fascism establishing an incoherent set of ideas that cannot be implemented.

The sixth feature presents the transit to the desired future. All socialist experiences end in authoritarian regimes demonstrating that the population is forced to accept the socialist point of view. There are at least two possible paths to take power, the revolutionary and the democratic paths.

The seventh feature is the declared aim of building socialism as the ultimate, legitimizing goal. Absurd socialism has an important place in the official ideology and motivational and inspirational significance for a substantial number of party activists. The final stage of absurd socialism is communism which would eliminate the need of the state.

This legitimizing goal is the justification for all the toil and hardship that might be encountered along the way. If the goal is abandoned, absurd socialist regimes are in danger of being judged based on their incapacity to deliver more immediate results. Without the goal of communism, the 'leading role' of the state would become far harder to legitimize.

The eighth defining feature is the existence of, and the sense of belonging to, an international socialist movement. The existence of that movement is of great ideological significance. The notion of a strong state is fundamental in the absurd socialist ideology. It is the supposed internationalism of socialism that attracted many of its adherents. For individual members of socialist parties, the consciousness of belonging to a great international movement is of huge importance.

Absurd socialists believe in a universe where every other country would be socialist. They are not satisfied with a humble socialist country isolated in a specific region, they want to install socialism all around the globe. For socialists themselves, 'socialism' has two different meanings. It refers both to an international movement dedicated to the overthrow of capitalism systems and to the new society which would exist only in the future when Marx's higher communist stage had been reached.

## Pragmatic Sphere

The first feature of absurd socialism practical sphere is distracting the population from the miserable reality. For absurd socialists, the importance of gaining the consent of the population and such of the elites is fundamental. Many ideological socialist characteristics are unnatural, therefore, the system must devise mechanisms to keep the population out of the temptation of protest against the status quo. One of the strategies of the socialist state is to keep people begging to survive, they must remain submissive to opt for basic goods and services. The elite stays submissive receiving many opportunities to have a better life than the rest of the population.

The second feature is the understanding of the idiosyncrasy of the nation and the population. The absurd socialist state spends many resources on the understanding of the culture and traditions of the country to maintain its power. Ideology is not the whole thing, the absurd socialist state must understand the history of the country and what makes people accept unacceptable policies. The state identifies historical events or external enemies to gain popularity.

The third feature is the understanding of the physical characteristics of the country. Understanding the economy and what natural resources are available is a must for communists but absurd socialists are bad pupils. Central planning, utilized to define the industrial projects and the exploitation of natural resources is poorly managed in absurd socialism. To guarantee full employment, communists devise a huge template to organize the population near factories and mines, absurd socialists are incapable of devising a prosperous infrastructure.

The fourth feature is the tendency to mismanage financial resources. Even though some absurd socialists can be good administrators, those that dare defy the system are punished. There are many cases of corruption that are penalized. However, with all the power at their disposal, absurd socialists use to stay unaccountable and capable of amassing a fortune, diverting funds toward buying consciences, and to buy the elite and those that produce wealth to maintain a submissive order.

The fifth feature is related to regime survival. One technique is "coup-proofing." Being surrounded by "family, ethnic, religious, ideological or corrupt loyalties" makes absurd socialist survival possible.

The sixth feature involves the use of terror. Absurd socialism is characterized as an exploiter of human emotions and fear is one that is permanently at its disposal. The population is subject to all sorts of pressures to make them understand that the party-state is the one deciding their future. The population suffers constant indoctrination to avoid any thoughts about complaining.

The seventh feature is the utilization of security forces to repress the dissidence. Absurd socialists use special forces to combat any danger against the status quo.

The eighth feature is related to the violation of the laws and the Constitution. Absurd socialists tend to maintain the criteria expressed in the Constitution but they can define new rules according to the needs of the state. Their governance is characterized by the rule by law, where laws are defined according to the needs of the party-state. For example, forgetting about egalitarianism and welfare to maintain the dictatorship of the party-state was a practical decision in China.

The ninth feature involves staying eternally in power. Absurd socialism is not a doctrine that accepts its failure. Absurd socialism's main objective is to govern the whole human race, therefore, the approach to follow is perpetuating its government in power. For experience, absurd socialists know they are not capable of solving the problems of their societies, therefore, their explanation is to convince people that over many centuries they are going to finally produce the best system for humanity.

The tenth feature is to identify the enemies and incarcerate political dissidents. Internal and external enemies of absurd socialism are identified, attacked, and eradicated. Some internal enemies are used for propaganda purposes or to instill fear in the population. External enemies are important for socialists because they are a source of confrontation and exaltation of hate emotions against the common adversary. Sometimes, absurd socialist countries start wars against neighbors or the Empire to gain popularity.

The eleventh feature refers to the management of protests. Absurd socialism does not care about protests provided they don't affect their popularity. Absurd socialist countries have hundreds of protests per month, lack of services such as water, electrical energy, propane. It is when people protest because of the government that things start to become ugly. Hundreds of death because of protests are not uncommon in those countries.

## Globalization Dimension

Venezuela was a country that had been traditionally aligned with the West but today it is aligned with communism and fascism. Because Venezuela is an important oil producer, its main ties were with the United States. However, since absurd socialism took power, there has been a major shift in political allies. Venezuela has been flirting with totalitarian regimes such as Cuba, Russia, China, Syria, Iran and political organizations such as Hezbollah.

The situation in Venezuela today represents one of the most serious political, economic, social, and humanitarian crises the Western hemisphere has ever endured. Once a sophisticated country during the mid-twentieth century, Venezuela has now collapsed under the narcostate regime of President Nicolas Maduro – a collapse characterized by hyperinflation, widespread scarcity of food and medicines, and high-speed disintegration of institutions. Today, Venezuela ranks last in most global rankings for economic, security, and social well-being indicators. And the continuous increase of civilian deaths and misery depict a country with a level of destruction resembling those in war.

Latin American Region

The following paragraphs present a summary of the main sociopolitical characteristics of the Latin American region. Daniel Zovato presents his article called: 'Latin America: political change in volatile and uncertain times.' 17/09/2019

https://www.idea.int/news-media/news/latin-america-political-change-volatile-and-uncertain-times

It is possible to identify the following trends:

1. **The elections.** Almost all of the elections are characterized by a high level of citizen unrest concerning politics and the incumbent political forces, referred to the "election of anger." In several countries, this sentiment of unrest generated an anger vote, a vote rejecting the government and traditional parties tied to the emergence of anti-establishment candidates with a strong personalist slant. Jair Bolsonaro in Brazil, Andrés Manuel López Obrador in Mexico, and Nayib Bukele in El Salvador are the three main examples of this trend.
2. **Weak political institutions with low levels of credibility and legitimacy, especially political parties and legislatures,** increase the possibility for the emergence of candidates with a populist and anti-traditional elites discourse, highly personalized, a sort of "messiahs" or "saviors" who would supposedly come to fight against "old politics and its vices." In many countries, traditional parties are quite depleted and worn down.
3. **High levels of uncertainty, volatility, and polarization** resulting in centrist options not viewed as an attractive alternative in the vast majority of elections (as happened in Brazil and Colombia, and may also occur in Argentina).
4. **The middle class** – demanding, impatient, and more pragmatic than ideological – played a key role by supporting and voting for candidates in tune with their demands that promised fast concrete results.
5. **The vote to punish ruling parties prevailed over continuity.** Power alternated in the three main economies of Brazil, Colombia, and Mexico, as well as in Chile, El Salvador, Guatemala, and Panama (seven of the 12 elections held to date), while the ruling party **retained power** in Costa Rica, Ecuador, Paraguay, Honduras, and Venezuela (the last two by way of reelection).

6. **Consecutive reelection** only occurred in two countries, and in both cases, it exacerbated or triggered severe political crises and was unable to generate unquestionable legitimacy. The first was the electoral farce in Venezuela, where Nicolás Maduro was reelected in a general election completely lacking legitimacy, and the second was in Honduras, where the reelection of Juan Orlando Hernández was also very much questioned due to the high number of serious irregularities. In two of the three elections held in October, the current presidents did not get re-election, Evo in Bolivia and Macri in Argentina.
7. **Runoffs are becoming more frequent for determining who will be president.** Seven of the 12 elections seemed likely to require a second round, and in six of these seven elections (Brazil, Chile, Colombia, Costa Rica, Ecuador, and Guatemala) a runoff was needed to choose the president, El Salvador being the only exception. In two of these elections, Costa Rica and Guatemala, there was a reversal of results in the second round, i.e., the winner of the first round was defeated in the runoff.
8. **Governments with legislative minorities.** Except Mexico, where Andrés Manuel López Obrador obtained a majority in both legislative chambers, and Panama, where President Laurentino Cortizo enjoys a majority thanks to an alliance with MOLIRENA, **no other presidents elected have a legislative majority**. We anticipate that this will make governing more complicated and the approval of strategic reforms (fiscal, employment, pension, etc.) that many of these countries urgently need more difficult.
9. The serious **corruption scandals** throughout the region (aggravated in some countries by Lava Jato and Odebrecht) frequently tied to irregular political financing, and **high levels of citizen insecurity** were two issues present in almost all campaigns.
10. **The normalization of lies (fake news) and disinformation in electoral campaigns.** In several of these elections, **social media played an increasingly important role** (for example, the intensive use of WhatsApp in Brazil), progressively taking the place of traditional media. This presents new and important challenges in terms of regulations and the oversight that electoral authorities should carry out.

11. **Evangelical groups are gaining more influence,** as seen in a significant number of these elections. In 2018, the most notable instances were in Brazil, Costa Rica, and Mexico.
12. **Backsliding as regards gender parity among the presidents of the region.** With the conclusion of Michelle Bachelet's term, plus the fact that in none of the 15 elections of the election super-cycle has any woman been elected (nor will any be elected in the remaining elections), there has not been a woman president in Latin America since March 2018.

Economic Globalization

Hugo Chavez came to power in Venezuela in 1998 and, because Venezuela is a petrostate with the largest oil reserves in the world, his socialist government was able to successfully implement its plan to provide subsidized goods and services to the Venezuelan people. Venezuela, home to the world's largest oil reserves, is a case study in the perils of petrostates. Its oil dependence signifies that oil sales account for 98% of export earnings and as much as 50% of gross domestic product (GDP). Besides that dependence, production has been falling, oil output has declined for decades of socialist rule, reaching a new low in 2018.

PdVSA, the Venezuelan oil company, went from being one of the most efficient and important oil companies in the world to a disaster on the verge of bankruptcy. From their financial statements, it appears that the government drained up to 12 billion US dollars in some years to finance political spending, destroying the cash-flow, balance sheet and the future of the company. These funds have disappeared in a network of clientelistic interests and offshore accounts of regime leaders.

Chávez was an innovator in how he *spent* money, but he did little to improve how Venezuela *makes* money. He paid no attention to diversifying the economy or investing in domestic production outside of the oil sector. The country relies on imports for many of its most basic goods and services, including foods and medicines. Since its discovery in the 1920s, oil has taken Venezuela on an exhilarating but dangerous boom-and-bust ride that offers lessons for other resource-rich states. However, years of economic mismanagement and corruption under Chavez led to Venezuela's almost complete dependence on oil exports, and the collapse of global oil prices in 2014 led to a rapid economic decline.

Decades of poor socialist governance have driven what was once one of Latin America's most prosperous countries to economic and political ruin. The spiraling economy is declining population prosperity restlessly. In 2018, the GDP shrunk by double digits for a third consecutive year and 2019 remained without improvements. The soaring debt is impossible to be reduced. Venezuela has missed billions of dollars in payments since defaulting in late 2017, damaging the savings of millions of investors.

Huge hyperinflation hits the pockets of the poor incessantly. Annual inflation is running at more than 80,000%. Inflation is known as the tax of the poor. The Chavez regime economic advisers repeated, "printing money for the people does not cause inflation"... Money supply has been increasing exponentially, by 3,000% in a single year, 2018, destroying the purchasing power of the currency.

If Venezuela can emerge from its tailspin, experts say that the new government must establish mechanisms that will encourage a productive investment of the country's vast oil revenues for at least 50 years.

Political Globalization

As Venezuela's economy has collapsed, Maduro's popularity has also plummeted, and protest movements have rocked the country. The Maduro regime has become a growing autocracy. President Nicolas Maduro has violated basic tenets of democracy to maintain power. The Venezuelan government has jailed political opponents and disqualified them from running for office. At the time of writing, Venezuelan prisons and intelligence services offices held more than 400 political prisoners, according to the Penal Forum, a Venezuelan network of pro-bono criminal defense lawyers.

In February, International Criminal Court (ICC) Prosecutor Fatou Bensouda announced a preliminary examination to analyze whether since at least 2017 crimes occurring within the court's jurisdiction have taken place, including allegations of use of excessive force against demonstrators and detention of thousands of actual or perceived opponents, some of whom claim to have suffered serious abuse in detention.

Political Non-alignment

It is also no secret that Chavez and Maduro have angered the US by seeking stronger economic relations with Iran, China, and Russia. Beginning under Chavez, Venezuela helped create multilateral bodies that excluded the US, such as the Community of Latin American and

Caribbean States (CELAC), the Bolivarian Alliance for the Peoples of Our America (ALBA), the Union of South American Nations (UNASUR), and PetroCaribe, through which socialists offer oil at a preferential rate to various countries in Latin America. "These bodies are part of a broader effort to limit Washington's influence in the region and support progressive governments, for example, in Bolivia, Ecuador, Honduras, and El Salvador."

The systematic attack against property rights and nationalization of the means of production as established in the National Socialist Plan 2007-2013, expropriate companies, use the box of state companies to political purposes, impose intervened prices and print money massively. The Center for the Dissemination of Economic Knowledge (Cedice) estimates that more than 2,500 companies have been expropriated by the Chavez-Maduro regime. Of these companies, the vast majority are now bankrupt and have been devastated by socialist management. The NGO Transparencia Venezuela, in its report Property Owned by the State in Venezuela, describes as "terrible" the management of expropriated companies using ideological and political criteria: "Instead of increasing production, it has decreased."

Social Globalization

Severe shortages of medicines, medical supplies, and food leave many Venezuelans unable to feed their families adequately or access essential healthcare. The massive exodus of Venezuelans fleeing repression and shortages represents the largest migration crisis of its kind in recent Latin American history. Other persistent concerns include poor prison conditions, impunity for human rights violations, and harassment by government officials of human rights defenders and independent media outlets.

In 2014, extreme poverty was 23.6% and in 2017 it was 61.2%. Total poverty exceeded 87% in 2017 (according to a study by the Central University of Venezuela and the Simón Bolívar University). Venezuela's economic freedom score according to the Economic Freedom Index of the Heritage Foundation is 25.9, making its economy the 179th in terms of freedom in the 2019 Index.

Refugee Crisis

The political, economic, human rights, and humanitarian crises in Venezuela combine to compel Venezuelans to leave and make them unable or unwilling to return. The United Nations High Commissioner for

Refugees reported that, as of November, more than 3 million of an estimated 32 million Venezuelans had fled their country since 2014. Many more not registered by authorities have also left.

Money-laundering

A web of former Venezuelan officials and businessmen was charged in the U.S. with operating a massive $1.2 billion international money-laundering racket funded with stolen government money that was invested in South Florida real estate and other assets. The defendants are accused of embezzling funds from Venezuela's vast oil income and exploiting its foreign-currency exchange system to amass illegal fortunes in the United States and other countries, according to a federal criminal complaint.

How did the embezzlement work? It took advantage of Venezuela's currency exchange rules. "There are two exchange rates in Venezuela: the national currency, the bolivar, and the US dollar." "The rate of the bolivar to the US dollar was fixed by the central bank." But not everyone can convert bolivares into dollars, and vice-versa. Only a few companies can operate an official conversion from bolivares to dollars – including PDVSA. All those who don't have access to official exchanges must operate on the black currency market, which has very different rates than the official ones. Bolivares have a much higher value at the official exchange rate than at the black market rate – and the group of fraudsters reportedly exploited both the official and unofficial currency exchange systems.

"The fraudsters had dollars." "With the dollars, they bought bolivares on the black market. They then gave a loan to PDVSA, which paid them back at the official exchange rate" – which resulted in them having many more dollars than what they started with. This allowed the group to increase its initial investment tenfold. The operation began in December of 2014 and was meant to embezzle $600 million (about €534 million). By May 2015, the group had been able to double the amount to $1.2 billion (€1.07 billion).

The complex money-laundering scheme

According to investigators, starting in 2016, one launderer was tasked by one of the co-conspirators to launder a portion of the embezzled money. He reportedly was able to clean $60 million (€53 million) and received $600,000 (about €534,000) in commissions for it. This launderer was not the only person involved in money laundering for the group – an operation that involved different means and countries.

"A great many different models were chosen." "We know that a very large part of the money first went to Malta, namely to shell companies which had 'nominee shareholders,' strawmen to whom the companies belonged – but only on paper." "From Malta, they then reportedly invested this money in different businesses. For example, they invested in bonds issued by a company, or they reportedly invested on a grand scale in real estate in Spain. Or they transferred it through so many banks that the sender was no longer recognizable."

Money-laundering destination countries

In February, after a tip-off from US investigators, authorities in Bulgaria blocked transfers from a series of suspicious bank accounts that received millions of dollars from PDVSA. The case appears to not be directly related to initial launderers. The bank accounts were opened by an individual with multiple citizenship, including a Bulgarian one, at a small, unnamed Bulgarian bank. According to sources, people looking to launder money usually look for countries with weak banking supervision and stable currency to clean their dirty funds.

"Countries like Bulgaria, but also countries like Germany, are target countries for this kind of money," Malcher explained. "If you have to hide money gained through corruption somewhere in the world, of course, a lot of countries come to mind." Investigators are now looking at all transfers in and out of the suspicious accounts.

Alliances between international criminal elites and Venezuelan government officials have become common and widespread. In July 2018, operation 'Money Flight' revealed how a network of Venezuelan elites and international bankers from Germany, Portugal, Uruguay, and Colombia allegedly laundered more than $1 billion from the state-owned oil company Petróleos de Venezuela S.A. (PdVSA).

Nicolas Maduro's embattled Venezuelan regime, desperate to hold onto the dwindling cash pile it has abroad, was stymied in its bid to pull $1.2 billion worth of gold out of the Bank of England, according to people familiar with the matter. The Bank's decision to deny Maduro officials' withdrawal request comes after top U.S. officials, including Secretary of State Michael Pompeo and National Security Adviser John Bolton, lobbied their U.K. counterparts to help cut off the regime from its overseas assets, according to one of the people, who asked not to be identified.

### U.S. Sanctions

For more than a decade, the US has used sanctions against the Venezuelan government and nearly 100 individuals in response to what the US has called activities related to terrorism, drug trafficking, trafficking in persons, anti-democratic actions, human rights violations, and corruption.

"In the months ahead ... the United States will announce even stronger sanctions on the regime's corrupt financial networks," The U.S. added. "We will work with all Venezuelans to find every last dollar that the regime stole and work to return it to Venezuela."

These sanctions follow years of similar moves by the US designed to pressure on Maduro, who enjoys the support of Russia, Turkey, and China, among other countries, as well as state institutions including the military. Maduro accuses the US-backed opposition of staging a coup.

The sanctions on PDVSA freeze the company's assets in the US, as well as prohibits US firms and citizens from conducting business with PDVSA. According to the Treasury Department's guidance, purchases can be made from PDVSA or its entities provided that the payments are made into a blocked account that Maduro's government cannot access. After that date, no purchases can be made. The sanctions also target key individuals linked to Maduro, including some of his ministers.

The main characteristics of absurd socialism have been presented. It is a sociopolitical system that takes the worse recommendations from socialism, communism, fascism, and anarchism.

# Chapter 16: Sociopolitical Preference

The sociopolitical systems presented in previous chapters have certain ideological characteristics that distinguish one from the others. Societies adapt their administration to several characteristics, selecting and combining attributes to fit their needs. Eventually, the objective would be to define a set of questions for each feature to produce an index indicating the preference for sociopolitical systems.

The sociopolitical systems considered are:
- Communism
- Socialism
- Anarchism
- Absurd Socialism - 21$^{st}$ Century Socialism
- Social Democracy
- Liberalism
- Conservatism
- Capital Democracy
- Fascism

## Preference of Sociopolitical System

A sample set of questions for sociopolitical systems is used to produce an index of preference. The questions have been associated with one or more sociopolitical systems. Each question in quotation marks should be answered using a scale of 1 to 10 (1: strongly disagree and 10: strongly agree).

POLITICAL SYSTEM

1. This sociopolitical systems considers that authority arises from below, through the consent of the governed. Therefore, "Authority must be rational, purposeful, and limited. There must be a preference for legal-rational authority and public accountability." ( )

2. These sociopolitical systems are suspicious of decentralized authority, which is oppressive and linked to the powerful and privileged. Therefore, "The society must endorse the authority of a collective body as a means of eliminating individualism and greed." ( )

3. This sociopolitical system proposes a multiplicity of centers to decentralize power in all its manifestations. Therefore, "There must be a strong support for the federalization of society which visualizes that there shall not be any single authority, rather, there shall be multiple centers of authority." ( )
4. These sociopolitical systems regard themselves as a creative force, a means of constructing a new civilization through 'creative destruction.' Therefore, "The charismatic authority of the leader should be absolute, unquestionable and totalitarian in character." ( )
5. These sociopolitical systems are influenced by libertarian ideas concerning authority. Therefore, "The notion of authority should be built through parliamentary politics and political pluralism." ( )
6. This sociopolitical system has expressed reservations about democracy, not only because of the danger of the majority rule but because political knowledge is unequally distributed due to limitations of education. Therefore, "The uneducated are more likely to act according to narrow class interests, whereas the educated are able to use their knowledge and experience for the good of others." ( )
7. This sociopolitical system embraces the ideas of totalitarian democracy. Therefore, "Genuine democracy should be an absolute dictatorship because the leader monopolizes ideological knowledge and is able to articulate the 'true' interests of the people." ( )
8. For this sociopolitical system, electoral or representative democracy is merely a facade that conceals elite domination and the oppression of the masses. Therefore, "Direct democracy with continuous popular participation and radical decentralization is the future of humanity." ( )
9. This sociopolitical system is based on democratic centralism, "People can participate giving their opinion about society issues, however, it is the elite who decides the path to follow and their decisions must be obeyed without questioning." ( )
10. These sociopolitical systems are convinced of the need for government but they also know the dangers that governments entail. All governments are potential tyrannies against the individual. Therefore, "The government must be limited in its

scope and decisions through the establishment of constitutional constraints and democracy." ( )
11. These sociopolitical systems exhibit some measure of internal fragmentation applying the doctrine of separation of powers. Therefore, "Constitutionalism must introduce internal constraints to disperse political power among a number of institutions and create a network of 'checks and balances.'" ( )
12. These sociopolitical systems have been always prone to support the possibility that "The state can define new rules according to its own interests, independently of the opinion of the population, and the new legislation represents what is called the rule by law that must be obeyed." ( )
13. This sociopolitical system supports the imposition of "The party is in control of the state, it is the party who decides what path to follow." ( )
14. These sociopolitical systems promote parliamentary democracy. Therefore, "The state must guarantee the balance between free enterprise and government intervention." ( )
15. This sociopolitical system considers that society should be viewed as an organism, a living entity. Therefore, "The state is defined by history, tradition, authority and a common morality. Authority develops naturally, as it has done during centuries, guided by the wise hand of government." ( )

ECONOMIC SYSTEM
1. This sociopolitical system has always manifested the idea that "Workers are alienated from the product of their labor because they work to produce not what they need or what is useful but 'commodities' to be sold for an economic profit." ( )
2. These sociopolitical systems have always supported the idea that "The entrepreneur is the only one who benefits from the worker's labor and gets accordingly a profit that the worker deserves as well." ( )
3. These sociopolitical systems consider that humans are motivated by moral incentives and not only by material incentives. Therefore, "The moral incentive to work hard is founded in the desire to contribute exclusively to the common good, and not for individual profit, which develops uniquely out of sympathy and sense of responsibility for fellow human beings." ( )

4. This sociopolitical system has never said that the individual is a completely isolated unit and selfish. Therefore, "Human beings are rather cooperative minded and with strong individual drivers but they are capable of favoring a society of small enterprising cooperatives to benefit the individual and the population." ( )
5. This sociopolitical system has placed faith entirely in history, culture, and the idea of organic community. Therefore, "The national community has to be viewed as an indivisible whole, all rivalries and conflicts being subordinated to a higher, collective, even mythical purpose, directed by the elite in power." ( )
6. This sociopolitical system has influences from public ownership and free market. Therefore, "Partial collective ownership of the means of production should be implemented and combined with acceptable free market's policies." ( )
7. Under this sociopolitical system, national interests supersede all other societal needs. It subsumes common people and businesses into a vision of the good of the state. Therefore, "The state must direct and control all the factors of production, it includes all public companies and those private entities that may own part of the factors of production." ( )
8. This sociopolitical system is influenced by entrepreneurship. Therefore, "Collective ownership of the means of production must be drastically limited, giving preference to private entrepreneurs." ( )
9. This sociopolitical system considers that "Social justice should emphasize primarily commercial entrepreneurship and free market, instead of welfare to the needy." ( )
10. These sociopolitical systems have always supported the idea that "The state should be in charge of all the means of production." ( )
11. These sociopolitical systems promote the idea that "Private property must be respected under any circumstance." ( )
12. These sociopolitical systems consider that property reflects merits. Therefore, "Only those who work hard and have talent will, and should, acquire wealth." ( )
13. These sociopolitical systems support the idea that "The laws of demand and supply should not operate in the society, only needs should determine what people can own." ( )

14. These sociopolitical systems promote a non-materialistic approach to the economy. Therefore, "Acquisitiveness is morally corrupting, human happiness or fulfillment should not be gained through the pursuit of wealth." ( )
15. These sociopolitical systems consider that "Competition among human beings is natural and, in some respects, healthy." ( )
16. These sociopolitical systems consider that "Central planning cannot take in consideration the diversity of the population and it requires a simplification of reality that harms the individual more than it helps." ( )
17. These sociopolitical systems consider that "The state must be the only one in charge of planning the economy to define and guarantee the production and distribution of goods and services which benefit the population." ( )
18. This sociopolitical system is primarily motivated by capitalistic concepts. Therefore, "A society should be oriented on commodities' production where wealth is predominantly held on private hands. Material self-interest and maximization of profits should be the main motivators for enterprising and hard work." ( )
19. These sociopolitical systems have always sustained that "Social classes are originated by the divisions between 'capital' and 'labor,' that is, between the owners of productive wealth (the bourgeoisie) and those who live off of the sale of their labor power (the proletariat)." ( )

PERSONAL INFLUENCE

1. For these sociopolitical systems it is convenient that "The poor must receive preferential treatment over the middle and rich classes on all aspects of life." ( )
2. This sociopolitical system considers that human beings are essentially limited, security-seeking creatures, drawn to the known, the familiar, the tried, and tested. Therefore, "Humans are rationally unreliable and human corruption is implicit in each individual." ( )
3. These sociopolitical systems regard humans as essentially social creatures, their behavior shaped by society rather than by birth. Therefore, "Humans are prone to cooperation, sociability, and rationality to attain social development; ambition, greed or envy are not in the human spirit." ( )

4. These sociopolitical systems propose that "Human nature is defined by culture and not by nature, it is 'plastic', can be modified and molded by the experiences and circumstances of social life." ( )
5. These sociopolitical systems give priority to the 'right' over the 'good.' Each group or person is free to pursue the 'good' as it wishes, without defining what is 'good,' or accepting an imposed 'good.' Therefore, "The individual ability to act freely at his own discretion, without state constraints, should be guaranteed by society." ( )
6. This sociopolitical system considers humans imperfect, understood as psychologically limited and dependent creatures. Therefore, "People are drawn psychologically to the safe and the familiar, and, above all, seek the security of knowing 'their place.' People give importance to social order and are suspicious of the attractions to liberty." ( )
7. These sociopolitical systems consider that "The group is more important than the individual, therefore, the individual must accept the decisions of the group even if the group is mistaken." ( )
8. These sociopolitical systems consider that "The individual must be limited in its decisions, it is the state that determines individual's independence." ( )
9. This sociopolitical system has a pessimistic view of the capabilities of ordinary people. Therefore, "The masses are weak, inert and ignorant, requiring a strong leadership and the help of an elite of 'warriors.'" ( )
10. For these sociopolitical systems individual liberty, with few limitations, is the supreme political value. Therefore, "Liberty is the main condition in which people are able to develop their skills and talents and fulfill their potential." ( )
11. These sociopolitical systems regard freedom as an absolute value, rejecting any form of political authority. Therefore, "Freedom is the achievement of personal autonomy, allowing people to become self-willed and self-directed." ( )
12. This sociopolitical system rejects any form of individual liberty. Therefore, "True freedom means unquestioned submission to the will of the leadership." ( )

13. This sociopolitical system considers that "Equality is only acceptable because the objective of its society is to make everybody poor." ( )
14. These sociopolitical systems deviate from the total-equality concept. Therefore, "Equality of opportunity is a feasible aspiration compared to the unattainable social equality." ( )
15. This sociopolitical system is obfuscated by entrepreneurship. Therefore, "Equality only makes sense in the commercial context, people are absolutely free to establish any enterprise with the purpose of making a living." ( )

SOCIAL INFLUENCE

1. These sociopolitical systems oppose the conception that people are equal, they agree with the statement "All human beings are different, reality shows us a captivating treasury of humans, the exuberance of an evanescent play and alteration of behavior." ( )
2. These sociopolitical systems consider that immoral and criminal behavior is rooted in the individual, humans are selfish and greedy. Therefore, "Crime is not the result of inequality or social disadvantages, it is a consequence of basic human instincts and appetites." ( )
3. These sociopolitical systems propose a broad range of political and economic views for a society. Therefore, "Society requires a commitment for equality and the collective ownership of the means of production combined with the acceptance of market efficiency and individual self-reliance." ( )
4. These sociopolitical systems consider that "All governmental actions must be for the benefit of society as a whole, the individual is unimportant." ( )
5. These sociopolitical systems are primarily influenced by notions of freedom. Therefore, "Freedom in all its manifestations should be supported by the state but entrepreneurial freedom must take precedence over other types of freedom." ( )
6. These sociopolitical systems have endorsed meritocracy on both economic and moral grounds. Economically, there is a need for incentives, and morally unequal individuals should not be treated equally. Therefore, "The society should be ruled by those with merit, meaning, intelligence, and capable of effort. To build a

society in which social position is determined exclusively by ability and hard work." ( )
7. This sociopolitical system considers that the emphasis on the nation or race implies that all the people are equal, at least in terms of their core social identity. Therefore, "Humankind is marked by radical inequality, both between leaders and followers and between the various nations or races of the world." ( )
8. These sociopolitical systems support the idea that "Social rewards should be distributed entirely on the basis of need and not on the basis of capability." ( )
9. These sociopolitical systems are committed to the individual. Therefore, "Society must satisfy primarily individual's interests to allow them to achieve fulfillment, society is benefited indirectly." ( )
10. These sociopolitical systems consider a society just as a collection of individuals. Therefore, "Society only exists out of voluntary and contractual agreements made by self-interests human beings." ( )
11. These sociopolitical systems consider that society is naturally hierarchical, characterized by fixed or established social gradations. Therefore, "In society, there must be leaders and followers, there must be managers and workers, there must be those who go out for work and those who stay at home and bring up children." ( )
12. This sociopolitical system considers that a society should be viewed as a living organism. Therefore, "Society exists above and prior to the individual, it is held together by the bonds of history, tradition, authority, and a common morality." ( )
13. For this sociopolitical system, human beings can be 'good' or 'evil' depending on the political circumstances in which they live. Therefore, "People who would otherwise be cooperative, sympathetic and sociable become nothing less than oppressive tyrants when raised up above others by power, privilege and wealth." ( )
14. For these sociopolitical systems, human beings are social creatures willing to use the power of the community rather than simply individual effort. Therefore, "Humans must work together for collective action instead of striving for personal self-interests." ( )

15. These sociopolitical systems have often seen class issues as an expression of the interests of the working class. Therefore, "Class inequalities should be substantially reduced, workers should emancipate themselves from capitalist exploitation to become fully developed human beings." ( )
16. This sociopolitical system abandoned the idea of a classless society. Therefore, "Classes exist naturally in society, the objective must be to ameliorate the conditions of the less favored through welfare facilities." ( )

IDEOLOGICAL SPHERE

1. This sociopolitical system establishes that the proletariat receives the fundamental debt. Therefore, "Any decision taken by the state must be oriented to the well-being of the proletariat." ( )
2. These sociopolitical systems establish that the society as a whole receives the fundamental debt. Therefore, "Any decision taken by the state must be oriented to the well-being of the society." ( )
3. These sociopolitical systems establish that provided the individual receives the fundamental debt, the society receives it indirectly. Therefore, "Any decision taken by the state must be oriented to the well-being of the individual because indirectly the society benefits." ( )
4. These sociopolitical systems have an open mind about the issues affecting the world. Therefore, " To understand the current world-view, the state needs to understand both the nation and the rest of the world." ( )
5. For these sociopolitical systems, according to their ideology, provide an unclear model for a new society. Therefore, "Ideologies don't need to be precise or define how their new proposed society will function, improvisation is the best approach to solve problems." ( )
6. These sociopolitical systems provide a clear path from the current situation to the new proposed society. Therefore, "A new society will be build with few sacrifices, using best practices will guarantee success, trial and error is not an acceptable strategy." ( )
7. These sociopolitical systems define a mixture of ideologies that recognize diversity. Therefore, "Society must evolve towards a conglomerate of people, each with a defined identity, that

recognize the specific conditions and necessity of wise interchanges." ( )
8. This sociopolitical system is based on an ideology using slogans and full of unattainable aspirations, claiming it is the future of humanity. Therefore, "An ideology can be perfectly based on empty slogans, and does not need to provide any convincing explanation of how to transition from the old to the new society." ( )
9. This sociopolitical system is based on ideologies proposing many nice human aspirations that are unfeasible. Therefore, "An ideology based on unattainable aspirations such as 'Extending democracy to the economy' or 'Democratizing every aspect of society,' does not need to be supported by an institutional framework which fulfills those aspirations." ( )
10. These sociopolitical systems are based on ideologies suggesting that "A feasible aspiration would be 'Everybody will work happily for the good of everybody.' Egoism is not allowed in a society." ( )
11. These sociopolitical system are based on an ideology sustained on moral and religious beliefs instead of materialistic conceptions. Therefore, "A society must maintain a balance between a free market economy and the intervention of the state." ( )
12. This sociopolitical system considers that collectivization is more important than individualization. Therefore, "Collective human endeavor is of greater practical and moral value than individual self-striving." ( )
13. This sociopolitical system takes cooperation to the extreme by identifying the social classes to be allowed to cooperate and exclude the rest. Therefore, "The poor and the excluded workers are the only ones allowed to participate in society; the only way for the rest of people to participate is by becoming poor or excluded workers." ( )
14. This sociopolitical system has always considered that "The natural relationship among humans is one of cooperation rather than competition." ( )

PRAGMATICAL SPHERE
1. This sociopolitical system proposes a society with three kinds of people, the supreme leader, the 'warrior' elite of fighters and the

ignorant masses. Therefore, "Society should be intrinsically based on propaganda, interested in ideas only to elicit an emotional response, and spur the masses into action." ( )
2. These sociopolitical systems support the idea that "The masses must support the regime, therefore, people's street demonstrations are constantly called for to support the regime." ( )
3. This sociopolitical system considers that "Indoctrination is a necessary and constant activity, several hours a week must be dedicated to learning how to please the state." ( )
4. These sociopolitical systems support the notion that "Those who dare to oppose the state should be rapidly purged and restrained of their access to basic surviving goods." ( )
5. This sociopolitical system punishes the opposition using harsh methods. Therefore, "The state must identify the enemies and offer them to obey or else go to prison or concentration camps." ( )
6. This sociopolitical system has been always in favor of the statement that "A good government is one that spends the money giving parties and promoting fairs to make people believe they are living a happy life." ( )
7. These sociopolitical systems implement harsh mechanisms for controlling the Press. Therefore, "The Press must be controlled to avoid criticisms to the state, a unique standard viewpoint is communicated to the population such that they don't get confused by multiple sources." ( )
8. For these sociopolitical systems, once they get the power, it is important to stay eternally in power. Therefore, "Once in power, the regime must retain power by any means, including the use of force to neutralize dissidents." ( )
9. These sociopolitical systems manipulate the needs of the population on their benefit to stay longer in power. Therefore, "Taking charge of the means of production is a way of controlling the population, people need to survive and must accept the status quo independently of how miserable it is." ( )
10. For these sociopolitical systems staying eternally in power and manipulating the needs of the population are not valid objectives because of their orientation to individual self-realization. Therefore, "Taking charge of the means of production should not

be an objective for a society. The society needs entrepreneurship to accomplish a multifaceted productive administration." ( )

11. These sociopolitical systems mismanage financial resources for the benefit of its partisans and to buy consciences. Therefore, "Mismanaging the sources of income and placing partisans in charge of the administration guarantees the survival of the regime." ( )

12. For these sociopolitical systems, society must devise a mechanism for self-control. Therefore, "Mismanagement of financial resources must be penalized even if accountability or independent controls are not implemented." ( )

13. These sociopolitical systems allow widespread corruption in the state to control the dissidence. Therefore, "Partisans should be allowed to make a living by mismanaging the resources of the state and participating in irregular activities which guarantee their complete submission to the regime." ( )

14. These sociopolitical systems consider that political knowledge is not important for society. Therefore, "The population only requires survival knowledge, giving them the possibility of knowing too much puts in risk the safety of the regime." ( )

15. These sociopolitical systems distract the population from the miserable reality to retain power. Therefore, "To retain power, the state must implement mechanisms to distract the population from the harsh reality. For example, offering free goods and services; making people stay in long lines to get food at regulated prices; negating the access to necessary services such as water and electrical power; attacking Imperialism and the opposition; praising sport event's stars and long gone partisan idols; waging war against other countries." ( )

16. For these sociopolitical systems, knowing the idiosyncrasy of the nation and the population must be exploited to stay longer in power. Therefore, "Knowing the weaknesses of the population must be exploited, a mechanism of domination to stay longer in power must be implemented." ( )

17. For these sociopolitical systems, the idiosyncrasy of the nation and the population is useful to help the population. Therefore, "Knowing the weaknesses of the population provides a path to improve the lives and performance of citizens." ( )

18. These sociopolitical systems exploit natural resources for their benefit and not for the benefit of the population. Therefore, "A country with huge reserves of natural resources presents the ideal environment to keep the population submissive. An unjust regime must be giving away large amounts of income instead of investing in better services." ( )
19. These sociopolitical systems stimulate the use of terror to guarantee their political survival. Therefore, "Terror is a deterrent of dissidence and must be established as a way of life." ( )
20. These sociopolitical systems maintain a constant violation of the laws and the constitution. Therefore, "The best way to maintain a submissive population is to control the judicial system. Defining new laws and violating the constitution becomes a legalized way of perpetuating in power." ( )

The author completed the questions and produced the average for each sociopolitical system. The results were as following:

| | |
|---|---|
| Liberalism: | 8.7 |
| Conservatism: | 8.1 |
| Social Democracy: | 7.5 |
| Capital Democracy: | 7.4 |
| Anarchism: | 7.2 |
| Socialism: | 1.9 |
| Communism: | 1.7 |
| Absurd Socialism: | 1.5 |
| Fascism: | 1.2 |

The results demonstrate that for this set of questions associated with sociopolitical systems, the author has a preference for the moderates (Liberalism, Social Democracy), some unprogressive (Conservatism, Capital Democracy), and one extremist (Anarchism) leaving the rest of extremists (Socialism, Communism, Absurd Socialism) and Fascism quite behind. Another consideration is that no sociopolitical system got the maximum or the minimum points, meaning that most questions don't represent an absolute reject or complete approval by the author.

## Final Notes

The song of Charles Aznavour, Emmenez Moi, explains how people react in front of life fantasies. The following lyrics demonstrate why people accept a wrongful approach believing paradise on earth will be attained.

Moi qui n'ai connu toute ma vie<br>
Que le ciel du nord<br>
J'aimerais débarbouiller ce gris<br>
En virant de bord

The English translation is the following:

I, who knew all of my life<br>
Only the northern [grey] sky<br>
I would like to wash away the grey<br>
In setting sail

It demonstrates that people are ready to risk their life believing that moving South to a warmer country will solve all their problems. They don't give it a thought before plunging into the unknown. The lyrics applied to sociopolitical systems would look something like this:

I, who lived all my life<br>
In a capitalist country, without any hope<br>
I would be ready to risk my life<br>
And accept doomed Socialism

It is a pity that people accept passively all socialist disgraces, it is as if people wait patiently to be cooked down in the socialist's cannibal casserole.

I definitively like the song Emmenez Moi. It has good rhythm and interesting lyrics, quite different from the usual popular folklore. As usual, songwriters try to bring up emotions in their songs and Aznavour succeeded in his effort.

I hope readers would get the message and adore songs like this one but abhor sociopolitical systems such as absurd socialism that don't deliver what the population need. Regrettably, some people make emotional decisions based on aspirations and propaganda, supporting failed sociopolitical systems that are non-viable.

Aspirations must be evaluated to determine their viability. Utopian aspirations can produce unexpected results affecting the population. It is the responsibility of citizens to identify non-viable aspirations and fight against their implementation because the consequences can be catastrophic.

Absurd (21st. Century) Socialism is a sociopolitical system proposing too many non-viable aspirations, a summary of its characteristics follows:

Political System

Totalitarian state with poor criteria.
Authoritarian through a charismatic leader.
Favors populism leadership.
Favors democracy of the poor against the rich directed by the elite.
Uses the constitution as a subterfuge.
Uses one party to influence the state.

Economic System

Expropriates private property.
Promotes the poor and excluded workers against the middle class.
Promotes the common good for the elite.
It is welfare oriented but to benefit the elite.
Uses planning for propaganda purposes.
Promotes price controls to create shortages.

Personal Influence

Favors collectivization directed by the elite.
It is oriented to cooperation just to stay in power.
Nurture oriented, anybody is capable of leading.
Considers everybody must be poor.
Accepts the freedom of its partisans only.

Social Influence

Favors regulation to benefit only the poor.
Favors rewards based on how poor you are.
Expects people to conform to a bad government.
Favors the loyalty of the masses obeying the elite.
Builds upon the absurd elite and the excluded masses.

Ideological Sphere

Pragmatical, to consolidate the poor class.
Increases unproductive institutions to build a bureaucracy.
Considers only the poor, the excluded, and the elite.
It does not understand the world.
Believes in a transition based on trial and error.
It has no ideology, improvisation is common.

Pragmatical Sphere
Attacks the opposition and the empire.
Uses indoctrination to convince the poor.
Threatens the press and gets rid of it.
Imprisons enemies and destroy producers.
Uses corruption to buy political consciences.
Distracts the population from the miserable reality.
Uses terror to punish the opposition.
Uses the judicial system to stay in power eternally.

All this journey confirms how distorted is the knowledge about sociopolitical systems. People are a mix of ideological beliefs choosing the features that better describe their position on each topic. People can agree on some liberal arguments and also accept conservative positions. For example, I prefer to be conservative when choosing a government that proposes unfounded transformations to society. A socialist government, willing to change society upside down does not guarantee stability, therefore, I prefer the status quo.

The following evaluation statements divide the spectrum of ideologies into advanced and idealistic viewpoints in one extreme, progressive and balanced viewpoints in the middle, and obscure and retrograde viewpoints at the other extreme. Each range could be associated with sociopolitical systems, however, it is not a precise association, it gives an idea towards what type of ideas a person is biased.

Each statement can be associated with a continuum scale from 1 to 10 that helps to identify personal preferences.

(1: a proposition in one extreme) <--------> (10: a proposition in the other extreme)

Adding all the evaluations and getting the average gives a result that gives a rough idea about a person's ideological tendency. It is a simple tool that positions yourself in such a complex territory.

1. (Totalitarian state) <--------> (No state as of today)
2. (Totalitarian authority) <--------> (Authority absolutely decentralized or not at all)
3. (Leadership centralized from above) <--------> (Leadership decentralized from below)

4. (Radical democracy, totalitarianism) <-------> (Decentralized democracy)
5. (Disrespect to constitutional values) <-------> (Constitution used as the reference guide)
6. (Party dominates the state) <-------> (Rejection of party domination of the state)
7. (Only public property accepted) <-------> (Primarilly private property)
8. (Workers benefited by loyalty to the state) <-------> (Workers benefited by merits)
9. (Orientation to the common good) <------->( Orientation to profit)
10. (Imposing welfare as a social right) <-------> (Welfare as complementary help)
11. (Total central planning approach) <-------> (Distributed planning)
12. (Total interventionist price control) <-------> (Price control based on supply and demand)
13. (Forced collectivization) <-------> (Individual free participation)
14. (Only the poor get benefited) <-------> (Only the capable get benefited)
15. (Happiness defined by the state) <-------> (Happiness defined by the individual)
16. (Nurture-only defines behavior and personality) <-------> (Nature-first defines behavior and personality)
17. (Outcome-oriented social equality) <-------> (Opportunity oriented equality)
18. (Limit freedom to the population) <-------> (Complete freedom to the population)
19. (Altruist behavior is forced by the state) <-------> (Altruist behavior is individually decided)
20. (Disrespect on human rights) <-------> (Total respect on human rights)
21. (Society defines who the individual is) <-------> (Individuals define society)
22. (Social justice rewards according to needs) <-------> (Social justice rewards based on merits)
23. (People's total submission to the state) <-------> (People obey only just laws)

24. (The leadership is imposed from above) <-------> (Leadership comes from below)
25. (Society uninterested on knowledge) <-------> (Knowledge oriented society)
26. (Promoting conflict and force to resolve class struggle) <-------> (Accept a natural propensity to the existence of classes)
27. (Ideology based on fantasy or Utopia) <-------> (Ideology based on reality and facts)
28. (Promote aspirations without institutional support) <-------> (Institutions are built to support aspirations)
29. (Fundamental debt-oriented to the collectivity) <-------> (Debt oriented to the self, the individual).
30. (The current world is wrong) <-------> (Overcome world defects)
31. (Revolutionary or harsh transition) <-------> (Slow and secure transition)
32. (Total improvisation) <-------> (Well thought approach)
33. (Promoting ideology through propaganda to maintain a submissive population) <-------> (Convince the population through reasoning)
34. (Use indoctrination to avoid apposition) <-------> (Use regular education channels approved by the population)
35. (Total control of the press) <-------> (Total free press)
36. (Bad treatment to enemies) <-------> (Using the just rule of law)
37. (Using corruption to buy consciences) <-------> (Fighting corruption of any kind)
38. (Using distraction measures to forget people's misery) <-------> (No need of using distraction, there is no misery)
39. (Totalitarian use of terror) <-------> (No need of using terror)
40. (Total judicial control to stay in power eternally) <-------> (Independent judicial system applying the laws)

An evaluation below 3 indicates a totalitarian and retrograde viewpoint on ideology. An evaluation above 7 indicates an idealistic, optimistic or Utopian viewpoint on ideology. An evaluation between 3 and 7 indicates a moderate and progressive viewpoint on ideology. Know thyself ideologically!

# Bibliography

[Adler 1992] Alfred Adler, "Understanding Human Nature – The Psychology of Personality," Oneworld Publications, 1992.

[Albright 2018] Madeleine Albright, "Fascism, A Warning," Harper Collins, 2018.

[Bethell 1993] Leslie Bethell, Editor, "Cuba, A Short History," Cambridge University Press, 1993.

[Boloix 2017] Germinal Boloix, "Socialist Bingo: Knowledge Distorted Knowledge," Germinal Boloix Editor, 2017.

[Boloix 2018] Germinal Boloix, "Socialism is Dead, Nietzsche is Eternal," Germinal Boloix Editor, 2018.

[Boloix 2019a] Germinal Boloix, "Socialism and Failed States," Germinal Boloix Editor, 2019.

[Boloix 2019b] Germinal Boloix, "Human Nature against Socialism," Germinal Boloix editor, 2019.

[Brown 2009] Archie Brown, "The Rise and Fall of Communism," Doubleday Canada, 2009.

[Bueno 2011] Bruce Bueno de Mesquita, Alastair Smith, "The Dictator's Handbook, Why bad behavior is almost always good politics," PublicAffairs, Perseus Book Group, 2011.

[Fleming 2008] Thomas Fleming, "Socialism," Marshall Cavendish Corporation, 2008.

[Freeth 2011] Ben Freeth, "Mugabe and the White African," Lion Hudson plc, 2011.

[Fukuyama 2011] Francis Fukuyama, "The Origins of Political Order," Farrar, Straus and Giroux editors, New York, 2011.

[Fukuyama 2014] Francis Fukuyama, "Political Order and Political Decay: From the Industrial Revolution to the Globalization of Democracy," Farrar, Straus and Giroux editors, New York, 2014.

[Gaona 2018] Jose Mauricio Gaona, "Democratic Blending: The New Model of Dictatorships in Latin America," Journal of International Affairs, June 12, 2018.

[Harari 2014] Yuval Noah Harari, "Sapiens, A Brief History of Humankind," McClelland & Stewart, 2014.

[Hayek 1994] F. A. Hayek, "The Road to Serfdom," The University of Chicago Press, Chicago 1994.

[Heywood 2003] Andrew Heywood, "Political Ideologies: An Introduction," Palgrave MacMillan, 3rd. Edition, 2003.

[Huenemann 2009] Charlie Huenemann, "Nietzsche: Genius of the Heart," Talking Donkey Press, 2009.

[Lopez 2018] Margarita Lopez Maya, "Populism, 21st-century socialism and corruption in Venezuela," Sage Journal, https://journals.sagepub.com/doi/full/10.1177/0725513618818727, 2018.

[McRaney 2011] David McRaney, "You are Not so Smart," Penguin Books Ltd. 2011.

[Niemietz 2019] Kristian Niemietz, "Socialism: The Failed Idea that never Dies," IEA, Institute of Economic Affairs, London Publishing Partnership Ltd. 2019.

[Nietzsche 1998] Friedrich Nietzsche, "Twilight of the Idols," Oxford University Press, 1998.

[Scruton 2017] Roger Scruton, "On Human Nature," Princeton University Press, 2017.

[Steele 2017] Graham Steele, "The Effective Citizen," Nimbus Publishing Limited, 2017.

[Wilson 1978] Edward O. Wilson, "On Human Nature," Bantam New Age Books, 1978.

# Epilogue

The main characteristics of absurd socialism have been presented. It is a sociopolitical system that takes the worse recommendations from socialism, communism, fascism, and anarchism. The Venezuelan population is suffering while many partisans, disguised as officials and capitalists, are getting rich without remorse doing doubtful business. The government is still in power but 2020 is the year of victory, the country would regain honest administration rejecting failed absurd socialism.

An interesting note is that the European Parliament has produced a resolution to combat totalitarian regimes such as communism (socialism) and Nazism:

http://www.europarl.europa.eu/doceo/document/TA-9-2019-0021_EN.html European Parliament resolution of 19 September 2019 on the importance of European remembrance for the future of Europe (2019/2819 (RSP))

One of the resolutions "Calls on all Member States of the EU to make a clear and principled assessment of the crimes and acts of aggression perpetrated by the totalitarian communist regimes and the Nazi regime."

It would be important for the world to impose harsh sanctions to all those recently born absurd socialists countries that intent to implement communism (socialism) and Nazism.

www.ingramcontent.com/pod-product-compliance
Lightning Source LLC
Chambersburg PA
CBHW051751040426
42446CB00007B/319